Establishing a
Leadership Mindset

Establishing a
Leadership Mindset

A Guide to Using
the Power of the Human Brain
to Motivate Learning

Tony Holland

AMERICAN
ASSOCIATION OF
COMMUNITY
COLLEGES

ROWMAN & LITTLEFIELD
Lanham • Boulder • New York • London

Published by Rowman & Littlefield
An imprint of The Rowman & Littlefield Publishing Group, Inc.
4501 Forbes Boulevard, Suite 200, Lanham, Maryland 20706
www.rowman.com

6 Tinworth Street, London SE11 5AL

British Library Cataloguing in Publication Information Available

Library of Congress Cataloging-in-Publication Available

ISBN: 978-1-4758-6364-2 (cloth : alk. paper)
ISBN: 978-1-4758-6365-9 (paper : alk. paper)
ISBN: 978-1-4758-6366-6 (electronic)

♾™ The paper used in this publication meets the minimum requirements of American
National Standard for Information Sciences—Permanence of Paper for Printed Library
Materials, ANSI/NISO Z39.48-1992.

Contents

Foreword

Upon the completion of my master's degree, my first assignment was at the Borough of Manhattan Community College, teaching biology and general science. Most of my students were slightly younger than me but not by much. I was twenty-four years old. One of these students was an African American young man, let's call him Steven, who was doing well but, suddenly, stopped coming to class. At first, I thought he was ill, but after two weeks I decided to call his home. I asked how he was doing and why he seemed to have dropped out of my general science class. He responded: "Well, Professor Marti, the truth is that I don't want drop out. I enjoy your class and I miss the interaction with other students." I inquired about why then did he stopped attending.

Steven's response truly changed my life.

He said: "You see, live in Harlem and I have lived there all my life. The first time I ventured downtown was when my buddy and I came to register at the college. We always travel together to protect ourselves in this area of NY. It is dangerous to be black in NYC." I could not believe my ears! I know that this was 1966 and the Civil Rights Act was no more than two years old, but for a kid to be afraid of traveling by himself to Manhattan was almost impossible for me to fathom. But there was real fear in his voice.

It was 1966 and I had just completed my courses toward my PhD in biology. I fully expected to dedicate my life to the exploration of basic research in cell biology. But Steven's response made me realize that through teaching I could change peoples' lives, and the rest is history. This experience made me grasp that teaching in a community college is much more than transmitting knowledge; that community college teachers must consider all the factors that impact the learning experience. There is an inherent beauty in researching how students learn. To what extent must a teacher counsel students in life-impacting decisions? How do we nurture the learning process in an environment that has a double normal curve of students' preparation and ability? How do we keep prepared students engaged and how do we help those who lack the preparation to meet the rigor of the curriculum?

Teaching at highly selective institutions with well-prepared students is very different than teaching at less selective colleges and universities. Faculty members teaching at any higher education institution are not required to take courses in pedagogy, classroom management, or leadership. Faculty members at less selective colleges and universities generally have larger teaching loads and their task is greater than simply translating knowledge in an elegant manner. As the graduation and retention rate in nonselective colleges is low, "all hands-on deck" are needed to ensure that the American Promise of better life after completing college is kept.

The fact is that at less selective colleges and universities much of the institutional commitment is at the periphery of the classroom activities. To scale up the successes achieved in some colleges we must engage the members of the faculty, the people at the frontline of the learning process. Yet, they are asked to do so much more than they bargained for when they applied to be considered for the job. This book addresses an important way to assist faculty members attain leadership skills necessary to achieve the promise we make to entering freshmen. In addition, administrators, trustees, and staff can benefit from a better understanding of what is needed to meet the Completion Agenda.

Training programs are short in duration and highly focused. Some colleges have adopted centers where faculty meets and discusses the latest techniques. This informal process, a well-designed "teachers' lounge," can serve as a haven for teachers to discuss matters affecting the very difficult problems encountered in the classroom. In some cases, there is a formal set of lectures that provide continuing education units. In others, the informality of the "lounge" is conducive to creating mentor-mentee relationships.

Colleges and university hold members of the faculty accountable by conducting classroom observations of untenured professors, chairman end-of-year evaluations, student evaluations and peer reviews. It would seem that these processes are sufficient to maintain accountability in the classroom. However, it is clear that even the best teachers are faced with the almost impossible task of remediating all the factors that contribute to a student dropping out or failing the course. It is clear that leadership is an important ingredient for success. Mr. Holland makes a good case that teachers must be leaders and provides an excellent example of how the Instructional Leadership Academy (ILA) in his state has been used to develop this leadership mentality throughout the faculty ranks.

In this book, the question of the type of leadership needed to thrive in a nonselective environment is addressed. Accountability is ultimately measured by student success, although nonselective institutions that are not homed in on the Completion Agenda goals seem to accept the inevitability of student failure. All of us have heard faculty members say: "I will not lower my standard to accommodate the wishes of the administration" or "I have lectured this way for over twenty years, and you can't make me change." These are the very faculty member that must be held accountable.

In the academic world, it is peers who can most effectively influence recalcitrant faculty members. There are many protections, from Academic Freedom to Union contracts, to university traditions that make it very difficult to convince a tenured member of the faculty to change their methodology. But good institutional leadership creates an environment wherein all members of the faculty come together as group to ensure that the greatest number of students succeed without lowering standards, as evidenced by the ILA data and testimonials Mr. Holland shares. This book is a good tool that can spark discussion among the "functional circles of power" of the faculty and not the traditional lines of authority.

The administration must consider the classroom instructors as "partners in the enterprise." The traditional ranks could be translated as assistant professors being junior partners, associate professors as being associates, and full professors as full partners. If one considers members of the faculty in this manner, and not as employees, the need for support becomes obvious. The responsibility of the institution is to provide the support needed by junior partners to be good enough to become a Master Teacher or a Full Partner (Professor). We are all in this together and there are no superior ranks but simply less experienced partner. And the most important support that any institution can provide is to have a safe environment that encourages experimentation, corrects mistakes, and enhances leadership skills. Clearly, there are members who don't fit and, after receiving due process, must be held accountable. But the vast majority of faculty members want their students to be successful and they will welcome any support that is provided by the peers or the administration. In this book, Mr. Holland provides strategies to achieve this higher level of collegiate development.

Teaching is a difficult profession. Most people think of college as it is depicted in popular culture: young people crazed by sexual desires, drinks, and partying. When I hear someone criticizing faculty members because they *work* "only" fifteen hours, nine hours, six hours per week, I cringe. When I hear people demeaning the profession because we have summers off, or are eligible for sabbatical leaves, I fume. A college professor must lead insecure young adults and not-so-young adults through trying times. Think of a woman living in a trailer in the mountains of your state without a car and, literally, risking her life to come to the local community college. This is a true case. Her boyfriend, in a rage of jealousy, beat her because she was trying to be better than he. She finally got her nursing license and was able to leave the trailer and take her two kids away from him. When I was teaching her anatomy and physiology, I was able to help her get protection and psychological help to get through the curriculum. This is just an example. I already mentioned Stephen who needed to feel secure enough to attend my classes.

These types of situations are what teachers of nonselective institutions and community colleges face on a daily basis. And, in addition, they may be required to perform research, attend a myriad of meetings, and publish in order to be promoted. Good institutions recognize this difficulty of the profession and provide mechanisms to support all the faculty through their tenure. This does not end with the full professorship, for the highest ranks also need encouragement to stay fresh and not get jaded by all they have seen through the years. I believe that this book addresses the issue of faculty development in an excellent and practical manner.

Mr. Holland's description of Improvement, Constant And Never-ending (I-CAN) practice at Wallace Community College—Dothan (WCCD) is effective in relating how an institution can scale-up support services and faculty development that result in increased retention and student success. KAIZEN or continuous improvement is essential to a well-organized, well-accepted institutional program designed to enhance the chances of success for under-prepared student. But the thread that weaves together programs such as I-CAN is leadership—the actions that inspire a college community to collectively embrace innovation without fear or coercion. That is what makes this book so very important. This book posits that a culture that encourages effective faculty leadership is an essential component of a successful institution.

The COVID-19 crisis has caused teachers to re-examine the profession. For some, this was a time for inspired innovation, while for others, it was a time for despair; in either case, the crisis has made us look at what we do in very different ways. Leadership in the classroom is an essential ingredient for student success and for a very long time we have blamed the student, the family, and/or the household situation. All these are valid, but a good faculty member must find ways to address each individual student as a particular case and treat them as their own offspring. For, after all, we are to one degree or another *in loco parentis*. Regardless of one's chosen field of study, the overarching discipline in a teaching college is pedagogy. This book clearly addresses these issues in a clear and effective manner and will inspire you to adapt your strategies and techniques to achieve maximum effectiveness.

Eduardo Marti
Author of *America's Broken Promise: Bridging the Community College Achievement Gap*

Preface

In a time where the Completion Agenda has been described as *"the most important reform of our lifetime"* (T. O'Banion), it is imperative that we look beyond the promise of boutique programs and small-scale initiatives to inspire meaningful change for all students. Although these programs may provide the support needed to increase student success for participating students, they seldom result in substantial increases in retention and completion across the institution. Adopting a more at-scale approach requires instructional leadership, but more importantly it requires more leadership *within* our faculty ranks—something that directly leads to enhanced engagement, collaboration, and innovation.

Although it is understood that a book should have a clear and defined audience, I argue that leadership is an *action*, not a position or title. Instructional leadership, therefore, must come from within the faculty ranks and with the unwavering support for instructional innovations by the institution. Leadership and lifelong student should be synonymous.

Starting with the premise that *all great teachers lead and all great leaders teach*, readers can see the benefits of practical and direct discussions grounded in basic concepts applicable for administrators, teachers, coaches, and parents—basically anyone who has an influence over others. For this reason, this book is written to deliver fundamental insights which support learning with a myriad of examples and strategies that can be immediately implemented to support equity in opportunity for all. It is written in honor of all those educators before us who inspired us to seek more effective ways to enhance learning and establish values and behaviors that can lead to more opportunities in life for our students.

Whether you are a faculty member, department chair, divisional director, instructional dean, parent, counselor, or coach, this book is designed to persuade you that teachers lead and leaders teach. Training our focus on the teacher-leader connection uncovers the values, attributes, and strategies common to each of these positions. It also reveals their common goal: inspiring others to do what they need to do even when they may not want to or feel they cannot do it.

This inspirational goal of providing a learning environment which moves others beyond their self-perceived limitations is shared by all leaders, whether they lead students, athletes, employees, soldiers, or others. By viewing learning through the lens of constant improvement, and improvement through the lens of positive change, we can begin to implement the comprehensive change that will activate the Completion Agenda at scale and in community colleges across the nation.

Understanding your time is too valuable and the mission too important; this book is written to maximize the benefits of your time. This book will not only inspire you to action but will provide a return on investment through your personal empowerment of others that will well exceed the time you spend reading this book. You are encouraged to highlight those areas that resonate with you and seek additional research for any areas you may question.

The approaches discussed in this book are transferrable to the classroom, the boardroom, the ball field, the battlefield, and life itself. These applicable approaches have been practiced in the crucible of the classroom, the department, then division-wide, college-wide, and ultimately, system-wide and are discussed in a practical manner to facilitate action. Your willingness to learn more about instructional leadership by reading this book speaks volumes for your desire to serve others!

It is prudent at this point to clarify what this book means by "leadership," as well as to explain the argument that teachers should continue to develop the art of leadership while ensuring it is grounded in the science of human behavior. It has been said that management requires persuading people to do things they may not want to do, while leadership requires *inspiring* people to do that which they may never have thought they could. Teachers provide leadership on a daily basis to their students—as do parents to their children—by inspiring them beyond their comfort zones and self-perceived limitations.

When teachers embrace constant learning and growth for themselves through self-reflection, they become better prepared to provide leadership for both their students and their colleagues. They become better able to motivate a group of people toward achieving a common goal. When, on the other hand, teachers do not embrace constant learning, or when an institution or department does not have enough buy-in for innovation and constant improvement, then it is very difficult to foster effective leadership.

Over the years, the traditional silos that have existed among faculty have hindered opportunities to expand positive influences team-wide. When silos are removed and intentional and positive interactions are created among a department or team, the members initially operating with a greater degree of vision, purpose, and positivity become evident. Although these members may not have a leadership title or position, it is through their optimism and encouragement that they inspire others to action—whether intentional or unintentional.

This "lead-by-example" approach can be the most effective at inspiring children, students, new teachers, and seasoned faculty alike, and it can also be applied to the committees on which you serve. This approach requires the use of initiative and is a reason you should never ask permission to lead as you will know when it is time. There is a magical power in boldness, especially when it sends a positive message of hope for a better tomorrow.

To effectively influence colleagues, as well as students, it is necessary to understand obstacles to growth inherent in human nature. Therefore, for each scenario, strategy, activity, or approach mentioned in this book, you will be asked to use self-reflection to assess your answers to three questions. First, you will be asked *whether you are already doing the described action*. If you feel you are already doing it or have done it, the question becomes how you can *more intentionally produce the desired action*.

The final question asks how this action can be *promoted throughout your team*. This team may be your department, your division, or your entire institution, although starting with a more manageable and progressive team can then inspire action in larger teams. You can approach this work through frequent brainstorming sessions focused on what can be done to enhance the intellectual and emotional rigor of learning in the classroom. It is through activities such as this, and with accountability for the goal of the team, that leadership can be developed. This is the goal of leadership, whether in the classroom or departmental meeting—to develop more leaders.

According to *Inside Higher Ed*, wholescale innovation is never easy to implement: In the past, other than a few exceptions, major institutional innovation only occurred "where . . . the institution faced the prospect either of taking direct action or of losing accreditation or of being forced to close. Innovation, in almost all of these instances, was a matter of survival." (Diamond, 2006). Too often, survival conditions provide the forcing function to ignite change and innovation. What is required to support change when the stakes are not quite so high is a broadly implementable program based on learning that seeks to provide equity of opportunity through education, rather than inequity through an initiation process.

Such a program depends on leadership development. This may push readers beyond their limitations, but history has shown that these limitations are usually self-imposed and can be overcome, sometimes in surprising ways, by encouragement. This is why the power of encouragement is used to inspire readers to move beyond their comfort zone to become more effective leaders who inspire others.

As stated by Paula Rothenberg, "If education is about learning to see the world in new ways, it is bound, at times, to leave us feeling confused or angry or challenged. And this is a good thing. Instead of seeking to avoid such feelings, we should probably welcome a degree of discomfort in our lives and feel short-changed if it is not present."

This book is designed to challenge the reader's existing paradigms. Although we may find comfort in those who agree with us, we can find growth in those who do not. This not only applies to our approach to teaching, but it is also applicable to the core competency of critical thinking—a prerequisite to problem-solving—for both students and teachers.

In addition, this book focuses on the one variable that is absolutely crucial to meeting the goals of the Completion Agenda: educator involvement. Educators, after all, are the ones who can and must implement effective instructional and support strategies for a deeper and more meaningful learning experience (and for a more diverse group of students). The teacher's ability to enhance learning is powerful and has been helpfully articulated by Terry O'Banion: "If we are to improve on our record of student success, the role of the teacher in creating learning must become the primary focus of the Completion Agenda." This book was written to argue for a primary institutional focus on creating and supporting teachers in and out of the classroom: It is essentially a guide to help faculty successfully navigate their work in becoming teacher leaders.

Research consistently shows that quality of teaching matters more to student achievement than any other aspect of schooling (Sanders and Rivers 1996; Opper, 2019), although peer tutoring offers another effective form of "teaching." Unfortunately, community college and university teachers are not required to have formal training in leadership, pedagogy, or support strategies. Although this book provides numerous activities to inspire and facilitate intellectual rigor among educators, the primary focus is on offering educators and instructional leaders a powerful fundamental educational philosophy and communicating the neurology of learning and its impact on teacher—and therefore student—success.

Along the way, this book also offers high-impact teaching strategies informed by philosophy and neurology that can be immediately implemented to increase student learning and close achievement gaps. For those of you who may already be familiar with or are using some of these strategies, it is important to focus efforts on becoming more intentional in your approach to these strategies. This book makes the most of research indicating that the "human factor" is the most significant common factor among effective teachers.

***

A K–12 teacher, college instructor, division director, dean, and president have one thing in common: They are each responsible for inspiring people to operate at a higher level of effectiveness. Because of this crucial role of instruction, anyone who serves as a source of inspiration should be considered one of the most important leaders on campus. This is perhaps more true of educators than anyone else: Their efforts have more of an impact on closing achievement gaps and aiding student learning and success than any other aspect of schooling.

For educators, learning to become effective leaders means being able to navigate change and being ready to take advantage of a powerful influence on students and colleagues. This, in turn, typically requires people to do that which they may not *want* to do but *need* to do. We can help teachers become leaders by providing an environment conducive to constant improvement and growth and by leading—and encouraging everyone else to lead—by example.

"Navigating change" means undertaking a journey. The journey is not straightforward but filled with different options that require a number of decisions on the way to a final destination. It also requires a mindset of constant improvement fueled by a sense of positive restlessness. This mindset uses mistakes as opportunities to improve, but it strives to allow only new mistakes. In the context of higher education, this mindset allows for maximum improvements in a minimum amount of time in the journey to providing equitable learning opportunities for all.

However, as with any journey with multiple routes, a clear plan and path to begin this adventure will ensure the travelers meet their destination. Just as in life itself, the path of least resistance requires the least amount of energy because it has the least number of challenges and frustrations. However, it also usually leads to the least amount of progress and personal fulfillment.

For teachers, personal fulfillment is directly proportional to student learning, empowerment, and increased confidence. In other words, the route teachers decide to take has a profound impact on the options and opportunities available to students, as well as the children or future children of students. Of course, it also has a profound impact on the teachers.

This book guides readers along a route filled with spectacular views on the way to becoming a trailblazing educator. The views may appear to constantly shift, but that's always the case—only the lead dog on the sled sees the changing views! In fact, the path is *so* enlightening and empowering that it must come with a warning: If you do not wish to experience the overwhelming personal satisfaction that results from directly impacting learning for all students, and especially the most underserved students, this book may not be for you.

Also, if you do not wish to experience immediate and overwhelming student motivation to learn, especially from those with limited past success, the information in this book may not be for you. If you do not wish to expand your influence in a way that can transform education, create more opportunities in your community, and enhance social justice, simply disregard the proven strategies and concepts provided in this book. In addition, if you do not wish to empower your personal and professional life with a purpose and passion reserved only for the most determined and committed, now is the time to stop reading.

If, however, you are looking for information *guaranteed* to expand learning and growth for both you and your students, you have come to the right place! Chapter 9 will provide evidence that shows when faculty are provided an environment with high expectations and a positive, respectful application of training, accountability, support, and encouragement (TASE), they respond with amazing degree of innovation and passion. The testimonials in chapter 9 indicate the abundance of faculty who can confirm the profound impact the information in this book has had on both their personal and professional lives. It can—and will—impact you, too.

The acronym TASE is one example of many that conveys the need to strive for balance in our strategic approaches. The high level of training needs to be balanced with a high degree of support in order to maximize learning. Since accountability can sometimes be perceived as less than positive, balancing it with an abundance of encouragement is crucial to maximizing buy-in and performance—for both teachers and students.

In this book, educators are provided with proven high-impact strategies supported by recent advances in cognitive science and brain physiology. These are universal strategies that can be adapted to any subject matter at any level. Furthermore, because these strategies support productive neuronal growth, they ensure maximal learning for a greater diversity of students. Combining the strategies with a positive can-do growth mindset and a whatever-it-takes attitude creates a dynamic learning environment where mistakes become opportunities to learn, and where teaching and learning become mutually rewarding, as well as fun. This leadership mindset allows educators to foster a culture of inquiry and constant improvement.

> If education is about learning to see the world in new ways, it is bound, at times, to leave us feeling confused or angry or challenged. And this is a good thing. Instead of seeking to avoid such feelings, we should probably *welcome* a degree of discomfort in our lives and feel short-changed if it is not present.
>
> —Paula Rothenberg

It is important to acknowledge that higher education faculty did not invent the current system of education, but they adopted it. The old system, which served us well in the past, is not as effective for meeting the demands of the twenty-first century. This past system focused on the transmission of knowledge, which was needed in a world with limited access to information, so the approach of "covering content and testing" was deemed sufficient. Today, however, educators need not just new tools but a new mindset. In fact, the educator's mindset can significantly increase learning, attendance, retention, and completion.

Today's research on learning offers overwhelming evidence that, in higher education, it is not a matter of knowing *what* to do but *how to do it*. Because we can only do better once we know better, this book provides the information needed to "know better."

COMMUNITY COLLEGE TEACHING

Because teaching in higher education does not require previous formal training in teaching and learning strategies, many instructors are left to determine which strategies *they* are most comfortable using to reach their students. However, the community-college focus on learning demands instructors adopt the strategies by which *students can learn* most effectively. This can produce a disconnect.

Effective strategies are not always obvious, and holding faculty accountable for something they have not been trained to do is no more appropriate than holding students accountable for that which they have not been trained to do. Instead, the institution must ensure an environment of clear and high expectations, followed by the TASE needed to ensure constant improvement. This book can help.

Although the community college differs radically from the battlefield, the two environments have some things in common. Because of the battlefield's many variables and challenges, the military developed an acronym to assist during crisis and chaos. KISS—or Keep It Simple Stupid—reminded soldiers and company to stay focused on the simple by adding the emphatically demeaning term, *stupid*. In education, KISS serves as a reminder to always go back to basics when things seem to be in disarray. This is the reason for this book's many reminders for readers to KISS!

The approach is grounded in the basic fundamentals, which is where the word "simple" comes from. KISS is an approach that not only serves educators as they go through the transformations required to maximize student learning and meet the goals of the Completion Agenda but also provides a valuable skill for student success in academics and in the workplace.

However, in a team approach, complexity can actually create chaos and lead to apathy. Breaking problems into smaller steps and then focusing on the first step helps initiate action on all fronts. As it relates to learning, the more educators and students practice the fundamentals, or the basics, the more relevant the details become; conversely, without an understanding of the fundamental concepts and principles, details are irrelevant and quickly lost. This is another way this book focuses on KISS, by reiterating core concepts affecting learning throughout the chapters.

These core concepts support the insights shared in this book that were gained from my thirty-five-plus years in education, including the insights gained from the many professional educators with whom I have had the pleasure of working. Many of these educators provided the encouragement I needed to persist through the challenges of teaching, especially in the crucial first five years teaching chemistry and physics in the high school environment. Even though this time in K–12 was challenging, it provided an opportunity to work in industry for two summers, as well as to conduct research at a US Aeromedical Facility for two summers, and these experiences contributed to my growth as an educator.

Also, the contributions of those students and faculty who were more resistant to changes implemented to increase learning should not be overlooked. This resistance challenged us to seek more effective ways to inspire and facilitate learning for these students and faculty, with a heightened emphasis on using more data and research to explain the "why" behind the process. It was this "why" that created the relevancy needed to ensure buy-in, and ultimately, ownership.

Although twenty-seven of my years in education were served in the classroom, the number of extra classes taught over these years puts my full-time teaching *equivalence* at just over thirty-eight years. Yet, it was not the number of years or the variety of courses taught that truly contributed to my ongoing education—it was the variety of formats. The different formats required constant adjustments through adaptation and improvisation in order to be as effective as possible in the classroom.

These multiple formats are credited for shortening the learning curve in adopting more effective paradigms. Whether the courses were traditional, hybrid, online, telecourses, or correspondence, each required a unique approach to achieve maximum effectiveness; in fact, "maximum" became a rabbit that would be continuously chased (even if it could never actually be caught).

Differences in formats have also applied to the length of term, whether it be fifteen-, ten-, seven-, or five-week sessions, or one-, two-, three-, or four-days-a-week formats, or day, night, and weekend deliveries. It was truly a blessing to have taught in each of these environments: They provided the inspiration needed to avoid complacency. Such format diversity served as evidence for my belief that experience is much more correlated with the amount of change and constant improvements (another phrase for lifelong learning!) made over time than it is with simply adding the number of years on the job.

It is important to note that while the formats have differed, many of the classes required the same basic strategies and concepts. The differences were rather in the specific activities (or the details) necessary to reach as many students as possible. As reiterated throughout this book, details like these only become truly relevant after the basic concepts are in place: Just as it is for the student, so it is for the teacher.

While the classroom provided the training ground for a journey through constant improvement in teaching strategies, learning was also significantly enhanced outside the classroom. Ten years of coaching basketball at the high school and community college level provided much-needed lessons on teaching and motivation, and I learned that players who may not have had much success in the classroom could learn multiple and complex offensive and defensive plays. In some ways, I saw on the basketball court what I already knew from the classroom—we are not dealing with students incapable of learning.

Prior to entering the field of education, four plus years of military training as a paratrooper and commissioned officer in the US Army also contributed significantly to my insights and development as an educator and leader. Just as in coaching, many soldiers who had limited success academically were able to learn and perform at a level well beyond the average person, and under some of the most stressful conditions imaginable.

Lessons learned from both these fields were valuable in the classroom setting and reiterated the importance of holistic student development—enhancing learning outside the confines of the actual course content. Observations as a military officer and as a coach confirmed that the "basics" that support growth and development are common to military, sports, business, and education. Starting with these commonalities can open the door for more effective collaboration between different fields or disciplines.

This short time in the military provided exposure to some of the most effective leaders and highest-performing teams in the country. As anyone who has been a part of a highest performing team—whether in the military, sports, business world, or any other organization—can attest, core values are perpetuated. These values, especially personal responsibility and accountability, are the foundation upon which constant improvement, innovations, and true excellence can thrive.

The successes of these teams do not rely on just one leader; training and preparation is such that leadership permeates throughout the entire team, creating an environment rich in adaptation and innovation. All that is required for readers to begin the journey to achieve results that may be elusive to the less prepared is a mindset cultivated by a desire and commitment to help as many students as possible have a maximum opportunity for success in the twenty-first century. It is this mindset and commitment that forms the foundational definition of a "professional" educator.

In describing my own leadership journey, the most valuable part of my life training and experience cannot be omitted: my parents. Their insistence to "say what you mean and mean what you say, without being mean saying it" taught me the importance of discipline, integrity, and treating everyone with respect, virtues crucial to success as a leader in inspiring others to action.

The core values instilled by my parents were invaluable in establishing a foundation upon which future training could be maximized. This advantage provided the motivation to help those who may not have had the love, support, experiences, or encouragement needed to increase their chance of success. As with all educators, using our training and experiences to help the less fortunate is our way of serving our communities.

It was this desire to positively impact as many students as possible that prompted acceptance of a division director position, which I served while being a faculty member. Eleven years later there was an opportunity to serve as instructional dean at this same college, providing a chance to impact even more students. Although it seemed like a major move from faculty to administrator, the basics, again, were similar: Simply put, teachers lead and leaders teach.

Working with one of the most effective leaders I have known in higher education, Dr. Linda Young, contributed greatly to my growth as an administrator. Using her thirty-plus years of experience as a college president, Dr. Young had assembled a team of some of the most committed and competent deans and directors in higher education. This time as dean was an enlightening experience that contributed greatly to my growth as an administrator. It was in this intense growth environment where I was challenged once again to move well beyond my comfort zone and expound upon the lessons learned in the classroom—it was a stark reminder that leaders never quit learning!

Six years later, there was yet another opportunity to work with an even greater diversity of faculty serving as Vice Chancellor for Teaching and Learning for the Alabama Community College System (ACCS). The primary focal point for this position was on creating a program which provides the supportive environment faculty need to inspire a greater degree of innovation in instruction, increase in performance indicators, and closure of achievement gaps. Using proven foundational strategies that had already been successfully implemented at the classroom, departmental, divisional, and institutional level, the Instructional Leadership Academy (ILA) was created and implemented across Alabama.

Although these strategies had already been shared with faculty members all across the country through workshops and conferences, ILA provided a format by which a year-long collaborative program provided faculty members with constant training, support, and encouragement. By tapping into the power of diversity of thought from cohorts of twenty-four faculty each, positive collaborations across disciplines spurred additional innovations. The added advantage of the program was that it allowed for data to be shared and celebrated regularly for leading indicators of learning, as well as analyzed and targeted for improvement in the case of the lagging indicators of course success, retention, and completion.

Prior to the formation of ILA, division directors at Wallace Community College—Dothan, AL (WCCD) implemented similar strategies through an at-scale philosophy and system called I-CAN: Improvement, Constant And Never-ending. This instructional initiative, which was first practiced throughout the science division, resulted in closing socioeconomic student achievement gaps while increasing retention and completion, with a 29 percent increase in fall-to-fall retention rates and a 49 percent increase in graduation rates in just four years.

It was through these courageous faculty efforts, combined with committed institutional leadership, that WCCD was selected as the top community college in the nation for student success in 2017 by the American Association of Community Colleges (AACC) due to the closing of socioeconomic student achievement gaps. This Award of Excellence by AACC was not due to implementation of a boutique program, or even a magical set of strategies unique to this institution but was the result of team approach to an intentional growth mindset focused on the primary reason for instruction—learning.

Two other community colleges in the state also followed this approach. The retention and completion results were strikingly similar for all three institutions: The average increase in retention and graduation rates at these three colleges was fifteen percentage points. Due to the low rates prior to the initiatives, retention rates at all three colleges increased an average of over 30 percent and graduation rates over 80 percent. WCCD saw a doubling of the graduation rate after just six years. These results speak volumes about the impact on motivation through sharing strategies and celebrating successes—especially when data can be quantified.

Our common approach to focus initial efforts on the top-ten enrollment courses and developmental courses also led to significant financial gains—the three colleges gained almost $4.5 million per year in additional combined tuition revenue due to increases in retention rates. Despite the fact that the average number of additional students successful in these courses was less than two per section, the at-scale approach resulted in a one-year total of over 2,400 additional successful students for the three colleges combined.

Although all too rare in higher education, these improvements are exactly what can be expected when a common group of people make an uncommon commitment to the goal of learning for both faculty and students. The key to the I-CAN initiative was not with each instructor using all the strategies discussed in chapter 6, but that each instructor was implementing something new to enhance learning for their students and sharing the results of these additions in divisional collaborations.

Action plans submitted to division directors provided the accountability needed to ensure participation by all, while also serving as motivation for future improvements through the sharing of results for the newly implemented strategy or activity. The increases in leading and lagging performance indicators surpassed all expectations and serves as a reminder of the power of faculty-driven innovation on student learning.

Reflecting on these experiences, it became apparent that the greatest advantage teachers can have in the classroom is the expectation of constant improvement for both themselves and their students—after all, when teachers quit learning so do students. Approaching each lesson, subject, position, and year as a kind of research project can instill a sense of positive restlessness which constantly seeks more effective ways to inspire learning in a greater number of students.

For me, this advantage stemmed directly from experiences prior to entering education, experiences where change was not something to be avoided but was a welcomed part of the growth process. This adapt-and-improvise approach was grounded in KISS, used mistakes as opportunities to improve, and required a constant reminder to Quit Taking It Personal (otherwise known as Q-TIP)!

When an interaction is taken personally, there is often an emotional reaction as opposed to a logical action. An emotional reaction is an obstacle when it is focused more on rectifying feelings than on taking advantage of a teaching/learning moment. Just as addressing a problem too aggressively may lead to hasty and careless decisions, so is it true for emotional reactions.

Leaders must allow time for more effective observations which in turn, produce more effective decisions. Applying the KISS acronym to this—teacher/leaders must model this approach by acknowledging mistakes when they happen and then taking ownership of them by making the necessary adjustments to improve. To maximize the impact of a teaching/learning moment, learn to Q-TIP.

Q-TIP may seem like an idiosyncratic method, but it can be a helpful guide to effective problem-solving. By using Q-TIP, we can focus on what can be changed to improve the situation, which is why it should be the default anytime leaders feel the need to emotionally respond. It is important, however, to recognize that change can be uncomfortable for some and physically painful for others. As Dolly Parton says, "If you want the rainbow, you've got to put up with the rain!" Since rain and storms are enough to discourage most people, it also helps to remind students (and ourselves) that they may need to do what they have never done in order to achieve that which they have never achieved.

Since we are wired to accept ideas that confirm our existing beliefs and reject those that do not, intentional effort is required to avoid personal biases and implement fundamental strategies for maximizing growth, and less emphasis on finding excuses to satisfy personal feelings. Q-TIP serves as a reminder of how much growth can occur when accepting responsibility to change, as opposed to excuses and blame.

This acceptance of personal responsibility is a basic premise to change and growth, and therefore, hope—it is not about what we are doing "wrong" or whose fault it is, but about what we can do to improve the situation. The default for a growth mindset always comes back to the same question—What can I do to improve?

Knowing that change, like grief, has a natural sequence of phases that must be traversed can help leaders avoid judgmental reactions. Although anger follows the initial phase of denial, we can celebrate the fact that we are no longer in the first phase—we are making progress! Following the anger phase, bargaining, depression, acceptance (buy-in), and ownership complete the traditional phases of change. The highest performing teams also go through an additional phase of "extreme ownership," in which team members accept 100 percent responsibility for anything impeding their attainment of the goals.

Some may be further along the phases of change, maybe a little closer to buy-in and ownership. But most of us started at some point with the first step—denial. Even though we may each move through the phases at different rates, we cannot remain in the denial phase because it undermines growth and improvement. This book provides strategies designed to help facilitate progress out of denial and through the remaining phases, while foregrounding the fact that the most important determinant of successful movement through the initial phases is mindset.

The television series, *Kitchen Nightmares*, is an excellent visual and auditory depiction of transitioning from denial to ownership in a very short period of time. Gordan Ramsay, a world-renowned chef and restaurant chain owner, has only one week to transform failing restaurants. This short time frame for change is a reason for a warning—the initial meeting is not about making personal connections, but about shocking the owners out of denial and into the bargaining phase as soon as possible. It is this strategy that prepares them mentally to be more receptive to suggestions, training, and change. The overwhelming degree of confidence, combined with a positive mindset, that is built through this process is evident in the final celebration stages of the show. Observing the transition through the phases of change in one episode can help leaders better recognize each phase.

Whether it is an administration expecting change from faculty, or faculty expecting change from students, it is helpful for those working to implement change to view any resistant behaviors as a part of a natural progression through the phases of change rather than a character flaw or lack of commitment. A positive mindset can enact—and withstand—major change. The minimum acceptable standard for a growth/leadership mindset is a commitment to "maximum effectiveness." To KISS it: If we desire to either promote or achieve a degree of diversity in completion well above the average institution, we must be willing to develop a level of commitment and persistence well beyond the average institution.

Although this level of commitment to growth and improvement will no doubt require more work initially on the part of all stakeholders, the work is in the service of developing a more effective system of teaching, which ultimately results in less work and frustration. Our responsibility as professional educators means we have an obligation to develop this commitment and persistence. In fact, we must use data and observations to constantly improve our system's effectiveness at inspiring and facilitating learning.

This book can help.

To develop commitment and persistence, you must ask two questions:

1. Do I want to improve?
2. Am I willing to feel uncomfortable while going through the changes required for improvement? Am I willing to put up with the rain in order to have the rainbow?

If you answered "yes" to both of these questions, you already have an understanding of the natural growth/change process and the initial insecurities and uncertainties that may accompany this growth. Realizing that the phases of change are a *natural* process can help provide the motivation we need to persist through the discomfort associated with change.

Next, you will need to *commit to persistence*. Since most instructors, and even administrators, chose to enter the field of education in order to make a difference in the lives of students, ask yourself if you have a quota on the number of lives you would like to positively affect. If you are reading this book, you probably already know there is no quota, that *constant improvement* is a core (and minimum) requirement, just as it is for a professional in any field. This is even more true in education, in which the end goal is all about learning.

Because constant learning leads to constant improvement, committing to persistence is required to develop the leadership mindset necessary to maximize results in the classroom. We need not spend time discussing what is wrong with our current efforts; we need to spend time learning what we can do to become more effective at training students for the twenty-first-century workplace.

By concentrating on what can be done to improve our situation, we will take advantage of the neuronal aspects of a growth mindset, which helps keep the negative emotional center of the brain disengaged. Since the latter portion of the brain undermines progress, our effort is intended to shift from blame and excuses to a more positive, proactive approach that plans for and expects future challenges and improvements. The small and immediate successes of this approach serve to further inspire additional changes and improvements while instilling a greater sense of hope for faculty and students. After all, isn't this the purpose of a high-quality education?

As a note, the topics in this book are not mutually exclusive. You will gain a deeper understanding as you progress through the chapters because the basic concepts gain new details, meaning, and relevancy.

***

A child born in poverty in the United States today is more likely to remain in poverty than at any other time in the history of this country. This is one reason family income is the best predictor of future life success for four-year-olds. If this country is to achieve the goals of the Completion Agenda, as well as a greater degree of social justice, we must provide a learning environment that intervenes in the lives of *all students*.

This learning environment must support the skills and values our students need for success in the twenty-first-century workplace, regardless of the circumstances of their upbringing. Being born into an environment that does not support attainment of these skills and values should not be a life sentence for our students. For professional educators and aspiring teacher-leaders, seeking and using more effective instructional and support strategies should not be an option but a moral imperative.

I hope that through reading this book, you will not only activate this imperative, you will—like a rookie learning fresh new ideas and practices—be activated by the excitement of new learning. To quote an old saying on the farm, "If you're green, you're growing. If you're ripe, you're rotting!" This book is written to help you always feel a little green and growing!

The following serves as a review of a few key concepts from this preface:

- In education, KISS serves as a reminder to always go back to basics when things seem to be in disarray.
- Great teachers lead and great leaders teach!
- As Dolly Parton says, "If you want the rainbow, you've got to put up with the rain!"

Acknowledgments

In addition to the many educators that inspired each of us, this book is also written in honor of Scott Dukes, a dear friend whose humor and passion for life continues to inspire me to this day. Although he left this world much too early, his endearing spirit lives on. It is also written in honor of my lifelong mentor and dad whose love of people, combined with a relentless work ethic, integrity, and solid values, has reminded me to *keep it simple, stick to the basics, harness the power of boldness, treat everyone with respect, and never, ever give up*—because if it is worth having or experiencing, it is worth sacrificing for.

I am forever indebted to the faculty of the Science Department at Wallace Community College—Dothan (WCCD) who courageously addressed student equity by adopting a learning-centered mindset focused on confronting each obstacle to student learning with the question—What am I doing about it? With the only unacceptable answer to this question being "nothing," these science instructors served as trailblazers for the college-wide I-CAN instructional initiative that was implemented several years later. These faculty aggressively reimagined a learning environment where academic success is not determined by how well students can compensate for ineffective instructional strategies and limited support, but where a more active and engaging learning environment backed by early, intrusive interventions empower students to persist to completion.

It was in those earlier years serving as division director for the sciences where there was a cultural transformation made possible by the adoption of a leadership mentality throughout the division, a culture founded on extraordinary levels of accountability and support. I had not witnessed such an extreme level of ownership since my early days of military service. The early efforts of these science faculty—Ann McCarty, Bob Speed, Cindy Robison, Julie Fischer, Janet Bradley, Kara Danner, and Todd Tolar—served to inspire others to action through their lead-by-example approach to teaching.

I am also indebted to all my colleagues at WCCD for their support and encouragement in the transition from twenty-seven years in the classroom to serve as their Dean of Instruction through their bold and transformative approach to instruction. Operating with a passion and purpose reserved for true professional educators, their insightful suggestions and criticisms helped drive an initiative focused on maximum improvements in a minimum amount of time, achieving the uncommon results expected when a group of common folks make an uncommon commitment to a common goal and mission of inspiring and facilitating learning. Their efforts were a testimony to the adage, *teamwork makes the dream work!*

A special thanks to those WCCD general academic division directors—Bob Speed, Chris Joiner, Delmar Smith, Rosemary Hunter, David Cobb, Kevin Meadows, Zack Kelley, Tara Estes, Lisa Sanders, Julie Fischer—who provided crucial leadership during the initial phases of our at-scale approach to instructional standards that focused on the top enrollment courses. In addition, the leadership provided by the associate deans—Kathy Buntin, Bill Sellers, and Leslie Reeder— served as an inspiration for others to follow. Backed by an instructional support staff of Holly Byrd and Tomi Sherlock, this instructional division provided the support needed to solidify the effectiveness and efficiency of adopting a leadership mentality throughout the organization. There are many examples offered throughout this book that would not have been possible if not for the efforts of these faculty and staff members, *as well as many others.*

I am truly appreciative of several others who provided assistance and encouragement in my early years in education. A special thanks to basketball coaches Jim Golden, Larry Easterwood, Eddie Barnes, and Johnny Oppert for allowing me the opportunity to coach in a sport I love, while also learning valuable lessons about learning and motivation outside the confines of the classroom. Imogene Mixson, Jim Kinney, Alan Borland, Elsa Price, John Michaels, Robert Tucker, and Gerald Bryant all served as mentors in my early years in the Science Department at WCCD and inspired both their colleagues and students with their passion for learning. A special thanks to

John Fergus for allowing me the honor to serve as a division director and for his contagiously enthusiastic approach to leadership through his deep love for people. I would also like to thank Stan Aman, who as dean of instruction provided the motivation for me to make a move from the classroom to administration.

The Aspen Institute states, "Every high-performing community college has a first-rate president," and this is especially true for WCCD where the president—Linda Young—has served as a president for over thirty years. Dr. Young, along with our state chancellor, Jimmy Baker, displays an unwavering commitment to student success and a willingness to do whatever-it-takes to develop a culture of teaching, learning, evidence, and leadership. I am forever indebted to these leaders, both of whom operate with an extraordinary level of purpose and passion for student success. Their ability to balance the administrative, political, and leadership aspects of their positions is second-to-none in higher education, and I am fortunate to have had the honor of serving with each of these transformational leaders.

I would also like to thank the deans at WCCD—Ashley Wilkins, Jackie Screws, Mark Shope, and Lynn Bell—each of whom served as a mentor in my early years as dean of instruction and provided the institution with a level of leadership all too rare in higher education. The lessons I learned by serving with this group are priceless. A special thanks to Dr. Wilkins for her patience as she provided valuable editing for my early articles on instructional and support strategies, as well as my mom, a retired English teacher, for her assistance in providing insights and edits for this book. I am also appreciative of the value Molly Gage has brought to this project through her relentless and insightful edits, as well as her understanding of the challenges faced by community colleges.

For the over 500 Instructional Leadership Academy (ILA) participants, as well as the ILA facilitators, I extend my utmost appreciation for their efforts to lead a transformation in instructional and support strategies at their respective institutions. Wendy Wood has been instrumental in assuring the ILA is working to constantly adapt and improvise for maximum effectiveness and is yet another reason for the success of this program.

Serving as a compensator for the mental stresses of personal and professional challenges, I would like to thank those on the morning basketball group for allowing me the opportunity to continue playing after thirty-plus years. Their humor and love for the game have provided an environment where physical activity, although a 5:30 a.m. commitment, has provided a much-needed outlet to the daily mental activities required of educators. A special thanks to my Army Paratrooper teammate, Tom Ziegenfelder, for his messages of inspiration which remind me that *"we don't stop playing because we grow old, we grow old because we stop playing!"*—George B. Shaw.

A special gratitude is extended to all those participants in my conference forum sessions over the years that have shared their desire for me to write a book, although this may have been more from the overwhelming amount of information shared in these sessions. However, it is my dear friend and mentor Dr. Terry O'Banion who first encouraged me to write more, and for that I am forever indebted. His messages of student equity and holistic student development through a learning-centered approach resonated with me and provided the inspiration to continue scaling-up effective practices. I would also like the thank Dr. John Roueche for the insightful conversations that always left me inspired and in awe. His wealth of knowledge, combined with a deep commitment to equity through higher education, has inspired me out of my comfort zone on many occasions.

I would like to thank my family for their patience and support over the years as it may have often seemed as if my responsibilities to them were overridden by my personal responsibilities toward education. To my daughter Anna and son Beau, I am truly grateful for your patience in adapting to the long hours required in those early years of teaching and coaching, while also providing me with your love and encouragement to continue serving others.

To my wife, Gloria, who accepted the responsibility of raising three grandchildren as she was approaching her last semester in nursing school, and at a time where I had just accepted a new role as dean, I remain amazed at her ability to provide the support, encouragement, and sacrifice needed for our household to flourish. Her willingness to return to school after over twenty-plus years in business is a testimony to her commitment to lifelong learning and serves as a reminder of the challenges our nontraditional students face, especially those single mothers and fathers working to provide a better life for their families while also pursuing their formal education.

Take care, stay well, and . . . Lead On!

. . . or as a 70's song is adjusted for clarity, *"Lead on. Lead on. Lead until your students' dreams come true!"*

Chapter 1

Mindset for Success

Many arguments are made in this book, but only one is truly fundamental: Your success depends more on mindset than skillset. This principle of leadership distinguishes the great leaders in almost every area of life, including the workplace.

MINDSET OVER SKILLSET

Understanding the power of mindset separated Coach Vince Lombardi from the rest of the pack. Lombardi, the head coach of the Green Bay Packers during the 1960s, led his team to three straight and five total NFL Championships in seven years, in addition to winning the first two Super Bowls in the 1966 and 1967 NFL seasons. All these accomplishments took place after the Packers won only one game in 1958, despite five future Hall-of-Famers on their team. In his first team meeting after assuming the head coach position at Green Bay in 1959, Coach Lombardi said, "If you aren't fired with enthusiasm, you will be fired with enthusiasm." He knew that maximizing attainment of any skillset required a positive mindset.

In sports, the concept of mindset over skillset is responsible for the underdog. The underdog is the competitor who plays but is not expected to win. They may be less fit than their competitors, less skilled, and they are certainly assumed less likely to win the prize. Yet, underdogs constantly surprise us. They play a game in which the odds are stacked against them, but they still stand a chance to win it all. If it were not for underdogs, the arena would lose

its meaning: They bring the madness to the March NCAA basketball tourna-
ment—anyone who has ever watched "One Shining Moment" knows it is the
underdogs that inspire sport.

Witnessing any situation—in sports or life—in which the human spirit
prevails over all odds can be rejuvenating. This kind of rejuvenation has
been experienced in many community college classrooms across the country. It can also be seen on the part of the students, who are typically underserved, underprepared, and under-supported. But it can also be seen on the
part of community college teachers. While it is easy to see how educators at
community colleges, frequently responsible for educating up to 300 to 400
students each year, are the most important leaders on campus, they are often
underdogs, too.

This is precisely why the first two chapters of this book are dedicated to
discussing ways to build leadership throughout the organization, which leads
to proactive problem-solvers throughout the organization. With a system for
leadership in place, innovation becomes the norm, and silos are abandoned in
pursuit of maximum learning—for both students and faculty.

GROWTH MINDSET

A mindset-over-skillset philosophy works best with a leadership mindset.
This kind of mindset is a contagiously enthusiastic growth mindset, and the
person who has it is focused on constant improvement and operates with a
positive, proactive, whatever-it-takes approach.

A commitment to constant improvement (lifelong learning, growth mindset, positive restlessness, etc.) is part of the definition of a professional in any
field and is key to maximizing effectiveness as a leader. As will be discussed
in chapter 4, the Japanese implemented this approach as a national movement after the devastation of World War II and moved from dead last in
economic performance among industrialized nations to second place in fewer
than ten years. The unprecedented growth depended on each citizen asking
themselves each day what they could do to improve something in their lives
or community—a concept called Kaizen ("change is good").

Two of the most successful coaches in college football and the NFL this
century, Nick Saban and Bill Belichick (University of Alabama and New
England Patriots, respectively), have used the Kaizen philosophy of constant

improvement with relentless intentionality in every aspect of performance. Working together, Saban and Belichick took a Cleveland Browns team, which, in 1991, had given up the most points in the NFL, to one that gave up the least number of points just three years later. Although all coaches may preach this philosophy of constant improvement, a culture of quality is not built around what is preached but what is practiced.

In education, the relationship between taking personal responsibility and a unified team effort should be constantly communicated with a courageous commitment and crystal clarity (CCs). This concept, which I refer to as CC'ing the mission, values, and purpose (MVP), serves educational leaders well. It is the responsibility of institutional leadership to obtain buy-in for the MVP of the institution, allowing for a more enthusiastic and purpose-driven approach to transformation.

The institutional leadership cannot expect faculty to buy into something they themselves have not fully committed to. The lack of at-scale commitment to constant improvement in instructional and support strategies hinders significant improvements in higher education the most, especially in those highest enrollment, first-year courses so crucial to building core competencies.

Achieving a culture of quality and inquiry requires not only a growth mindset and buy-in for constant improvement but a higher sense of responsibility—ownership. Achieving this level of accountability is much more natural when the "why" or relevancy is obvious. Dr. Terry O'Banion's book, *Launching a Learning-Centered College* (1999), emphasized the importance of focusing on learning as the primary gauge of effectiveness. This was a revolutionary idea to the old paradigm, whereby less prepared students are weeded out and the system was focused on knowledge transmission.

Constant improvement applies to every member of the team because the leader's ultimate responsibility is to develop more leaders. When a team adopts this growth mindset and mentality, it significantly enhances efficiency because problems are solved at the lowest level possible. This allows faculty to solve student issues and problems at the classroom level, leaving administrators the time to provide valuable training, accountability, support, and encouragement (TASE).

One of the most astonishing examples of solving problems at the lowest level possible occurred at Wallace Community College—Dothan, AL

(WCCD), when the secretary for the Allied Health division, who also handles student issues/problems for the Instructional Affairs division, made an observation about the lack of excitement in her position. Instructional departments had begun to make proactive approaches to student retention. As a result, she said, she rarely had the opportunity to deal with student issues because faculty were solving student problems. Looking for a more quantitative description, I asked her about how many students she used to see, to which she replied, "about three to five a week." Prompted for her current count, she said she was now seeing "about two or three all semester!"

DEVELOPING A GROWTH MINDSET

Training for a growth mindset means focusing on building confidence through early, small, and multiple successes, both individually and as a team. All highest performing team members have an extraordinary degree of accountability to each other and their collective mindset is always searching for a more effective approach. Leadership for these teams is evident throughout the organization, and not just in those with a leadership job title.

An environment conducive to this empowerment and development of students and faculty is one with crystal-clear expectations, an abundance of encouragement and support, and a high degree of personal and team accountability. In this environment, mistakes are opportunities to improve; therefore, only new mistakes are allowed. This is a place where inaction is met with encouragement and accountability, action with appreciation, and results and successes with celebration.

Words matter in this environment. Something as simple as adding the word "yet" to the end of every statement about what someone has not mastered does wonders in developing a growth mindset. What a powerful message this can be when students hear—and repeat—that they can't do math . . . "yet!" The word "yet" provides a quick reminder to students (and teachers) that accomplishments are processes that require practice, and, sometimes, more practice is all that is required.

Developing a growth mindset begins by asking ourselves the same question in response to any problem or issue: "What am I doing about it?" The only wrong answer is, "Nothing." Although skillsets are built over time, your mindset sets the limit for skillset development. By taking the lid off this limit to growth and assuming 100 percent responsibility for everything that happens or does not happen in your area of responsibility, skillset development is *maximized*. Once again, total responsibility does not equal total control, as there can be many unpredictable variables when dealing with people. But to achieve *maximum* growth, a leadership mindset means taking responsibility and making things happen, not waiting for them to happen.

With this kind of growth mindset, you are always looking to improve. Because you are always looking to improve, you approach problem-solving positively, which keeps the brain proactive and feeling more in control. The reduced stress that results from this neuronal perception of control allows for quicker and more focused action, leading to further improvement. The people with this mindset realize their efforts control their level of success (internal locus of control) and are more likely to persist with additional efforts to achieve additional successes. Acceptance of personal responsibility is a result of this mindset and is crucial to maximizing personal development.

Keep in mind, however, that the research referenced in this area of behaviors, habits, and mindsets is from a *cognitive* approach and does not address underlying issues of causation. Realizing students learn more effectively when their unique strengths and personal identities are supported, educators can take advantage of the vast amount of neurological and pedagogical research supporting more effective strategies for teaching and learning.

It is much easier to make connections with students when there is a basic understanding of the challenges they face, something essential to inspiring change. As it is with most natural processes, the more information educators have regarding the cultural challenges of generational poverty and a greater understanding of the realities of a survival environment, the less judgmental they will tend to be.

When it comes to habits, which are formed by behaviors and mindsets, there is just one question that must be asked—How productive are your habits? This self-reflection question may very well be a prerequisite to igniting change and developing more productive behaviors and mindsets. Although even small changes can be difficult for some, changing an entire mindset or system and any unproductive cultural behaviors that may accompany that mindset/system may seem overwhelming for most people. As with any change, the focus is on small, continuous steps fueled by a burning desire and motivation to improve.

Education was changed forever after Dr. Carol Dweck's research revealed that motivation and achievement were driven by peoples' underlying beliefs about their ability to learn. Those most likely to persist and put in more time and effort were those who understood that effort leads to higher achievement, while those with a more fixed mindset tend to believe that their efforts do not control success and intelligence.

As you can imagine, the fixed mindset is a major deterrent to accepting more responsibility for action since the focus is more on the seemingly overwhelming obstacles that are outside the internal realm of control. A Brookings Institute study from 2012 found that 30 percent of Americans did not think their efforts controlled their success, and the percentage was even greater in European countries. This study reiterated the need for leadership which encourages action and celebrates growth and successes.

According to Dr. Ruby Payne, in her book *A Framework for Understanding Poverty* (2005), those among the lowest third of income levels in the United States identify common attributes and behaviors associated with a fixed mindset. For example, a belief in destiny, that efforts do not control success, was one of the beliefs common to this group.

It is evident that closing student achievement gaps require developing a growth mindset in students, as well as in faculty and staff. Much of this mindset depends on understanding how to study and learn effectively—for both students and faculty. Having the additional tools and ability to work more effectively leads to an increase in performance, which in turn leads to a greater sense of internal control that constant improvement is personally achievable. These insights can provide the empathy and understanding needed for teachers to seek more effective approaches to learning as they realize beliefs, behaviors, and mindsets are a *natural* result of a student's environment but can be changed with consistent and intentional strategies.

"Just 57 percent of America's children graduate from high school with decent grades and having avoided teen parenthood and criminal conviction. By the time children can be reasonably held accountable for their choices, many are already behind because of choices their parents made for them" (Brookings, 2012). How will students know what a good choice/decision is if they are not educated on the facts and evidence of successful mindsets and behaviors?

A greater sense of hope comes from understanding there are things they can do to improve their success in life, just as there are strategies faculty can use to improve student success. On the other hand, a message that variables outside the control of students will dictate their success in life is one of misery, despair, and hopelessness. As it has been since the beginning of time, when the human brain is faced with factors it truly cannot control the human spirit must find a way to compensate. This is the essence of hope—there is always a way to improve, although it may require adopting a new system of behaviors and beliefs, something much easier said than done.

According to 2013 research from the Brookings Institute, people who follow three rules have a 98 percent chance of avoiding poverty. The rules? Graduating high school, getting a full-time job, and being at least twenty-one and married before having children (Haskings, 2013). In a personal polling of over 1,000 high school students from 2012 to 2014 in orientation sessions at WCCD, not a single student raised their hand when asked if they had ever heard of these three rules. It is no surprise that stacking the odds against success starts with poor decisions earlier in life that lead to an external locus of control where students feel that their personal efforts do not impact their success.

Should a "high-quality" education withhold information that can help students make better decisions that lead to increased chances of success in life? After all, how can students be expected to make better decisions in life if they are not provided the information that would allow them to do this? With so many odds stacked against many of our students, our goal should be to maximize their chances of success by maximizing the effectiveness of the learning environment in teaching critical thinking skills.

A simple activity to engage students in relevant conversations on how to increase their chances of success in life is to have them work in groups to determine a top ten list of behaviors that do not require talent or academic expertise in order to be effective. This empowering activity can provide a starting point for students becoming better students, parents, employees, and people. Knowing there are things they can do daily that can significantly improve their chances of success in life can provide the hope many students need to accept more responsibility for their decisions and behaviors, also moving them closer to a growth mindset.

A recent study by Vanderbilt University (Salisbury, 2012) labeled people with a growth mindset "go-getters." The dopamine bursts in these folks followed a path leading to areas of the brain (striatum and ventromedial prefrontal cortex) responsible for reward and motivation. Their natural high occurred with progress, even just the perception of progress. In essence, "go-getters" brains were addicted to the dopamine-induced euphoric feeling of accomplishment.

This Vanderbilt study even explained ways we can train our brains' dopamine neurological pathways to be more like those of go-getters. For example, we can create to-do lists chunked into smaller tasks, or we can learn new material by using 3 × 5 cards with information chunked into smaller segments on each card. The cards make it much easier to take short study breaks throughout the day, allowing for multiple study sessions and constant review. This method further enhances learning, or the perception of progress because the number of cards yet to be learned is constantly decreasing, and this provides motivation for further learning.

For the "slackers" in the study, the dopamine took a different neurological pathway. It went to a part of the brain (anterior insula) responsible for emotions, feelings, and risk perception. These folks got their natural high from avoiding a problem—the fear of failure prevents a more aggressive approach to problem-solving. This helps explain the natural tendency for these people to make excuses and place blame. Dopamine in the insula was also associated with a decreased desire to work, even if it meant the subjects would earn less money. In the real world, "slackers" tend to be more minimum-minded and are more concerned with the minimum required to maintain employment, and not the more aspirational focus of a growth mindset.

A greater sense of hope comes with an understanding there are things students can do to improve their success in life, just as there are strategies faculty can use to improve student success.

Unfortunately, when people take a victim mentality approach and blame others for their problems, the initial high of not feeling responsible to act is followed by longer-term feelings of disappointment and/or increased anger toward the system or person(s) perceived as responsible for their problems (external locus of control). This reduces motivation for action and is associated with the fixed mindset belief that effort does not control success and that external factors outside their realm of control determine success.

Since a brain in a fixed mindset state tends to have a much lower sense of control, the brain is held hostage to its surroundings and is much less likely to implement positive action. It is much more likely, when forced into action, to be emotionally reactive and not logically active. Emotions are more quickly satisfied with excuses than action, especially when that action carries with it a perceived degree of risk. This is the case unless the brain is trained to assume more responsibility for its own health and well-being.

The growth mindset of go-getters encourages them to always seek solutions to problems in their life (and thus make continual progress). Those with this mindset understand there is a solution to every problem whether they have found it yet or not, and they are constantly working to find solutions through continued efforts. However, putting forth constant effort is a by-product of realizing that if you want more than the average person has, you must be willing to do more than the average person is willing to do. By focusing more on the goal, go-getters are less likely to be distracted by those frightful little things (obstacles) that hinder progress.

The growth mindset is in contrast to the fixed mindset of slackers who are more prone to resort to making excuses; in their mind they are clearly not responsible for their own success because they do not perceive their efforts control this success. This mindset, if not trained differently, can lead to a perpetual cycle of despair. That is why teachers must intervene. Because eliminating socioeconomic achievement gaps in higher education is the first step toward reducing and reversing the cycle of poverty, educators' efforts must be directed toward providing an environment more conducive to self-motivation and relevant learning.

Students' feeling of despair can be turned into a feeling of hope when educators teach behavior skills and values essential to success in life. Many students need to be taught that it takes discipline to do that which others find too uncomfortable: "You can suffer the pain of disappointment or the pain of discipline—the choice is yours," writes Jim Rohn.

Of course, teachers can easily fall into the trap of a fixed mindset when they realize archaic practices of the past are not effective for an increasingly larger number of students. The emotional attachment to a system can be difficult to break, especially for those more prone to a fixed mindset themselves.

As opposed to the growth mindset, the fixed mindset does not strive to learn and identify ways to improve as this would require more effort.

To KISS this concept, the continued use of only traditional methods of instruction for nontraditional students is a recipe for disaster. The increasing percentage of underserved students requires the most effective learning strategies that support natural neurological functioning. In other words, when we teach the way the brain naturally learns, learning becomes easier and more motivating.

A recent study by EAB's Student Success Collaborative found in their interviews with students that the students want advisors and faculty to support them in cultivating grit and a growth mindset, while also cultivating life skills that can enrich their experiences. It is imperative faculty practice and model these same mindsets, skills, and behaviors in order to more effectively teach these principles. However, it is important to note that some people may have more of a growth mindset in a certain area even if it is not practiced regularly in other areas of their life.

One of the biggest self-imposed barriers students place on themselves is believing they are not cut out for college. This should not come as a surprise as the traditional environment of higher education was typically designed for those already prone to a growth mindset and supported by an upbringing and resources designed to promote this mindset, making an education seem more like an initiation for those attempting to compensate for their shortcomings without knowledge or training in how to do this.

Cultivating grit and a growth mindset in our most at-risk students and reversing their self-defeating mindset means training them to view early setbacks as challenges to overcome and not proof of their inferiority. Creating opportunities for early successes while focusing on developing supportive relationships can provide much-needed confidence for these students. Their need for early successes cannot be understated, neither can their need for an abundance of encouragement to accompany these early successes.

WHATEVER IT TAKES TO LOOSEN THE NUT

Years ago, three of our grandchildren came to live with my wife and me. With turmoil in every aspect of their lives, they had many bad habits that needed to be broken and growth mindsets that needed to be developed.

Homework posed a particular challenge, and their refusal to complete their homework, especially on the part of the eleven-year-old twins, drove my wife crazy.

One evening I was watching the original 1973 *The Exorcist* movie in our living room when one of my granddaughters walked behind me on the way to the kitchen. In a way, it was perfect timing: The actress in the movie was tied to the bedposts, hair in disarray, face cut, growling, with her head spinning. When my granddaughter asked, "Oh my, what movie is this?", I replied without even turning around that it was about "some 'ol girl who wouldn't do her homework." I continued watching the movie as she proceeded to get her water from the kitchen and return to her bedroom.

My wife came into the living room about thirty minutes later and asked what I had told our granddaughter. When I inquired as to why she was asking, she replied with astonishment, "She is in her room doing her homework!" After I told my wife what I had said, she replied that my response was just cruel. I informed her that she may call it cruel, but I call it effective—after all, where was our granddaughter now? In her room, doing her homework.

Of course, a certain approach may work at one moment and not work the next moment. What works with one twin may not work with the other. What works in the day class may not work in the night class, but if you are willing to do whatever it takes, you will find what works, at least for that moment. Little successes like this can fuel motivation for future success. In fact, a person with a leadership mindset holds that it is not always about immediately achieving an end result, but about accomplishing the *first step*, or, to put it another way, just getting the rusty nut loose from the bolt.

Although there was a powerful emotional *connection* made between the movie and my granddaughter, that connection was probably based on negative emotions. I do not advocate for using negative emotions as a first step because I prefer to invoke more positive encouragements. However, whatever works at the moment to make a stronger emotional connection increases the chances of success in this *collaboration* phase—even if that phase is about doing homework.

The *celebration* phase followed immediately when my wife and I latched onto my granddaughter's efforts and provided an abundance of encouragement and appreciation in an attempt to ensure future improvements in her willingness to complete her homework nightly. This example also serves to highlight the value of the three Cs to success for leaders—connect, collaborate, and celebrate.

Too many times in higher education we are quick to label strategies as spoon-feeding, entertaining, or high-schoolish. In reality there is only one question: Was the strategy or approach effective at inspiring and facilitating learning, at developing more of a growth mindset? This is the foundational question accompanying any activity, strategy, or decision, and it forms the basis of the learning-college concept. Labeling strategies in any way can stifle innovation and lead to an increased siloed effect among faculty, where they revert to isolationism and discontinue collaborations that could help other faculty improve their effectiveness. As the Lumina Foundation states, "It is not just that learning matters. It matters most of all!"

Sometimes the learning process cannot start with a simple warning or verbal directive; it must start instead with students (and/or faculty) doing something they may have never done before. Because this may be well beyond their comfort zone, the toughest part is simply getting started. It is imperative, therefore, to focus on the first step (meaning, it's time to KISS it—maybe with a more positive tone of Keep It Simple . . . Sweetheart!).

However, once the rust is broken loose and a new high-impact strategy is implemented, the intrinsic motivation of sensing improvements is usually enough to encourage continuation. Therefore, once the nut is loose, we can proceed to accomplishing the goal of removing the nut. For my granddaughter, the horrifying scene in *The Exorcist* was enough to get the nut loose and to provide the incentive needed to move beyond her comfort zone and accept responsibility for learning by doing her homework.

Developing a growth mindset requires the use of a term that may very well be one of the most underused aspects of learning: encouragement. The most impactful time a person can provide encouragement is anytime another person is learning a skill for the first time, regardless of the skill. Attainment of that first step, no matter how small, must be accompanied by an abundance of encouragement and appreciation.

When my granddaughter started doing her homework, my wife and I showered her with encouragement to continue and appreciation for taking the first step. In terms of homework, my granddaughter then realized that her efforts did control her success—what a great "rust protector" a growth mindset can be! This approach resulted in newfound confidence for her: She was motivated by her own success and our encouragement to build on her first step, and she proceeded to finish high school with an A/B average.

ENEMIES OF CONSTANT IMPROVEMENT

In higher education, administrators, educators, and other would-be leaders face many enemies to enacting their efforts of constant improvement. Often these enemies are simply modes of thought that hinder efforts to take the first step of getting the rusty nut loose from the bolt. Sometimes they are just words. Once they are identified as such, leaders—and those who seek to lead—can begin to develop and enact strategies to thwart enemies and activate effective solutions.

One of the biggest enemies to a commitment to constant improvement is three little words: *I will try*. When someone says this, it usually means they will try if it is not too difficult or too uncomfortable. The Marines understood the empty promise associated with trying and communicated it in their slogan, "We don't accept applications—only commitments." The slogan argues for an enhanced feeling of responsibility toward the mission and goals of the organization.

To assist with purpose-driven commitment, faculty leaders, as well as all other positions of leadership at the institution, should follow the acronym CC-MVP: Constantly Communicate with Crystal Clarity and Courageous Commitment to the Mission, Values, and Purpose of the Community College. The injunction is long, but it can help potential leaders keep a laser focus on the sacred responsibility bestowed upon educators as warriors for social justice. It provides a crystallized understanding and reminder of the "why" behind the community college mission.

The acronym is also pertinent to the committees upon which you probably serve because many committees are responsible for setting institutional standards. The word *constantly* cannot be understated. What has been said about teacher-leaders is true: If your folks cannot give a good impression of you when you are not around, you are not repeating yourself enough!

The next major enemy of constant improvement responds to the most used word in mission statements around the country: excellence. The enemy of the pursuit of excellence is the *good*. When, in response to redesigning courses with proven high-impact instructional strategies, an instructor says, "I'm good," it usually means they do not see a need or a reason to improve. After all, they are already "good." We often accept this response in education, but imagine telling a medical doctor about a new technique or strategy that would cut their mortality rates in half, only to have them respond with, "I'm good. I am comfortable with my own strategies and don't need to learn new ones."

Effective leadership is often uncomfortable. This is why it is important to ground leading strategies in data and evidence rather than personal feelings or comfort. Eliminating the option of responding with "good," or at least identifying *good* as a potential enemy to constant improvement, can help educators who want to lead hold themselves accountable. By avoiding the fixed mindset of *good*, educators practice the growth mindset of constant improvement, a leadership mindset where "maximum" *is* the minimum standard.

Often, educators face the common enemy of ignorance. They simply do not know what excellence looks like or how to strive for better than good. The grading scale used for decades in education clearly labels letter grades with a description: A—excellent, B—good, C—average, D—below average, and F—failure. Although an A is considered excellent, we have to ask what, according to data, "excellence" means. Sometimes, when we explore this question, we realize we do not really know what excellence looks like (either for us or for others). Sometimes our exploration reveals that our perception of our own excellence, or effectiveness, does not match the data.

Educators can begin to adopt a leadership mindset by simply acknowledging the discrepancy between perception and data or evidence and seeking easy or inventive ways to monitor progress. Leaders can begin this work by simply sharing data with colleagues. For many, it may be what loosens the nut from the bolt and gives others the courage to take the first step to transformational change.

The relative relationship between good and excellence is also clear in sports. Many players considered excellent in one league quickly realize there is another level of performance and competition in another league. I witnessed basketball players that were the top player on their high school team struggle in the high-octane environment of college basketball. Competition in sports, much as it is for the business world, provides the incentive for constant innovation and improvement. This is an incentive that must come from within for educators, as we internalize the importance of our mission. When we develop the leadership mindset throughout our team or department, we make accountability to the team an incentive for constant improvements.

The process of understanding our relationship to excellence depends on putting excellence in perspective. Consider the words of Cabrera and Phillips, who referenced Indian River State College and Miami Dade College ($1 million Aspen prize winners), in a 2019 article: "Being an excellent community college (or, for that matter, an excellent four-year college) means closing the persistent gaps in college-degree attainment that rob our communities, employers and our economy of needed talent." Miami Dade is an incredibly inspiring example of institutional excellence: By focusing on determined leadership throughout its institution, Miami Dade eliminated the completion gap entirely.

At Miami Dade, leaders are so focused on the mission that they are too busy doing what must be done to hear all the noise about how it cannot be done. They are too busy making things happen to be slowed down by those on the sidelines watching things happen (or even wondering what happened). Miami Dade shows us that uncommon results become common when a common group of folks make an uncommon commitment to a common goal and purpose, one step at a time. The multiplying effects of at-scale participation, no matter how small the steps, combine for the kind of uncommon results that qualify as excellence.

Building leadership throughout all areas of the college is the primary goal of the Community College Leadership Program (CCLP) at Kansas State University. This doctoral program is based on the work of John Roueche, whose pioneering efforts "created and managed the most substantive and most successful CCLP in the history of higher education at the University of Texas at Austin, which graduated over 600 leaders—one-third women, one-third minorities—and more than 200 presidents" (Kinnamon & O'Banion, 2021).

The program goal of CCLP of expanding a culture of leadership, and not just management, throughout all levels of community colleges is a formidable and worthy goal that is in direct alignment with the AACC's goal of preparing leaders at all levels within institutions. This book serves to inspire this leadership at the classroom level and in all areas of instruction.

The last major enemy of progress will be familiar to most because we have all used them, one way or another: excuses. In my classroom, successful life skills and behaviors were discussed by offering students a quote a week. The quotes opened up discussion on life skills (including collaboration and learning), and students were asked on the final exam to write down their favorite quote. In every term, the majority of students chose the same one: "You can make progress or excuses, but not both at the same time." This quote resonated with students and provided the inspiration they needed to become more positive and proactive.

Although excuses provide the temporary emotional relief of not having to endure the uncomfortableness of change, they are an obstacle to progress and growth. It is absolutely amazing what can be accomplished when excuses are replaced with a leadership (growth) mindset that never loses—it either wins or learns! Because this mindset is always seeking the next level of performance, learning occurs even in a "win" situation by using insightful reflections on what can be done to continue improving performance.

Two ex-Navy SEAL instructors, Leif Babin and Jocko Willink, who are now consultants for businesses on leadership and team building, once told a story. As instructors, they had teams engage in a constant string of boat races, requiring the teams to carry 200-pound World War II–relic inflatable boats atop their heads to shore, paddle the boat to a specific marker, dump themselves out of the boat and get back in, and carry through a path to the endpoint back on land. One crew seemed to win almost every race while another came in last almost every time.

Out of frustration, the instructors swapped the team leaders in each boat crew. Over the next hour, the once-losing team won nearly every race, while the once-winning team performed well, but never took first place. On the initially losing team, the toll of losing resulted in personal excuses and blame. But when these same team members were inspired to greater efforts by a more contagiously encouraging leader, they began to win. The transformation was so obvious that Babin and Willink tried the technique with subsequent classes, and they witnessed similar results.

When asked what accounted for the differences in performance, both instructors said it came down to two things: first, the new leader of the losing team was able to get his team to believe in themselves; second, neither team allowed for bickering. This, from my perspective, shows that amazing things can be accomplished when we disallow excuses and put a positive mindset in its place.

Babin and Willink described this profound lesson as directly as would be expected of Navy SEALS: "There are no bad teams, only bad leaders."

Adopting this mindset is paramount for leaders of *highest*-performing teams in any field where *extreme* ownership is an expectation, although it may well exceed the existing mindset of those who are not as far along the change (growth) spectrum. Internalizing "bad" as a situational and temporary state, the brain is motivated to focus on the more positive aspects of how to improve/grow that on the emotional and fixed mindset where feelings of insecurity may hinder growth efforts—hence, the acronym Q-TIP.

Babin and Willink pointed out the team's transformation was contingent on believing in *themselves*. But a leadership mindset can happen even when you do not have the faith and confidence to take your own performance to the next level. When surrounded by a team of positive, can-do people—or when motivated by a positive, can-do leader—everyone's mindset is more likely to change. Even when your belief in yourself is limited, your belief that your team can achieve anything can be a powerful boost to self-confidence.

To expound on an adage, "If you hang around three positive, can-do people—you will soon be the fourth!" Although no one teacher can change education in a community, the potential is unlimited when a group of faculty commits to a common goal of providing a more equitable environment for success through enhanced instructional and support strategies.

There are numerous examples in sports, military, business, and education where ineffective teams were converted to more effective ones by effective leadership, and the focus of these examples is usually on one leader initiating and championing a change in mindset. Although administrators or managers can help maintain the cultural environment of the institution, it takes a leadership mindset to move that culture to a higher level of effectiveness while leading faculty outside their comfort zone and well beyond self-perceived limitations. This is why Dr. Terry O'Banion (2015) refers to a need for "leaders who will disturb the universe."

In education, there are some instructors who can take the best strategies and find ways for them *not* to work, while others (teacher-leaders) can take much weaker strategies and find ways to make them work. Some can attend the best conferences and come back with nothing, while others can attend the worst conferences and come back with something positive to implement. The goal of leadership throughout the team is to develop mindsets that always seek to improve.

It will come as no surprise to hear that many believe the difference in effectiveness of these two kinds of people is a growth mindset focused on constant improvement, a mindset that seeks the next level of effectiveness. Although the skillset can be built over time, mindset sets the limit for just how much improvement can occur. This is also why educators often say that changes in education occur as fast or slow as the leadership allows. This is another reason faculty should be considered the most important leaders on campus—both for their students and their colleagues—as the efforts of teachers are the most crucial in improving learning.

If we take away the excuses, it becomes clear that the most effective teacher-leaders are the ones who do not wait for things to happen, they make things happen. They seek solutions, not excuses; they reinforce commonalities, not differences; they focus on positives, not negatives; and they see opportunities where others see crisis. Teacher-leaders empower others with their focused sense of urgency and purpose, while providing the support and encouragement needed to transform mediocrity into excellence!

Just as teachers must obtain buy-in from students for the learning process, it is the responsibility of instructional leadership to obtain buy-in from faculty for constant improvement. This instructional leadership may be in the form of more formal positions such as department chair, instructional designer, division director, associate dean, or dean, as well as the informal teacher-leaders who inspire others through their positive attitude and exceptional work ethic.

The impact that finding commonalities can have on a team or institution is conveyed by Gardner (1990) who observed that "leaders, whose task it is to keep a society functioning, are always seeking the common ground that will make concerted action possible. They have no choice. It is virtually impossible to exercise leadership if shared values have disintegrated." Finding this common ground with faculty requires the ability to inspire and motivate. As community college leader John Roueche said at a session of the 2013 annual American Association of Community Colleges (AACC) conference, "Can you motivate the faculty? If not, whatever you're trying to accomplish can't be done. Leadership is about motivation and inspiration." It is also about "tenacity and not giving up," he added.

When it comes to community college leadership, John Roueche should know because he has set the bar with his pioneering work of creating and directing the most successful CCLP in the history of higher education. At the 2013 AACC conference, Dr. Roueche commented on the importance of leadership skills throughout the faculty ranks—"Faculty may be well trained in their discipline, but community college teachers must also know how to motivate students who don't want to be there or are having academic issues. They need to collaborate with groups of students who have historically performed poorly in school."

Achieving this goal will require leadership mindsets that are always looking to adapt and improvise, while using the common ground of enhancing learning to facilitate more effective collaborations between departments.

Most readers know that the viability of the community college system depends on our *collective* ability to overcome the challenges of student learning and provide a skilled, educated workforce for the twenty-first century. A proactive leadership mindset throughout the faculty ranks is a prerequisite for meeting this challenge and maximizing return on investment for taxpayers, as problems are solved at the lowest level possible. Every leader's responsibility is to create an environment conducive to self-motivation with a high level of personal accountability for results and, of course, to express appreciation for the effort. This is as true for faculty as it is for those in an instructional leadership position.

To reflect on some key points from this chapter:

- A leader's ultimate responsibility is to develop more leaders committed to the community college mission.
- A growth mindset could also be called lifelong learning, constant improvement, or leadership mentality, and it defines a professional in any field.
- Growth mindsets are developed with TASE.
- All highest performing team members have an extraordinary degree of accountability to each other and a mindset that is always searching for a more effective approach.
- "You can suffer the pain of disappointment or the pain of discipline—the choice is yours."—Jim Rohn
- Achieving a culture of quality and inquiry requires not only a growth mindset and buy-in for constant improvement but a higher sense of responsibility—ownership.
- Little successes fuel the motivation for future successes. It is not always about achieving the end result immediately, but about accomplishing the first step—just getting the rusty nut loose from the bolt.

- As the sign says on the wall of a Chick-Fil-A restaurant in Atlanta, "How do you know someone needs encouragement? . . . they are breathing!"
- As has been said about teacher-leaders, if your folks cannot make a good impression of you when you are not around, you are not repeating yourself enough!
- Progress or excuses—the choice is yours.
- The most effective teacher-leaders are the ones who do not wait for things to happen, but make things happen.
- When we teach the way the brain naturally learns, learning becomes easier and more motivating.
- Although the skillset can be built over time, mindset sets the limit for just how much improvement can occur.

Chapter 2

Establishing a Leadership Ethic

When it comes to the Completion Agenda, boutique programs that do not have a laser focus on learning and constant improvement attempt to compensate for instructional ineffectiveness. Many times, this lack of boldness in enhancing learning also describes the accrediting process. Instead of requiring constant improvement from all employees, colleges attempt to compensate by highlighting policy compliances needed to achieve accreditation. The focus may become more on the tasks and less on innovation. The same checklist-of-tasks approach hinders learning in the classroom, as well as hindering innovation and at-scale improvements for the institution.

IT'S ALL ABOUT THE LEARNING

For the Completion Agenda to succeed, there must first be an institutional understanding that all institutional efforts are about learning. This will require a significant paradigm shift for higher education because, traditionally, the responsibility for learning has been left up to the students. In fact, in that traditional paradigm, if a student arrives at an institution without the tools, resources, or preparation to succeed, they are typically deemed "not college material"—a description that suggests to many students, especially the most underserved, that the process is more initiation than education.

In order to achieve equity of opportunity through higher education, educators must apply strategies that inspire and facilitate a deeper, more meaningful learning for a more diverse group of students. A failure to apply these strategies hinders social justice and deprives a segment of the population of the benefits of higher education, both economically and intellectually.

Developing a leadership mentality (through the growth mindset) throughout the faculty ranks is a prerequisite to modeling this same mindset for students, allowing for maximum student success. This mindset finds a possible solution to every problem, as opposed to the fixed mindset, which finds a problem with every solution. Leaders realize there is a solution to every problem whether one has found it yet or not, and this provides the motivation to continue adapting and improvising.

It would be prudent at this point to emphasize that the use of the word *leader* does not always indicate a titled position of leadership. It describes the mentality of accepting 100 percent accountability for everything that happens or does not happen in one's area of responsibility. This acceptance of accountability does not indicate 100 percent control but simply the responsibility to respond to any issue or obstacle impeding improvement and success.

There are many variables associated with learning that are beyond the control of the teacher. However, this does not save the educator from constantly seeking ways to maximize student learning and success. The essence of leadership is getting others to perform at a higher level long enough so they can gain the confidence needed to assist others in their journey to constant improvement.

Reaching the level of extreme ownership and accountability for action should be the goal of all leaders who strive to produce the highest-performing teams. They have an intentional plan for addressing variables within their control and devise a way to compensate for that which they cannot control. One may not be the fastest, strongest, or smartest, but can compensate by having a persistent work ethic. If one does not feel he/she is the most naturally talented, the chances of success can be increased by adopting more successful behaviors and habits.

Teachers may not be able to control the type of students in their classes or the prior preparation these students have received, but teachers can control the strategies they choose to use to compensate for a lack of prior skills training. This also relates to two very important life lessons: that life is not always fair and that you will not always have the advantage. However, what you can do is *create* advantages through more intentional use of proven strategies, better time management, and practicing a growth mindset.

As previously mentioned, leaders do not wait for things to happen, wish they would happen, or complain things don't happen—leaders make things happen through a willingness to compensate by creating advantages. The common denominator for compensating for variables outside our control is one psychology says is the best indicator for future life success at any age—the degree of self-discipline. In other words, the capacity to adapt and improvise (change) as needed to compensate for disadvantages and maximize successes is a key to success.

As pointed out in chapter 1, in response to any issue or obstacle impeding student learning, a leader always asks themselves the same question: "What am *I* doing about it?" The only wrong answer? "Nothing." This one question—and its forbidden answer—has the potential to transform higher education by forcing a more proactive mindset focused on expanding learning.

Instead of waiting for things to happen, to change, or to improve, a teacher-leader works to make things happen. If they do not know what to do, a teacher-leader asks what their colleagues are doing about the issue. Or, they research into what other colleges are doing. With the vast amount of information and research available online, not knowing what to do is no longer an option.

Accepting that *doing nothing is not an option* is the mandate that promotes the growth mindset needed to overcome the challenges of the twenty-first-century classroom. This is just another way to say *constant improvement*. Any attempt at all, whether by an educator or a student, and whether successful or not, is a stepping stone to further improvements: We never lose—we either win or learn.

In education, just as in sports, the only true losers are the quitters. Doing nothing is a way of quitting, quitting on students, colleagues, institutions, states, and the nation. Since faculty are on the front lines of student performance, they must be part of the solution—they must become leaders and adopt a positive mindset—or they are part of the problem.

MINDSET FOR EFFECTIVE LEADERSHIP

As has been said many times: One thing you need to know about leadership is that there is more than one thing you need to know about leadership. Combine this statement with the reality that leadership would be easy if it were not for the people, and you get a sense of the challenges associated with leadership. Because of the many variables associated with leading a diverse group of people, it is important to keep the discussion of leadership as simple as possible—back to basics and foundational principles. Just accepting the fact that there will always be issues when dealing with people can be enough to reduce the frustration of unexpected situations.

It is this extreme level of diversity (people, issues, problems, obstacles, etc.) in leadership that creates so many dichotomies for teachers. Trying to develop relationships essential for building rigor but not crossing the fine line of professionalism is one example. Balancing people and the mission requires leaders to care about both, but not so much that one is sacrificed for the other. The key to maximizing effectiveness is pushing the envelope enough for maximum growth, without pushing students into a survival mindset that undermines learning. This list below is only a fraction of the dichotomies or contrasts teachers/leaders must practice and balance on any given day.

- Covering essential content, but not so much content that the quality of learning is compromised.
- Providing hands-on guidance, but not so much that students become dependent on you.
- Providing activities that challenge the students, but not so much they resort to apathy.
- Providing grades to monitor learning, but not so much focus on grades that it becomes more about task completion and less about learning.
- Holding students accountable for the rules and boundaries, without being so rigid that it curtails learning and does not allow for adjustments based on the human factor.
- Having an aggressive approach to problem solving, but not so much that you overlook key variables and the impact on others.
- Providing enough information for students to solve the problem, without providing so much that it diminishes critical thinking.

Recognizing dichotomies and addressing old paradigms are keys to adopting a more effective leadership mindset for the twenty-first-century learning environment, followed by implementing more effective strategies. Most people respond to the possibility of change with denial, and this continues to exist until old paradigms, and the excuses that operate within them, are challenged. We challenge old paradigms with the same process we use to stimulate critical thinking in the classroom, by posing questions that challenge students to examine a problem from different viewpoints. It is also an essential step in self-reflection, reflection that is vital, but sometimes uncomfortable, to a teacher-leader's efforts to constantly improve.

Leif Babin and Jocko Willink's book, *Extreme Ownership* (2015), although referencing more business-oriented issues, address concepts directly related to maximizing improvement for all teachers, coaches, parents, and leaders. The same holds true for their follow-up book, *The Dichotomies of Leadership* (2018). It is here once again that Jocko and Leif apply principles of leadership that are directly related to everyone who has an influence on others, and especially teachers as they are responsible for building leadership for future generations.

In the conclusion of their book they point out that a good leader must be "confident but not cocky; courageous but not foolhardy; competitive but a gracious loser; attentive to details but not obsessed by them; a leader and follower; humble not passive; aggressive not overbearing; quiet not silent; calm but not robotic, logical but not devoid of emotions. . . . A good leader has nothing to prove, but everything to prove." What leaders are usually trying to prove is that the problem *can* be improved upon, providing much-needed inspiration for those yet to realize possible solutions.

Understanding that striving for this balance requires constant change and that resistance to change is part of a *natural* set of phases that must be navigated in order to achieve buy-in, and ultimately ownership, is key to avoiding judgmental responses attributing resistance to personal weaknesses. This natural process to achieving buy-in is as true for faculty and staff as it is for students.

The acronym Q-TIP reminds us to "quit taking it personal" when dealing with inevitable resistance, helping us avoid engaging negative emotion centers in the brain that are not productive to growth/learning. By "not taking it personal" teachers can maximize the teaching and/or learning moment, something much more difficult to do when emotional reactions override logical action. Sometimes, just helping faculty move out of their traditional silos and remember that quality of education is determined by *combined* faculty efforts is enough to remind instructors to Q-TIP.

Unfortunately, anger typically follows denial. This is usually an emotional response to a depletion of what we see as our logic (others further along the change spectrum may view emotional responses as excuses). Without an additional supply of logical responses, anger is directed toward the message or the messenger—often the one facilitating the change. This anger and the words that accompany it are a direct challenge to the commitment level of leaders and provide a reminder to Q-TIP.

The simple but profound saying, "sticks and stones may break my bones, but words will never hurt me," becomes more relevant when we internalize its broader meaning. Allowing the words of others to control us to the point where we cannot control ourselves is a recipe for misery. However, the good thing about the anger phase is that it signals progress: When we feel anger, we're no longer stuck in the first phase of denial!

The mindset for effective leadership and change management operates with a greater sense of purpose and passion for learning—a purpose that allows for a more naturally encouraging environment of growth. This mindset is always the default approach for leaders, as such positive boldness and restlessness are highly contagious and the epitome of leading by example.

THE COMMUNITY COLLEGE MISSION— ACTIVATING THE LEADERSHIP MINDSET

Community colleges are the only postsecondary institutions in this country that promise the opportunity of an education for all. Although open-access policies seem to provide an equal opportunity for all Americans to achieve the dream of maximizing opportunities in life through higher education, the socioeconomic achievement gaps leading to unacceptably low completion rates tell a much different story.

The very purpose of mission-led education is to effectively inspire and facilitate learning with a diverse group of students. It is not hyperbole to state that the strength and economy of our nation directly depend on the ability of community colleges to fulfill this mission. The challenge requires a commitment to constant improvement with a leadership mindset that uses the most effective and efficient instructional means possible to increase learning and close achievement gaps.

Addressing student success is much easier outside the instructional division, which is why so many more boutique programs have been created through student services. Many of these are designed to compensate for what is not occurring in the classroom. However, for institutions committed to closing achievement gaps, the instructional division is where the most significant improvements in student performance outcomes can be made.

Research in Tennessee (Sanders & Rivers, 1996) revealed that students placed with highly effective teachers for three years in a row significantly outperformed comparable students on a mathematics assessment (96th vs. 44th percentile). A Dallas, Texas study referenced by Peter Pillsbury in his 2016 article, *The Impact of Teacher Effectiveness on Student Achievement*, found that students who had an outstanding teacher for just one year remained ahead of their peers for at least the next few years. It also found that when a student had an ineffective teacher, the negative effect on achievement was not fully remediated for up to three years. This research is supported by additional data and should provide a crystallized understanding of the importance teaching strategies can have on the lives of our students.

The Rand Corporation's report, *Teachers Matter: Understanding the Impact on Student Achievement* (Opper, 2019), confirmed that teachers matter more to student achievement than any other aspect of schooling. This report found that a teacher is estimated to have two to three times the impact of any other school factor. It also found that effective teachers are best identified by their performance and not by their background or number of years of experience and that their impact is greatest on those students who suffer the most educational disadvantages in their background.

Given the outsized influence of teachers in the educational lives of students, it is surprising that so few initiatives seem concerned with promoting and refining instructional leadership. In 2019, Civitas Learning conducted an analysis of over 1,000 student success initiatives around the country, and classroom instruction and/or instructors were not even mentioned in the top five initiatives. This same study found that 40 percent of the analyzed student success initiatives had little or no measurable impact on student success overall. Of the 60 percent of initiatives demonstrating a positive impact, 20 percent were not effective for certain student groups. This apparent trend of institutions seeming to avoid initiatives directly related to classroom instruction is probably one reason why so few student success initiatives have produced significant results.

> Effective teachers are best identified by their performance and not by their background or number of years of experience, and that their impact is greatest on those students who suffer the most educational disadvantages in their background.

Since research overwhelmingly supports the impact of effective teachers on closing achievement gaps and creating a more equitable opportunity for success in higher education, we must implement more effective instructional and support strategies. To KISS it: Creating better students requires using better strategies, which in turn helps develop better teachers. The Civitas study that showed instructional initiatives were not even in the top five most common initiatives provides clear evidence for the lack of progress in closing achievement gaps.

It has been said that there are two types of colleges—ones that prepare students for the future and ones that allow faculty to live comfortably in the past. From a leadership standpoint, that second statement could include instructional leaders and administrators who sometimes also live comfortably in the past. Understanding the phases of change and what is needed to nurture a natural progression through the phases of adopting the growth mindset is one of the greatest assets for college leaders and one that can facilitate the move from the past to the future. As faculty begin to internalize and understand that it is all about the learning, they begin to accept constant improvement in instructional and support strategies as a natural process and adopt the growth mindset crucial to constant improvement.

But how can we foster and develop this mindset in ourselves and our students? The first step in implementation is clearly communicating the community college mission and philosophy and holding faculty and staff accountable to it. In this instance, Yogi Berra's words have proven true: "If you don't know where you are going, you probably won't get there." A maximum number of faculty committed to a common goal and purpose is essential to attaining the momentum needed to achieve uncommon results and close achievement gaps.

Once this mission is communicated and understood, the second step requires personal accountability from all team members. This can be as simple as asking faculty members to regularly share *new* activities or strategies they have implemented that enhanced learning. This "spotlight on learning" can be accomplished via email to all divisional members. The leaders in these discussions will surface with the most innovative, positive, or encouraging responses. Not only will these posts/emails provide evidence of constant improvement where it matters the most—in the classroom—they will also be a great motivator for those reluctant to try new strategies.

The third step in integrating a leadership mindset requires showing appreciation intentionally and persistently. To maximize the effectiveness of these appreciations they should be personal, specific, and sincere (also known as PSS). They should also be communicated regardless of the context. In this, we should remember the story of the NFL quarterback (QB) who, on an end-around sweep, gets a block from the running back (RB), allowing him to gain additional yards. On his way back to the huddle, the QB tells the RB how much he appreciated the great block.

A lineman nearby heard the QB and asked why his block did not get appreciated, especially since he flattened his defensive counterpart. The QB replied that the lineman "did that all the time." To this, the lineman replied, "Do you want me to keep doing it!?" This story reminds us that expressing appreciation—even to those who are already doing the work—is a great way to ensure desirable behaviors continue.

The most effective community college faculty, like those at Miami Dade, gauge their success by how effectively they work with their most at-risk, underserved students. For many of these faculty members, their passion for the community college mission—to provide a truly equal opportunity for success—acts as the motivation for their personal commitment to constant improvement. This passion and purpose for the mission can serve as an internal "forcing function" that initiates change and accountability to results. For others, however, an external forcing function, such as accountability to an accrediting agency, may be required.

Accrediting requirements can make resistance futile. Consequently, these requirements can serve leaders working to minimize the time spent guiding faculty and others from denial to acceptance to ownership. It is important to note, of course, that when faculty feels there is too much outside accountability regarding student learning, it is usually a sign that there is—or has been—too little accountability coming from within.

Integrating a leadership mindset is so important because a lack of leadership trickles down to the classroom. Often, faculty who do not act as leaders use ineffective teaching strategies in their classrooms. This is mainly because they do not require constant improvement for themselves, something that could result from a lack of understanding of the mission to inspire and facilitate a greater degree of learning. When faculty do not require it for themselves, they do not require it for their students, either.

A passive, teacher-centered learning environment focusing mainly on knowledge transmission challenges even the most motivated and prepared students, but it can be devastating for first-generation, low-income students. Research shows these students often lack the social, academic, financial, and/or moral support of the more affluent and better prepared students. In general, ineffective teaching strategies are most overwhelming for the first-generation, low-income, and minority students. Their success is further limited if the material is perceived as irrelevant to their life or life success.

Ineffective teaching strategies lead to one of the most destructively discriminatory practices in our country: They hinder empowerment and upward socioeconomic mobility for those who need it most. This has negative future generational effects. Evidence of the inequality is reflected in the socioeconomic student achievement gaps, which exist largely because of instructional effectiveness gaps, gaps which could be minimized by focusing on maximum engagement, relevant instruction, and supportive relationships.

Most of us already know that passive instructional strategies enlarge achievement gaps. What we do not always recognize is that these same gaps can be reduced with more active student-centered strategies. Implementing student-centered strategies is another effect of choosing mindset over skillset: It does not require complicated skills to implement a new, more engaging strategy in the classroom; it simply requires the courage to try something different and outside of our comfort zone.

Faculty skill develops as they assess their strategies and constantly adjust them based on data. Educators need not rely solely on lagging indicators such as program completion, retention, and end-of-term course success rates.

There are many leading indicators to assist the educator. Unit test averages, test score increases from one exam/assessment to another, number of assignments submitted, number of student-generated questions, and other signs of increased engagement and communication provide more immediate forms of data and observations that can be used to make future decisions concerning activities and strategies. These forms of data are also readily available to teachers, although there may need to be a more intentional emphasis on collecting this data.

It is important that teacher-leaders continue with proven strategies even if students initially resist. Many students have ample experience taking a more passive role and may resist strategies designed to engage them more in the learning process. In cases such as this, teacher-leaders must guide students through the phases of change, demonstrating relevancy and giving encouragement. In some cases, students perceive they are learning less even though final exam scores show increased understanding and performance. Teacher-leaders also need to make a concerted effort to avoid the pitfalls of overusing certain activities, which may lead to complacency through habituation.

Eliminating less-effective strategies is a priority from the perspective of a leadership mindset because a culture of quality is not determined by what is preached, but what is practiced and tolerated. This is why the RTAD report indicated a need to *"courageously* end ineffective teaching strategies" (emphasis mine). Just as with terms like *good* or *excellence, effective* and *ineffective* are relative terms. Strategies that some educators may label as effective in their early phases of change become less and less effective compared to higher-impact strategies for deeper learning.

This scenario is another classic case of "doing better once we know better." Starting with smaller, more impactful reflection activities proven to increase students' motivation to learn is a great way to gain the confidence needed for future improvements. The added advantage is that high-impact strategies such as the five discussed in chapter 6 not only increase retention of course content but also help develop those life skills and behaviors crucial to success in the workplace.

In general, the inability to scale up proven instructional and support strategies has stagnated completion rates and undermined diversity efforts, while failing to effectively meet the community college mission. Just as the requirements of accrediting agencies serve as a forcing function to potentially minimize broad resistance (and maximize collaboration and innovation), we may require a forcing function to end ineffective teaching strategies and maximize the use of more effective high-impact strategies.

Regular meetings or email collaborations to share newly implemented strategies for enhanced learning may be perceived as a less-mandated form of a forcing function. Many times, such as the recent COVID pandemic, there are sudden and more drastic situations that inspire educators to do what needs to be done, although those same changes may have been avoided in a previous environment. As with any personally stressful situation, the question is whether the situation left one bitter or better. For teacher-leaders, the latter supports constant improvement.

LEADERSHIP MINDSET DEVELOPMENT

Many of us are well aware that numerous hours of professional development activities have failed to produce a transformation in instruction. As already pointed out, some faculty strongly resist implementing changes to their pedagogy. A lack of focus on a unified goal and purpose (an inability to CC-MVP) to facilitate action will always hinder professional development efforts.

Because you are reading this book, you probably already know you can be the change you want to see in your department, your school, and your community. Your enhanced strategies may directly impact as many as over 300 students each year! However, by inspiring just five colleagues to action, you can raise the total number of students impacted to as many as 2,000 each year—that is 20,000 over a decade!

Even a single person dedicating themselves to developing a positive growth mindset of constant improvement and lifelong learning can make a difference. By adopting a positive, restless mindset, you begin to more effectively and efficiently develop new and adjunct faculty, as well as help ensure maximum learning for all students. Faculty development requires a team-oriented environment where learning permeates throughout the entire team. Regular collaborations become more intentionally focused on what has been done—and what can be done—to enhance learning across the department, division, or institution. Once again, the only mandate for this leadership mindset is to avoid doing nothing.

The impact of leadership mindset development became evident a few years after the implementation of the I-CAN instructional initiative at WCCD.

New faculty were required to submit end-of-term (as well as end-of-year) reflections on their experiences and observations, followed by a collaborative session with their mentor and department chair. One of the most mentioned observations involved the constant discussions in the hall, at the water cooler, or in the faculty lounge about student learning and success. These discussions often involved student success data because we deliberately accumulated as much data as possible to monitor improvement efforts, thereby meeting the basic requirement of all accrediting agencies—constant improvement based on empirical data.

Another common comment from these new faculty sessions was about the high level of positivity displayed by faculty at WCCD. A primary factor in developing a more intentionally positive approach was the emphasis placed on the course evaluation question regarding whether the student felt the instructor "truly cared for them as a student." In fact, this one question had double the value on the faculty performance dashboard as compared to the other questions on the survey. Although there will be more discussion of these course evaluation questions in chapter 5, the "caring question" resulted in the most favorable comments from students while setting the stage for a learning environment rife with encouragement, support, and appreciation— an environment where a leadership mindset could be taken to the next level.

However, it is not just about dedication. It is also about personal responsibility. By assuming ownership of decisions based on empirical data, the leadership mindset helps those who adopt it to avoid the pitfall of complacency that comes from basing decisions on personal comfort, feelings, or beliefs. The American College President Study (ACE, 2017) provided the longest-standing and most comprehensive study of presidency by reviewing the responses of 1,546 college and university presidents. Results showed an acknowledgment that performance indicators related to student progression and completion, as well as improving outcomes for the most underserved groups, were of greater importance than traditional indicators of status and prestige.

The surveyed presidents also indicated that improving student success through data-informed decisions would grow in importance. Yet, only 12 percent reported that institutional research data was important to their future. This disconnect hinders efforts to improve student learning. The lack of consistent data is one of the biggest obstacles to obtaining faculty buy-in to change. In fact, data must be constantly presented and analyzed for ways to improve.

A leadership mindset uses data to inform and course-correct, but when data suggests mistakes, teacher-leaders do not blame or fault. They take advantage of the opportunity to further improve the system by analyzing ways to ensure the mistake does not happen again (which, as we know, is learning at its best). This type of proactive and constructive default approach is the leadership mentality's greatest asset. The empowerment that comes from assuming responsibility for mistakes and coming up with a plan of action to prevent future mistakes allows faculty to reach levels of personal accountability reserved for true professional educators. This mindset does not lead to just identifying the problem, but it leads to implementation of a possible solution.

Solutions are a key part of adopting a leadership mindset. Identifying a problem without a possible solution is like dumping a problem in someone else's lap and expecting them to deal with it. It is more respectful for the person with the problem to identify a possible solution when presenting it. If a possible solution cannot be identified, they can request ideas and assistance.

It is important to note that mentally assuming 100 percent responsibility does not mean having 100 percent control. Accepting anything less than a leadership mindset of 100 percent responsibility leaves room for excuses, allowing us to justify inaction by claiming the situation falls into that small percentage that allows for some "wiggle room" on anything we do not want to address or initially feel cannot be addressed.

An example of this years ago was in class attendance, a problem that for years our WCCD science division claimed was out of their control—until faculty implemented frequent assessments. When the second highest enrollment course on campus, introductory biology, implemented frequent assessments, it resulted in a 31 percent increase in attendance. Over 900 students attended class each year who previously had not been attending.

Just as with students, faculty are more likely to accept responsibility for what they feel they have control over. In fact, this sense of control was the motivation for this book: when we have more effective strategies, techniques, and activities in place, we are more likely to feel in control. We can have a plan B, as well as a plan C and D, depending on how many tools (strategies/activities) we have in our toolbox. It is much easier to adapt and improvise with a range of high-impact and proven tools most effective for the task at hand. Our success as faculty depends on the tools we use—just as it does for those working on home improvement projects. Having the right tools for the job is absolutely crucial to effective and efficient outcomes.

When effectively instilled in the culture of the institution, a leadership mentality fosters total student development while closing student achievement gaps, increasing enrollment and retention diversity, and unlocking the gate to equal opportunities through a high-quality education. This culture of quality guarantees maximum success because *doing nothing is not an option.* Doing nothing, especially with overwhelming research in effective instructional and support strategies, is a major breach of academic and professional integrity.

It should be clear that success is not as much about specific strategies, but a specific mindset focused on learning, a mindset that accepts exceptional standards of self-accountability with a positive can-do attitude of whatever-it-takes, and does so with a contagious resilience and passion that inspires and encourages faculty and students alike. Although this mindset can be initiated by a passionate and committed leader, it takes an entire team operating with a leadership mentality throughout the ranks to accomplish that which eludes less committed teams. This is the mindset Babin and Willink spoke about when describing how SEAL trainees began believing in themselves *as a team.*

For most teacher-leaders, the need for leadership within a group is obvious, just as it is for students in a class. Maybe it is a continuous string of negative comments, silence in the room, or hesitation caused by a fear of failure. If you have identified this need, never, ever ask permission to take on the role—you will know when it is time. Many times, this can be as simple as interjecting a positive comment centered on what can be done to improve—in other words, providing situational leadership with words of inspiration. It has been said that "misery loves company," which is just as true for positive proactivity.

The ultimate goal of the most effective leaders is to inspire and create more leaders, and this is something that is easier to accomplish in a positive and supportive environment. This is the path to transformational change, which is more natural and continuous and less of a perceived personal threat. This leadership throughout the organization is effective for progress in departments and institutions, as well as for students in our classes. After all, most leaders do not set out to be leaders—they set out to make a difference with a purpose and passion for the mission that exceeds their own personal comforts.

The power of leading with initiative was reinforced for me on a trip with our grandchildren to Chattanooga, TN, to visit my daughter. We stopped at a swimming hole along the way where folks were jumping off fifty-foot cliffs. My grandson (twelve at the time) wanted to hike up the hill to watch them jump, followed by one of our twin granddaughters (thirteen). I agreed to walk up there with them while my wife and other twin granddaughter stayed at ground level. Upon reaching the top, my grandson said he thought he might want to jump. I told him we were going back down the hill and if he wanted to jump, he didn't need to think about it—he should just do it!

Well, he launched off the cliff! As we looked over the side of the cliff we could see him smiling in the water and telling his sister to "come on down." Since she was the most fearful of the three grandkids, I knew I was safe with someone to walk back down with me. As I ask her to walk with me back down the hill, she said she thought she may want to jump. "Yeah, right," I said to myself.

After telling my granddaughter the same thing as her brother, she was encouraged enough that she launched off the cliff, too! Now, there they were, both in the water, smiling and yelling for me to "come on down, Papa!" Just as I was about to start walking back down the hill, I hear, "Come on Papa. You can't think about it—just do it!" Using my own words against me was merciless encouragement. Against my better judgment—and with a total disregard for my age—I jumped!

Upon reflection after our return home (even in families—especially in families—reflection is crucial to learning), we discussed leading and following and how the best followers often make the best leaders. The first leader was my grandson, followed by his sister, who then took the lead in providing me with the encouragement I needed to follow her.

As you have no doubt noticed in this example, the power of encouragement cannot be overstated! Just as the word says, *encouragement* "puts the courage into" others. "When a brave man takes a stand, the spines of others are often stiffened," wrote Billy Graham. It is this courage that can propel the human spirit out of its comfort zones and beyond self-perceived limitations. These small, repeated successes build confidence for larger future successes.

One exercise my wife and I used to do with our four grandchildren after a family trip was to have them think of what they experienced that was new to them on the trip, what they tried or did new or what they saw that was new to them. The more ideas each one thought of, the more it stimulated responses from the other three. Not only did this reflection exercise generate more of an appreciation for our experiences, but it enhanced our ability to recall this information at a later time—extending warm memories much like photos or videos can do. More importantly, it sent the message that change can be good and that having the courage to try something new offers a chance at personal growth and empowerment.

Developing ourselves so we can better assist others in their development is an essential part of being a leader. While coaching ninth grade basketball in the late 1980s, I had a player I will call John. John was the star of the team in terms of ability and skills and did not miss an opportunity to remind the other players of that. He scored thirty-two points in an away-game loss just before Christmas holidays to a team we were to play again at our home gym after the holidays. The game required two practices over the holidays for preparation. John missed both practices without prior notification or reasons for the absences.

The next time I saw John, it was game day, and he was in the locker room getting dressed. I reminded him of the rule that for every practice a player missed, he had to sit out an entire half. He had missed two practices, so he would be on the bench for the game. After he replied that he might as well not even dress for the game, I reminded him of the rule that an unexcused absence from a game results in removal from the team. "It looks like you have a decision to make. I hope to see you on the bench supporting your teammates because they need your leadership and encouragement." A few minutes later, John emerged from the locker room to join his teammates.

John sat on the bench and watched his teammates play a hard-fought and close first half. By the second half, he provided more encouragement and motivation for the team. His encouragement must have worked because at the end of the game, we had won by twelve points to the team to which we had lost when John scored thirty-two points. From that point on, John began involving his teammates more in the games, even though it meant he scored fewer points. His sacrifice allowed the other players to become more confident and they began to believe in themselves as a team. John discovered the keys to leadership: sacrifice and encouragement. More importantly, the entire team realized how it feels when everyone is unselfishly focused on a common goal.

This should be the goal of every classroom—for everyone to learn as much as possible from each other in the time they have together. Constantly evaluating and reflecting on this learning help avoid mission fatigue and provide motivation for future learning. At any given time, anyone on the team or in the class can step up and provide a leadership moment with something as simple as turning a negative into a positive, a criticism into an appreciation, a crisis into an opportunity, a difference into a commonality, or even asking a question to generate thought and collaboration. Recognizing this leadership behavior is a great way to ensure it will continue, whether within a classroom, department, or institution.

It is time for community college faculty to raise the bar and seek a leadership mindset. Such a mindset results in a cultural transformation that abhors socioeconomic achievement gaps and provides encouragement and support for educational innovations. The change must be driven by a desire for a new status quo supported by the entire institutional administration, a status quo that accepts nothing less than constant and never-ending improvement in instructional strategies.

Within a culture of accountability that requires constant improvement and relentlessly communicates encouragement, professional development activities lead to real improvements—action. The first step requires taking on the leadership mindset. The next step requires practicing positive assertion, which sometimes means turning negatives into positives, differences into commonalities, and crises into opportunities. The last step requires developing a supportive, encouraging, and appreciative system of accountability for action, followed by celebration of successes.

These actionable steps lead to more collaboration and motivation, and they are driven by data. The cycle of *train* → *try* → *data* → *revise* directly aligns with accrediting bodies' primary requirement to "close the loop." In the next chapters, you will be shown how you can take these steps and implement this cycle.

Key points for reflection from this chapter:

- The efforts of teachers are the most crucial in improving learning.
- Most leaders do not set out to be leaders—they set out to make a difference with a purpose and passion for the mission that exceeds their own personal comforts.
- In response to any issue or obstacle impeding student learning the question is always the same for a leadership mindset: "What am I doing about it?" The only wrong answer? "Nothing."
- The one thing you need to know about leadership is that there is more than one thing you need to know about leadership.

- The essence of leadership is getting others to perform at a higher level long enough to gain the confidence they need to assist others in their journey to constant improvement.
- Educators often say that changes in education occur as fast or slow as the leadership allows.
- To maximize the effectiveness of appreciations they should be PSS.
- When faculty feels there is too much outside accountability regarding student learning, it is usually a sign that there is—or has been—too little accountability coming from within.
- Ineffective teaching strategies are most devastating for the first-generation, low-income, and minority students, leading to one of the most destructively discriminatory practices in this country today.
- If your institution or department seeks to obtain above-average results, then it must be willing to commit to doing more than the average institution or department.
- There are two types of colleges—ones that prepare students for the future and ones that allow faculty (and administrators) to live comfortably in the past.
- Although your enhanced strategies may impact as many as over 300 students each year, inspiring just five colleagues to action can raise this total number of students impacted to as many as 2,000 each year—or 20,000 over a decade!
- To KISS it: Creating better students requires using better strategies, which in turn develops better teachers.
- As with any personally stressful situation, the question becomes whether the situation left one bitter or better. For the teacher-leader the latter of these options supports constant improvement.
- It is much easier to adapt and improvise when using a diversity of high-impact and proven tools most effective for the task at hand.
- Never, ever ask permission to lead: You will know when it is time.
- Doing nothing, especially with overwhelming research in effective instructional and support strategies, is a breach of academic and professional integrity.

Chapter 3

Paradigms for Success

Although, over the decades, the pace of change in almost every area of our lives has been dramatic, archaic, and persistent, higher education paradigms continue to hinder efforts to meet the Completion Agenda and community colleges' promise to provide a high-quality education to all interested Americans. Allowed to go unchecked and unchallenged, these paradigms will continue to hinder the growth mindset needed to improve learning for both students and faculty.

Faculty did not invent the current educational system; they simply adopted the one already in place. However, it is our responsibility as higher education faculty and administrators to lead the change and innovation required to ensure a skilled and educated workforce. This can be difficult to do because of the resistance to change described in previous chapters. Faculty and administrators give many different reasons for the lack of at-scale instructional improvements, but the following represents a sampling of the statements from the archaic paradigm that holds us back.

"We are teaching *college* students; they should know how to . . ." (also known as, "We are teaching *adults*; they should know how to . . .")

Many of us have probably heard these statements from our colleagues. Some of us may have even repeated them—I know I once did! These statements hail from a traditional paradigm that viewed students as solely responsible for their own learning. This outdated view does not capture what it means to obtain an education at the twenty-first-century community college. It is important for us to remember that many instructors—many of us, in fact—were raised in a time where communication and critical thinking were required just to get through life. It is often difficult for some of us to relate to a generation where technology and society have decreased the use of these crucial core competencies.

It is not just a problem of technology. Successful life skills were more abundant and common in a time when knowledge was limited and therefore more valued. The easily accessible information of today combined with the decrease in life skills have created a challenge for traditional teachers. Understanding this on a personal level may help facilitate our own paradigm shifts and provide a greater degree of insight into our more resistant colleagues.

Inspiring our students, as well as our colleagues, to action sometimes requires understanding the obstacles they face. We must teach students how to *become* responsible adults and college students—to develop the total student, one who is prepared for the workplace and/or higher education. The faculty making the most significant gains are the ones capitalizing on proven effective instructional and support strategies, while incorporating essential life and study skills training.

To KISS this: We cannot continue to teach nontraditional college students using only traditional methods of knowledge transmission. The primary focus of traditional instruction focused on covering two topics: content and then testing. Unfortunately for educators reliant on these methods, real learning occurs with the reflection and review activities that connect these two topics. This work was traditionally left up to students to achieve on their own.

Today, we can do it differently. To start, a department or team can complete a simple exercise of listing what students should be able to do upon enrolling at college. This can provide keen insight, even if team members think many of these behaviors or skills should have been learned at a much earlier age. Often, faculty list simple skills such as following directions, reading comprehension, writing ability, proper study habits, and others. Then, ask your team the following powerful question: Do the majority of your students show up with these skills already in place? If the answer is no, ask your team for the plan of action to address the deficiencies.

To make sure the exercise is fully completed and serves to empower educators, take each skill and provide an activity or strategy to intentionally address deficiencies. Performing this as a team or department allows for more diversity of thought and innovation; it also provides an incentive for action which expands learning and reminds us we must teach the students we have and not the ones we wish we had.

"SO, YOU JUST WANT ME TO LOWER THE RIGOR/STANDARDS?"

This is a typical response given by many faculty when first addressing performance indicators such as graduation rates, retention rates, and course success rates. However, as high-impact strategies that lead to immediate increases in learning are implemented, faculty begin to realize the power of adopting a paradigm shift for this question. The shift also allows for reflection on where standards came from, how and why they are upheld, and what their purpose might be. This reflection is another one that benefits from diversity of thought and should be intentionally discussed as a department or team.

To maximize learning, we must shift away from a belief that adopting different standards is the same as lowering standards. If we focus instead on constant improvement in instructional strategies, we will find we cannot help but raise the standards of instruction and the quality of learning. In the classroom, this means we provide students with a level of TASE that exceeds the level of standards set in the course. Anyone can set high standards, but it takes a professional educator to provide a level of TASE well beyond those set standards. In sports this is called "practicing harder than you must play"— it is an old adage that applies to both teachers and students.

Although the topic of rigor will be addressed in the pages that follow, the paradigm question forces us to ask another question, which serves as a hypothetical for reflecting on the meaning of "high standards," as well as how these standards pertain to teacher and students. If instructor A constantly complains about poor student attendance, preparation for class, and motivation for learning, while instructor B teaches the same course with much higher rates of student attendance, preparation for class, and motivation for learning—which instructor has higher standards of performance/learning?

Things in nature tend to take the path of least resistance, that is why getting students to do what they need to do but do not want to do or know how to do is the essence of teaching/leading. The evidence this has been accomplished is directly related to the performance outcomes achieved, as indicated by instructor B in the aforementioned example. A paradigm that expects students to achieve learning and growth on their own alleviates the motivation for instructor A to implement more active and engaging instructional strategies that enhance learning.

This paradigm favors the students with effective prior preparation and has led to persistent achievement gaps, as successful students are the ones who already know how to self-motivate and compensate for less effective teaching strategies. It is possible that this instructor does not know what can be done to enhance motivation for learning, just as many students do not know how to learn.

The only way this question about lowering the standards would be a logical assumption is if there were not any strategies that could improve student success and lead to a deeper and more meaningful learning experience (or if one had reached the pinnacle of effectiveness and had no further room for improvement). However, the upcoming chapters offer a myriad of strategies, activities, and techniques that can significantly increase student learning and close achievement gaps. There is always more to learn and always room to grow.

"I *TOLD* THEM WHAT TO DO; IT'S NOT MY *FAULT* THEY DIDN'T DO IT!"

Faculty often offer this response to questions regarding student performance. The first problem with this statement is that telling is not necessarily teaching. We must provide a level of teaching well beyond just telling because many of our students are underserved and underprepared, both in life and in academic skills.

However, these students are not incapable of learning. With the vast amount of knowledge at our fingertips today, it is imperative we focus efforts on building critical-thinking skills and behaviors crucial to success in the workplace, higher education, and life itself. Effective teaching fosters effective learning, and effective teaching in the twenty-first century requires a much greater skill set and commitment to constant improvement in instructional strategies than simple knowledge transmission.

The second problem is that it misplaces fault. In today's community colleges, it is not about "fault." In fact, there are almost too many programs, policies, and people to blame. "Not my fault" is a defense mechanism set up to defy the need to change. Accepting change means accepting responsibility for improvement. Faculty who accept both typically experience much greater improvements in effectiveness regardless of their years in the classroom. These are faculty leaders.

A leadership mindset realizes constant improvement depends on constantly adapting and improvising for maximum effectiveness, a process that can lead to maximum growth in a minimum amount of time. Faculty can try this out for themselves. Instead of discarding an activity or strategy after the first use, faculty can ask what can be done to improve the technique—thereby practicing both the art and science of teaching. The sooner this process begins, the quicker the toolbox of effective strategies can fill.

Leading, teaching, parenting, and many other difficult tasks would all be easy if all it took was just "telling" in order to get compliance. Imagine a college football coach during the Monday morning news conference saying, "It is not my fault the players didn't play hard. I told them to. It is not my fault they were running around like they didn't know the plays. I gave them the handouts and told the players to study them."

What would we think of a pilot instructor offering the same excuse after his student crash-landed, or of an experienced phlebotomist explaining why students failed to successfully draw blood? We would see these excuses for what they are: excuses! If educators practiced the same level of intentionality and attention to performance in their teaching as many coaches do in analyzing every play, every practice, and every strategy used to inspire and motivate, student achievement gaps would be minimal.

Maximizing performance and developing discipline are what coaches are in the business to do. Teaching in the traditional sense may involve more instruction; coaching may involve more hands-on training and motivational techniques to inspire performance at a higher level. However, both teaching and coaching require leadership to facilitate learning and growth.

The focus for the teacher or coach is on getting the learner to reach a performance standard by designing backward from desired competencies, as well as fostering the self-discipline needed to succeed. In fact, self-discipline has been identified as the single best predictor of future academic success (and life success). Working *with* students creates a more effective learning environment, as well as provides the support and encouragement to develop even more self-discipline as faculty and students realize their efforts *do* control their success. Mortimer Adler (1982) describes the goal of coaching and the implications for teaching:

> Since what is learned (in acquiring core intellectual competence) is skill in performance, not knowledge of facts and formulas, the mode of teaching cannot be didactic. It cannot consist in the teacher telling, demonstrating, or lecturing. Instead, it must be akin to the coaching that is done to impart athletic skills. A coach does not teach simply by telling or giving the learner a rulebook to follow. A coach trains by helping the learner to do, to go through the right motions, and to organize a sequence of acts in correct fashion. He corrects faulty performance again and again and insists on repetition of the performance until it achieves a measure of perfection. Only in this way can skill in reading, writing be acquired. Only in this way can the ability to think critically—to judge and discriminate— be developed. (p. 27)

It is the responsibility of the instructor to constantly seek training and ideas for effective strategies, many of which may be obtained through a simple Internet search. However, it is the institution's responsibility to provide a support system of accountability and encouragement which assures all action is directed toward constant improvement. Implementing a new strategy in the classroom requires the courage (hence the need for en-*courage*-ment) to venture out of one's comfort zone and try something new, the same courage students must have in order to change their strategies.

The best professional development for faculty is implementing new strategies in the classroom, then adapting and improvising the activities to achieve maximum effectiveness. Committing to trying just one new activity each week would lead to approximately forty new activities by the end of the academic year. One of the best resources for active learning activities can be found with a quick Internet search on 280 active learning techniques (Kevin Yee, Interactive Techniques, 2019). Trying new strategies that enhance learning on a regular basis and then sharing these in a collaborative session with other faculty can enhance this professional development, as well as provide the internal motivation for continued improvements.

Teaching thirty students how to swim, even though some have never even been in a swimming pool, serves as another analogy for the outdated paradigm in which "telling" is considered the same as "teaching." We would never accept a swimming instructor pushing all students into the deep end and giving directives such as: "You're just not motivated enough. You're not trying hard enough. You should have read those chapters I told you to read. You should have looked at the PowerPoint I provided." According to the outdated paradigm, when fifteen of these students swim to the side of the pool and exit, the instructor takes pride in the fact that they have taught these students how to swim, and tells the others they could have learned had they been motivated enough.

An instructor from an outdated instructional paradigm does not look at the bottom of the pool and question whether something could have been done for those fifteen students. They do not ask themselves, "Could I have used more effective strategies to teach these students how to swim?" The instructor would not consider getting in the water with the new swimmers, or even holding their hands through the first few motions or providing encouragement so the new swimmers could relax in an unfamiliar environment.

Luckily, we are not bound to teach from within this outdated and ineffective paradigm. We now know that different strategies can teach more participants to swim. Anyone physically capable of swimming can learn to swim. Although many community college students have their issues and challenges, they are not mentally incapable of learning either. Once again, our responsibility is to teach the students we have and not the ones we wish we had; and if they cannot learn best with the way we teach, then why do we not teach the way they learn best?

"IT IS MY COURSE—I CAN DO WHAT I WANT"

This response can be common among many community college educators. It may be a consequence of the relatively few requirements (such as licensure) completed by community college teachers. It may also be a consequence of the lack of support typically given to community college teachers, as well as a lack of effective institutional efforts to disband the traditional silos that have hindered collaboration and innovation across departments.

However, the course taught by a community college teacher is, in fact, the institution's course. Evidence of this lies in the fact that the institution's name is on the college transcript of courses and not the instructors' names (even though teachers often have great freedom to do what they want within the boundaries set by the institution).

To ensure that instructors feel guided and supported, each department should uphold clearly communicated curricular standards. Administrators and department chairs likely already have such standards in place, but these are rarely situated as the backstop to course design. Providing a system of standardization ensures all students have access to the same basic high-impact strategies and resources that enhance learning. There is a reason health science programs are so standardized, and it is the same reason successful franchises implement standardization; to ensure the use of proven effective strategies that produce a consistently higher-quality product.

A system of standardization is much more efficient than simply waiting for each person, department, or college to figure it out on their own. The lack of standardization, or at-scale implementation of proven strategies, is a primary reason changes have occurred so slowly in education. To KISS it: If a department, college, or system does not have evidence of standardization in instructional strategies, then it does not have evidence of instructional standards.

The process of standardization can begin with a simple listing of problems associated with student learning and then—the most powerful reflection approach—what is being done, or can be done, to improve upon each of these problems. Because writing was considered the number one problem by faculty in WCCD's science department, all faculty in this department agreed to have at least three writing assignments each term for every course. Because attendance was the second problem, faculty agreed to implement frequent assessments for daily grades, which then improved attendance, as well as summative test scores.

These are just two examples of how little changes can lead to big increases in performance, as well as providing the motivation to continue with other issues that may have previously been perceived as too difficult to address. The success of these strategies made it easier to then implement across the entire institution, while also maintaining the freedom for faculty to choose the type of writing assignment and type of frequent assessments.

To KISS this paradigm, if students only write in writing class, only read in reading class, and only do math in math class (reading, writing, and arithmetic)—is it really a surprise they lack the ability to develop the skills needed to carry over to other courses or areas of their life? Deficiencies in the core competencies of communication and critical thinking also highlight the need for at-scale incorporation into every course.

High-impact and proven strategies used in response to issues, obstacles, and problems associated with student learning form the guardrails for educators' uphill and wavering climb to effective learning. Without boundaries, we are sending an instructor with a busload of students up a winding mountain road without guardrails. It may take several times of running off the cliff, sacrificing busloads of students, before the instructor eventually gets the hang of it. Why sacrifice students? We can simply put guardrails in place to virtually guarantee the bus reaches the summit in minimum time without ever driving off the cliff.

Community college leaders courageously putting the education and welfare of millions of often underserved students before the discomfort of dealing with resistance from faculty or unions are the true leaders and warriors for equity in opportunity and social justice. History has shown that although these efforts may be championed by one or a few individuals with a vision focused on learning for all, transformational change requires leadership throughout a department or institution.

Once again, these leaders must come from within the faculty ranks and must depend on the intent to develop as many leadership mindsets as possible. What is required of administration is an unwavering support of these efforts through funding, encouragement, accountability, and appreciation for efforts directed toward constant improvements.

Of course, freedom to choose one's own teaching strategies should not provide relief from the consequences of poor choices. The list of those adversely affected by ineffective strategies includes the students, the taxpayers, the college, the state, and the nation—none of which choose teaching strategies. This is precisely why a culture of quality is not determined by what is preached or expected, but by what is tolerated. All high-performing teams preach that without personal accountability for results there is no accountability.

Maintaining a high-quality educational environment means providing the TASE required to ensure constant improvement based on data—the basic requirement of all accrediting agencies. It is important for teacher/leaders to focus on this culture as they adjust their own paradigms in their own courses, and then make positive contributions to departmental collaborations in order to inspire others to action.

"I COULD TEACH THEM IF YOU WOULD SEND ME MORE MOTIVATED STUDENTS WILLING TO LEARN"

This is another common response to the frustrations of teaching in the twenty-first-century community college system and can be at least partly attributed to the competitive entry policies of universities. However, the community college is designed to provide a high-quality education to all, with the only prerequisite being a high school diploma or GED. Realizing that student motivation to learn is directly related to the relevancy of instruction and that the best internal motivator is progress/learning or the perception of progress/learning can be enough to reflect back on the usefulness of this paradigm statement.

Do doctors complain their success rates could be better if they were not required to treat patients who were really sick? Do deans say, "If I had more motivated faculty willing to do whatever it takes to constantly improve, I could be more effective?" Most of us recognize that this is just another way of saying, "Make my job easier and I could be more effective."

These types of questions can provoke self-reflection and provide more progressive insights into the challenges of teaching in the twenty-first-century community college. They are also a stark reminder of the uncomfortableness associated with profound growth. While others may lean away from discomfort and shortchange their own efforts to improve, this is not an option for those developing a leadership mentality that has the potential to impact so many—it is just another reason to remember Q-TIP!

It is important to understand that for many of our students, overwhelming family problems and/or a lack of previous life-skill training stands in for lack of motivation. Our underserved students may not be motivated because they may not see the value of the work. Part of our job, as administrators and educators, is to enable their capacity for internal motivation. This can be done by adopting the leadership mindset, which defines motivation through improvement. When we adopt the leadership mindset for ourselves, and—crucially—when we help our students adopt it, we go a long way toward helping our students become more willing to learn.

Research in psychology has shown that the best motivator is progress, or even just the perception of progress. We can put this another way: The best intrinsic motivator is learning or the perception of learning. This was reinforced when I asked my fifteen-year-old grandson to think of a time where he was excited about learning something new. After thinking for a minute, he said that it was when he learned to skateboard. When asked why, he said a friend brought a skateboard over and after a while he was excited about making progress on something that seemed difficult.

I followed this with more questions. "You mean you were not required to write a research paper on the history of a skateboard, and then memorize forty different parts and definitions for the skateboard, and then take a final exam on the physics of momentum, acceleration, force, etc. before learning to skateboard?" Looking at me like I was crazy, he replied, "Well, if I would have had to do all that, I probably would not have learned to skateboard!"

This scenario shows the power of stimulating motivation through curiosity and relevancy before new terminology, acronyms, or details. Students' understanding of basic concepts and principles leads to greater motivation for learning details, details that are less relevant before understanding concepts and principles. The motivation acquired by early successes provides the inspiration and desire for them to learn more. Just the simple interjection of more relevant and engaging activities prior to introducing a myriad of new words and terms can provide the incentive for continuous student learning/growth.

Studies consistently show that student achievement gaps are much more pronounced in classrooms where ineffective, passive, teacher-centered strategies are allowed to dominate. These gaps are significantly smaller (and sometimes nonexistent) in classrooms employing more active and supportive student-centered learning strategies. Active-learning strategies have been shown to support how the brain naturally learns, something it has evolved over millions of years to do very effectively.

It is very difficult for any student to be motivated to memorize massive amounts of material they perceive as irrelevant to their life or life success. Incorporating more relevancy and active engagement into the course will do wonders for motivation levels. The challenge, as always, is finding the appropriate balance between quantity and quality.

Taking time to implement more active and engaging learning activities requires a commitment to relevant learning as an ongoing process, as well as a willingness to sacrifice some details for increases in conceptual understanding and core competency attainment. Moving some of the knowledge transmission to lecture videos also helps free up more class time for engaging and reflective activities which facilitate transfer of information from short-term memory into working and longer-term memory.

Ultimately, compensating for less effective teaching strategies is most difficult for the most underserved students, especially those first-generation, low-income students with little or no support system in place. The consequences for these students extend well beyond their own personal success and into the realm of generational success of their children and/or future children.

Even though national reports have stressed more active learning for decades, the *Reclaiming the American Dream Report* (AACC, 2012) added emphasis with the directive to "courageously end ineffective teaching strategies." To KISS this: If we want better and more motivated students, then we must increase the use of more effective teaching strategies to promote a more meaningful, motivational, and relevant learning experience.

Of course, the law of mirrors is appropriate for all classroom issues (and often issues in life, as well). If we want more motivated students, then we must strive to become more motivating and encouraging teachers focused on learning. If we want students who are better prepared for class, then we must become better prepared teachers, using a clear and logical system to support preparedness. If we want to feel more appreciated, then we must convey a more intentional appreciation of others. Again, the reflection in the mirror points out the most important question I can ask about any problem: "What am *I* doing about it?"

Whether you are attempting to motivate students, colleagues, or yourself, appreciation serves as a source of encouragement—and it matters! I still remember when I, as a new instructor on campus, noticed a staff employee who was always upbeat, positive, and had a great work ethic. One day when he was scheduled to pick up a box of items from the chemistry lab, I wrote a note on a piece of torn-off notebook paper that mentioned how much I appreciated his positive attitude and work ethic. He thanked me a few days later.

Now, fast forward twenty-five years. One day, that same employee met my wife at the college. Upon realizing who she was, he immediately reached for his wallet and took out the yellowed, folded, brittle piece of notebook paper I had written more than two decades prior.

When I heard this story, it made me feel great! But my first instinctive warm feeling was quickly replaced with a sense of despair. I thought about how sad it was that someone who had worked for over sixty years of their life would treasure such a small gesture of appreciation. Let this serve as a reminder to intentionally recognize and appreciate the efforts of others—constantly!

The effectiveness of this approach does not depend on the age, position, or status of the recipient; it only depends on our sincerity of the sender and is a wonderful way to interject your leadership in building a team and class. In fact, our Instructional Leadership Academy (ILA) challenges faculty to provide one hundred *personal, sincere, and specific* appreciations to others in a thirty-day period. The comments from this exercise are overwhelmingly positive, for both the givers and the receivers.

"I ASKED THE CLASS IF THERE WERE ANY QUESTIONS AND NOBODY REPLIED. I EVEN ASKED THEM TO COME BY MY OFFICE IF THEY NEEDED ASSISTANCE"

This statement is often expressed by well-meaning teachers, but it shows a disconnect from the culture of many of our most underserved students. Expecting a low-income, first-generation minority student to walk up to a closed door with "Dr." or "Professor" on it and knock to ask a question they already feel is a stupid question does not reflect an understanding of the challenges our students face.

That is why faculty are encouraged to integrate frequent low-stakes assessments into their classroom activities. Such assessments take away any reluctance students might feel in proactively seeking out help. Just as important, low-stakes assessments help identify at-risk students prior to low scores on major exams. Identification is important because in many cases students mentally withdraw after failure on the first major exam, whether or not they have physically withdrawn. These students benefit the most from early, intrusive interventions. Ultimately, educators cannot assume that the absence of questions in class indicates complete understanding of all concepts by all students.

There are many other opportunities to reach students, too. In smaller classes, educators can create more supportive relationships through intentional use of student names, more aggressive intervention strategies, and more active and engaging activities that support total student development. All these strategies also help improve perceptions of approachability while creating a more collaborative learning environment where total student development is paramount. They also help educators take advantage of class size: After all, if teachers are just going to lecture as if they were talking to 300 students, then there might as well be 300 in the course.

Office hours can still be useful, but they may need to be rebranded. One strategy that can help with approachability is setting aside hours each week designated as "student hours," time in which students know they can seek assistance without an appointment. Research has shown that students perceive designated "office hours" as time where faculty members grade papers and/or prepare for another class. This perception is strengthened when students show up to a closed door and blinds. For "student hours," the door and the blinds are open, signaling an open invitation for student support.

"IT IS NOT MY JOB TO TEACH THEM BASIC LIFE SKILLS—THAT IS THEIR PARENTS' JOB"

In the state of Alabama there are over 116,000 children being raised not by a biological parent but by a grandparent or family member (and this number includes documented children only). The number is about the same in Mississippi, almost twice that in Georgia, and about three times that in Florida. This equates to almost *three-quarters of a million children* in just four states. And this does not include the number of children raised in environments that do not promote healthy life skills, nor those children in foster care.

Combining these statistics with the fact that the single greatest indicator for future life success for four-year-olds is family income makes our professional and moral responsibility clear: We must ensure all students—especially the underserved and underprepared—have the skills needed for success in the workplace and/or higher education. The generational impact of the opportunities available due to attainment of these skills for the most underserved can be transformational, both economically and socially. That is why there is simply no place in the community college of today, tomorrow, or any time in the future for a mindset of anything less than a willingness to do whatever it takes to facilitate learning with a diverse student population.

In fact, in addition to often difficult home environments, underserved students may face many other challenges. In research reported in 2019, the Association of Community College Trustees (ACCT) collaborated with the Wisconsin HOPE Lab to survey more than 33,000 students at 70 community colleges in 24 states. Of students surveyed, one in three reported going hungry while enrolled. In addition, half were housing insecure, and almost 14 percent were homeless.

The comfort of campus can be a pleasant relief from the disorganized, unstructured, and dysfunctional home environments many of these students experience. This alone can help students learn, and educators must be constantly cognizant of using strategies to decrease the likelihood of activating the survival mode in their students' brains because this is not conducive to learning. The following chapters provide more guidance on specific strategies designed to keep students' brains in control and out of survival mode.

Providing training and support in building these basic life skills for students is one of the primary ways community colleges can harness the learning power for many of our most underserved students. Once equipped with more effective and higher-impact strategies, students are better able to focus on deeper and more critical learning, leading to a closure of student achievement gaps. As a start, faculty can substantially increase their effectiveness at inspiring and facilitating learning by using proven high-impact strategies conducive to total student development.

The five strategies that form the foundation for implementing basic educational philosophy are covered in chapter 6. In some ways, how quickly student achievement gaps can be closed depends on how quickly faculty can adopt a more persistent growth mindset of constant improvement in instructional and support strategies when it comes to inspiring and facilitating learning.

"ARE WE SUPPOSED TO JUST GIVE OUT GRADES?"

When I hear this comment, I cannot help thinking back to my own university days, where it was common for a physics course (among others) to scale grades twenty to thirty points on average to compensate for the instructor's unwillingness to adjust instructional strategies. In these selective institutions, it was considered part of the rigor to have students figure things out on their own and then adjust the grade distribution at the end of term. Complexity and confusion were considered part of the rigor in academia, and although it may have provided an education for those well-prepared for that level of independence, it was more of an initiation for the less-prepared students. However, back then, I never heard of grade-scaling referred to as grade inflation.

In today's current workforce, the lack of basic life skills often causes employers to question what students are taught in the classroom. Students today may have degrees and grade point averages providing evidence of their ability to learn, but are still inexperienced in life skills crucial to workplace success. This perpetuates the general perception that grade inflation is a serious problem. Recent surveys support this perception, as employers consistently rate life skills above academic skills when searching for new employees.

A recent survey found that 67 percent of professionals in human resources (HR) say they withheld a job offer from a talented candidate applying for a job in the field of Information Technology (IT) due to a lack of soft skills (West Monroe Partners, 2018). In fact, estimates show that over 80 percent of all jobs (pre-COVID) are lost by a lack of life skills, sometimes called soft skills. It is no wonder that employers view grades as a poor reflection of the value employees bring to their organization.

There is a saying that goes a little something like this: People get hired based on their hard skills but fired based on their lack of soft skills. The results of Google's Project Oxygen (2008) came as a shock when it concluded that out of the eight top characteristics of their best performing employees, STEM (Science, Technology, Engineering, and Math) knowledge was last, and the top seven were all soft skills like interpersonal skills, emotional intelligence, being a good listener, and being a good critical thinker.

Soft skills encompass many nonacademic skills, such as the ability to communicate effectively and appropriately, resolve conflicts and recognize and respond to coworkers' emotions. In fact, *these "people skills" are better at determining long-term success in the workplace than academic/technical skills*, although there may be nowhere in the classroom grading system to allow for assessment of these life skills—again, fodder for the perception of grade inflation.

The topic of grade inflation forces us to ask another question: If, after implementing more effective learning strategies, student learning and grades significantly increase, does it mean grades were *deflated* prior to the change? The arbitrary nature of grades is just another reason why judging the past on today's standards is not productive for moving forward with constant improvement. Maybe one of the reasons grade inflation is mentioned so much today, particularly among educators who still operate in a traditional paradigm, is because many students graduate without basic success skills in place, a further indicator that courses need to be redesigned with more relevant competency development.

The answer to the question of grading depends on mindset. If a teacher thinks they have no further room for improvement, that could be rectified by introducing them to proven strategies designed to enhance learning. If, however, a teacher's mindset means they have no intention of changing or adjusting their strategies to improve learning, then that is more of a motivation problem.

The disconnect for many teachers is assuming there is no option to improve course success rates other than just giving away grades. This book is designed to convey many ways to stimulate learning, growth, and performance using small, incremental changes on a daily basis. But, once again, we can only do better once we know better—but once we know better we must do better.

By putting a primary focus on grades instead of learning, faculty hinder their own innovation and creativity. This is why faculty must not only tell students over and over again to "focus on learning and the grade will come," but they must also constantly remind themselves. To state this more generally, when anything other than learning is the primary focus, then learning is limited. This is precisely why the Lumina Foundation stated, "It is not just that learning matters, but that it matters most of all!"

Since faculty growth (and student learning) is hindered by self-imposed barriers, adopting a whatever-it-takes approach is necessary for helping remove these barriers and empowering educators to get closer to maximum effectiveness. "Extreme ownership" is the last step to phases of change and cements in the new paradigm in which educators display a committed effort to maximizing growth by accepting responsibility for all obstacles hindering the goal and mission of learning: buy-in → ownership → extreme ownership.

This "extreme ownership" mentality is required of all *highest* performing teams and provides a crystallized understanding of what it takes to succeed in the most challenging environment in postsecondary education: the community college. It also reminds us that when faculty quit learning, so do students.

This willingness to do whatever it takes benefited me greatly during my first few years teaching at the high school level. I remember a particular student, one of the smartest students I have ever taught. He won the state chemistry competition with ease and excelled in every science class he took. However, just one day before his high school graduation, two of his teachers informed me that he did not show up for his final exam in their classes. Although a poor final exam grade would still allow him to pass, the result of a no-show would be that he would not pass and would not be able to participate in the graduation ceremonies. Understanding the rapport I had with this student (he took general chemistry, AP chemistry, and physics from me), these teachers also informed me that he conveyed to them that he was not satisfied with his performance his senior year and was just going to repeat it.

I assumed there surely must be some misunderstanding, so I tried—and failed—to contact him via telephone. Since I had just finished giving my last final exam, I drove to his house to find out more. Although no one answered my repeated knocks on the door, I saw someone peeking through the blinds, so I continued with the knocking. To make a long story shorter, he answered the door, and I questioned his actions before making it clear I was not leaving without him. He finally agreed, and we drove to the school so he could complete his two final exams. To this day, he continues to thank me for helping to get him back on track.

Sometimes students just need to know there is someone who wants it more than they do at the moment. This is someone who can provide encouragement for the student to do that which they may fear. For some students, the confidence in your voice can be enough to give them the confidence they need to rise to the next level of performance. This is another reason why I do not agree with the aphorism I have heard many times in my career: "You can't want it more than they do." Although I understand its meaning, I have learned that sometimes we *must* want it more than they do, just so they can get to a point where they realize they should want it, too. This probably sounds familiar to many parents because it is something most parents find out, sooner or later, in the process of raising children.

"HOW WILL USING EFFECTIVE LEARNING STRATEGIES PREPARE THEM FOR UNIVERSITY?"

We have to assume this question refers to the common perception that universities expect students to compensate for any and all levels of instruction. However, students who have not learned how to study, critically think, and persist through obstacles do not have much chance of success in this type of environment. Therefore, it is crucial for those of us working at the community college level to focus on learning as it pertains to total student development. Too many times strategies acquire a negative stigma ("high-schoolish," "spoon-feeding," etc.). In actuality, the only defining feature of a strategy should be its ability to effectively inspire and facilitate learning.

Organizations such as the John Gardner Institute have been helping colleges and universities address some of the same issues that plague community colleges—enrollment, retention, lack of crucial life skills, completion, faculty training and accountability, and so on. By redesigning those essential first-year gateway courses, universities can provide a more engaging, relevant, and supportive learning environment for first-year students.

A basic component of this redesign is the creation of student learning objectives for every assessment or unit. These crystal-clear expectations for students are the very first step of the educational process. If this step is skipped (as with the first step of any process), every strategy that follows is simply an effort to compensate for the fact that the first and most important step was omitted. Chapter 6 will cover these course redesign standards in more detail.

The creation of these objectives allows faculty to reassess course content to ensure key concepts are given adequate practice and exposure. This process also helps eliminate much of the rote knowledge transmission in classrooms that can be more effectively covered through other avenues, or that is not essentially relevant to understanding course concepts. This is called content tyranny. It refers to the tendency of educators to try to cover too much material, typically leading to students absorbing less material at a more superficial level. By focusing instead on analyzing issues or problems rather than conveying information, students begin to adopt a deeper and more critical learning process.

One of the reasons given (what some people might call excuses) for not teaching these life and study skills is that community college students should be prepared for the next level of higher education. To address this misconception, I would like to point out that *preparing* for the next level does not require *being* at the next level. If it did, we would not call it the "next" level. Preparation, instead, is about providing the basic skill training students need to succeed in the workplace or the next level of higher education. More importantly, and as Dr. Terry O'Banion states, a goal of education is not always about the next level—it should be "about earning a good living and living a good life."

"I GUESS WE MUST BE ALL THINGS TO ALL STUDENTS"

This statement typically reflects an emotionally reactive response to the inevitability of change. Although we can never be "all things to all students," this does not mean educators can relinquish their responsibility to be as much as they can be to as many students as possible. This response is another example of why mindset is so much more important than skillset, and why removing self-imposed limitations is a way to maximize development of the skillset. By focusing on learning and total student development, student success is inevitable.

"THEY ARE NOT TRYING HARD ENOUGH OR ARE NOT MOTIVATED ENOUGH"

This statement is common advice given to struggling students, although without sufficient training in more effective study strategies students are more likely to resort to survival techniques more focused on completing tasks than learning. Like many of the other responses in this chapter, this statement shows a disconnect between the culture of many faculty members and the cultures present in our diverse student population. Although "diversity" is a good buzzword to stimulate warm feelings, it is difficult to practice strategies that lead to diversity in course success, retention, and completion without a deeper understanding of cultures outside our own and the empathy that results from this understanding.

To keep it simple, KISS it: If we use a limited set of instructional and support strategies, we can expect a limited set of students to be successful. If we diversify our instructional and support strategies, we are more likely to have a more diverse set of successful students. Maximizing diversity of strategies maximizes the diversity of completion. In fact, why would we continue to use only traditional methods with nontraditional students? This is especially pertinent at community colleges because the majority of community college students are considered nontraditional, whether by federal or real-world definitions.

For students with a limited set of effective life and study skills, "trying harder" is not always a productive solution. Instead, they require more effective skills they can only gain through a focus on learning and total student development. For many students, the classroom may be the only environment where they can learn and develop those skills.

By incorporating active-learning strategies that do not rely on simple "telling," educators can ensure effective skill development occurs through teaching, modeling, and practicing in a supportive environment, and one where training must rely on relentlessly attention to constantly applying the fundamental concepts throughout the course. This describes the roles of the educator—to teach, coach, mentor, counsel, and inspire!

As for references to motivation, we must ask ourselves just who determines the appropriate level of student motivation? How is this ideal level of motivation determined? Is it determined by how the student sits, looks, or responds in class? Could overwhelming family problems be misconstrued as a lack of motivation? Could frustration with the lack of effective instructional and support strategies practiced by the instructor be misconstrued as a lack of motivation?

Just using the term "motivation" indicates another disconnect with the culture of origin of many of our students. After all, the recent COVID pandemic resulted in many faculty feeling overwhelmed and underprepared for the changes they needed to make. Yet most faculty probably do not perceive their difficulties acclimating to COVID to be a "motivational" issue.

This is precisely why our responsibility as professional educators is not to just present the material but to inspire and facilitate learning. A focus on learning naturally involves more emphasis on course relevance, as well as on strategies to support motivation. Although students can "try harder" and be "more motivated," in a traditional classroom this results in about as much improvement as attempting to nail up a plywood wall with a screwdriver.

Provide students with a hammer, and watch their energy, motivation, and persistence rise to another level. Better yet, provide them with a nail gun, and see what they can build. Providing students with comparable tools in their tool kits allows for greater diversity in learning, which can contribute to closing student achievement gaps.

Although everyone seems to be an expert on evaluating others, one of the most valued assets for leaders is a constant self-assessment/evaluation. Simply put, "We find comfort in those who agree with us and growth in those who don't." Unfortunately, the continued reliance on the preceding statements in this chapter, which should by now sound archaic, contribute to a fixed mindset that undermines the growth needed to maximize learning for students *and* for faculty.

It is time to pass every instructional decision through the filter of the community college MVP to inspire and facilitate learning with a diverse student population and ensure maximum growth in a minimal amount of time for a maximum number of students.

To reiterate a couple of key points from this chapter:

- Putting students that do not know how to effectively learn in classrooms with teachers who do not know how to effectively facilitate learning is a recipe for disaster—TASE!
- Small class sizes in community colleges are only an advantage if they are used as an advantage.

Chapter 4

Kaizen Is Key to Transformation

Following the approach of leading colleges around the nation and our state, WCCD adopted an at-scale philosophy and system. Its results were recognized by the AACC, and it was named the top community college in the nation for student success in 2017. This Award of Excellence by AACC was not due to implementation of a boutique program or even a magical set of strategies unique to our institution but was the result of an intentional growth mindset focused on the primary reason for instruction—learning.

The program developed at WCCD is called the I-CAN program. Improvement: Constant and Never-Ending. It began in the fall of 2007 as a faculty-driven and data-inspired response to high withdrawals and failures in the science division. Identifying the top problems that were impeding student learning and developing a strategy to address each problem set the stage for integrating a growth mindset at the divisional level.

Our only requirement in response to an identified problem was that doing nothing was not an option—a challenge the science faculty accepted with a passion and purpose that was in direct alignment with our Professional Educator Commitment Statement at WCCD that was later adopted by our state ILA (Appendix A). The key to this document was not necessarily in what it conveyed as much as it was that *something* was conveyed—written evidence of a higher degree of standards and expectations from a group responsible for training our next generation of leaders.

The approach also incorporated a powerful question to help transform instruction through constant improvement: Every time we identified a problem, we asked, "What am I doing about it?" Many of the issues we addressed were previously considered out of our control, such as student attendance. However, once faculty began to see substantial results with small changes to pedagogy, their mindsets and confidence enriched, and they sensed a greater degree of control over student success.

This increased confidence led to departmental standards that addressed each area of concern related to student learning and success, both in the cognitive and affective domains. Strategies included improving student perceptions of the learning environment through more intentional use of survey results, providing detailed unit objectives and lecture videos, frequent low-stakes assessments, early intrusive interventions, and several pedagogical changes (more information is provided about specific strategies in chapter 6). These standards served as a lead-by-example approach which greatly benefited adjunct instructors as well.

Our results were immediate and substantial. With no additional funding, the next year saw a 31 percent increase in the number of students attending class, over 400 percent increase in the number of students showing up prepared for class, and a 47 percent increase in the number of successful students (C or higher) across all biology courses. A faculty mentoring program was also established. This, as well as monthly professional development focused relentlessly on student success combined with completely built courses available online, helped create a sustainable culture of quality in the science division.

Following the format that led to increases in student learning in the sciences, the same strategies were implemented for the top ten enrollment courses and developmental courses at WCCD in 2012. Analysis of data from these courses revealed the same deficiencies exposed in the science division five years prior. By focusing on the most common first-year courses, all full-time general academic faculty and over 90 percent of general academic adjunct faculty were directly involved. These efforts had a direct impact on all degree-seeking students, all of whom participate in several of these courses. This approach allowed a maximum number of students to be impacted as early in their college career as possible, and in a minimum amount of time.

The AACC's Reclaiming the American Dream report was released in April 2012 and was a blessing to our newly implemented I-CAN initiative, as we were in the early stages of change—mostly denial. This report reiterated almost every aspect of our initiative and was required reading by all faculty. This reading assignment was then followed by divisional meetings to provide collaborative reflection on the report. The report served as a crucial component in managing faculty resistance, as did the name of our initiative. Removing any logical opposition from educators was the goal of the I-CAN initiative's name because "constant improvement" is a logical core requirement for all professionals in any field.

The acronym was similar to the one that motivational speaker Tony Robbins used (CANI) several years ago in order to avoid using the term Kaizen. He felt a need to come up with terminology people in our culture could better identify with, but still keep the same fundamental meaning as Kaizen (discussed more later). At WCCD, we felt the need to send a more positive message to both students and faculty that conveyed the power of a growth mindset, hence the change to I-CAN. The goal was to develop a leadership mentality throughout the institution that would result in a more unified team approach to learning—an eventual conversion from I-CAN to We-CAN, harnessing the power of at-scale participation.

I-CAN was fully implemented in fall 2012, and it began to lead to substantial results in fall 2013. Ultimately, the program resulted in closing socioeconomic student achievement gaps, while also increasing enrollment, retention, and completion. Achievement gaps were completely closed in developmental studies, while over 75 percent of the gap was closed for the top ten enrollment courses. The most surprising statistic prior to implementation of I-CAN showed that higher-income minority students had almost a 50 percent greater chance of success in the top enrollment courses than the lower-income minority student. This supported national data showing a direct relationship between family income and test scores in math, reading, and writing.

In summary, institutional efforts resulted in a 27 percent increase in fall-to-fall retention rates at WCCD for the 2014 cohort compared to the baseline from 2011, and a 5.3 percent increase in enrollment for fall 2014 as compared to fall 2013. This enrollment increase was the highest in the state and earned WCCD a spot on the top-100 fastest growing community colleges in the nation. However, the biggest surprise was the increase in AA/AS degree completion rates, which depend on general academic course success.

After the first full year of I-CAN, the college also implemented a college-wide completion campaign focused on "Getting the Tassel." This campaign involved every employee of WCCD working to support efforts emphasizing student completion. Combined with instructional improvements, these efforts resulted in a 67 percent increase in the number of AA/AS completers for 2014–2015 as compared to 2010–2011.

The same growth mindset that supported the I-CAN initiative fuels a philosophy that has been practiced by Japanese businesses since World War II. The Japanese word "Kaizen" is by now a familiar term in the business world, and it simply means "change (kai) for better (Zen)." In the Western world, it is translated as "continuous improvement." Although Kaizen may sound fluid, it depends on data and statistics. In Japan, it is credited with moving the economy from last-place in the industrialized world after World War II to second-place in just ten years.

In general, and at WCCD, Kaizen is a daily process designed to be practiced by all employees. It demands a focus on small ideas and improvements that can be immediately implemented. The methodology includes making changes, monitoring results, and adjusting as needed—a process that mimics scientific reasoning (critical thinking) and that results in action. The key to its efficacy is that improvements are made using existing employees, technologies, and funds. This avoids the common excuses involving a lack of funding, inadequate technology, and lack of time, while igniting innovation at the individual level. The complacency resulting from these excuses is therefore avoided, placing the brain in a more positive and proactive mode of growth.

These improvements result from daily and immediate adjustments, as employees practice innovation prompted by constant communication and adherence to data. By focusing on leading data in the classroom (frequent assessments, test scores, assignments submitted, attendance, student engagement, etc.), faculty are able to make immediate changes in pedagogy and/or offer supportive interventions. The efficiency of the entire institution is enhanced as problems are solved at the lowest level possible. Frequent meetings used to share new improvements while brainstorming additional activities and strategies are a great way to maintain motivation and momentum through constant collaboration and celebration, a celebration inspired by the data.

The cycle of Kaizen activity involves planning → doing → checking → acting. For accrediting agencies this process is sometimes called "closing the loop," and it happens by analyzing data, implementing a possible solution, analyzing the newly implemented strategy for effectiveness, and then making the necessary changes to maximize effectiveness. This process is another version of the scientific method: We make observations, formulate a possible solution (hypothesis) based on these observations/data, implement the possible solution (experiment) while recording data, and then formulate a conclusion, which may indicate a need to repeat this process. This process does not result in a win or lose situation, as it is always focused on what can be done to improve—once again, we either win or learn, or both.

By implementing a program founded on the principles of Kaizen, the problematic conditions in the educational system associated with traditional educational paradigms, such as the long lag times associated with curriculum changes, the efforts to find funding resources, and the requirement to develop needed technologies, become a secondary focus. Instead, the primary focus is on innovations by individual employees.

It is important to note on the individual level anything that is a new strategy for a teacher would be considered innovative for that teacher, although it may be common with other teachers or other subject areas. It reminds me of a secondhand store called Nu2U. If a teacher is using case studies for the first time, it may be considered innovative, although the studies may be commonplace in courses such as nursing and psychology courses.

Successful innovations are then shared and disseminated through collaboration, resulting in additional documented action plans that are also implemented. Every committee meeting starts with the question, "What have you implemented that was new to you and increased learning?" This not only involves all employees in the mission of "inspiring and facilitating learning" but also takes advantage of the fact that innovation breeds innovation. After all, if you hang around three courageously innovative folks, you will soon be the fourth!

There are no ideas considered too small if they enhance the learning experience. Since research has determined that the most significant common factor among the most effective teachers is the "human factor," it is imperative that each instructor works to maximize the effects of these strategies through constant assessment within his/her content area.

Although the human factor distinguishes the learning process from the manufacturing process, there are many commonalities. These commonalities provide educators with learning opportunities (conversely, the lack of perceived commonalities hinders innovations across different fields or even between different institutional departments). The approach associated with manufacturing processes, such as Six Sigma, is in direct alignment with the Kaizen approach and the scientific method. Each of these processes shares in common the intentional approach to data-collecting and direct targeting for solutions.

Six Sigma methodology, another version of Kaizen, was developed in the mid-1980s by engineers at Motorola as a way to improve manufacturing processes. Successful implementation reduced product defects and improved profits, employee morale, and quality of products or services as a result of increased performance and decreased process variations. At its core, Six Sigma involves collecting and leveraging data to eliminate defects and waste in manufacturing, with the end goal of improving overall efficiency and quality.

Although this methodology is most effective with repetitive, assembly-line style operations, where individual steps can be isolated, examined, and improved upon, the concepts/principles are also applicable to our efforts to maximize effectiveness in the classroom. Just as meeting this goal for an entire academic department or institution requires participation from everyone involved, so, too, for the effective functioning of Six Sigma. This is why effective leadership is required.

In education, combining a focus on improving positive student perceptions with the implementation of proven instructional and support strategies produces synergetic effects that are much greater than a sum of individual parts. As in Six Sigma or Kaizen, analysis of these strategies allows for refinements to maximize effectiveness. This is a holistic approach, meaning, it addresses all areas affecting student learning and is designed to develop all aspects of the student that can lead to increased opportunities in life and the workplace.

Coupled with accountability for action, this process explains how WCCD was able to achieve maximum results in a minimum amount of time. For example, when institutions focus initial efforts on the highest enrollment first-year courses, a maximum number of students are impacted. For classroom instructors, this meant big initial efforts, such as course redesigns in their highest enrollment courses, but the work directly impacted the most students. Such improvements were not unique to WCCD: Two other community colleges in Alabama used the same approach as I-CAN and achieved similar results.

The growth mindset is a prerequisite to significant improvements associated with the human factor, and it is one reason why some instructors can take even the simplest of strategies and obtain significant results, while others can take the best strategies and obtain limited results. Because the human factor relies on feelings and perceptions, we use course evaluations (which are explained in more detail in chapter 6) to improve positive perceptions. These, in turn, have a powerful impact on student success.

A learning environment that encourages taking risks can produce the most innovation, creativity, and inspiration for both students and faculty. This environment can be cultivated in classrooms, departments, committee meetings, and entire institutions. Constantly communicating with crystal-clarity an expectation of a total focus on *inspiring and facilitating learning* can provide the safety needed from more vocal status quo groups resisting this change.

THE POWER OF AT-SCALE PARTICIPATION

The deeper learning and critical thinking that results from implementing effective strategies are its own intellectual rewards. However, maximum return on investment for the institution occurs as increases in retention, satisfaction, attendance, preparation for class, and completion are realized.

As with many other community colleges in the nation, WCCD did not have as much of an enrollment or budget problem as it did a retention problem caused by a lack of at-scale implementation of more effective student-centered instructional, support, and assessment strategies. This became more evident after at-scale implementation of I-CAN when WCCD had the greatest increase in enrollment of all community colleges in the state, as well as an additional $2.3 million per year in revenue due to the retention increases for full-time students only.

The at-scale implementation of these strategies occurs as a growth mindset realizes the question is not about whether an active learning strategy will work, but about how it can be adjusted to maximize effectiveness in each of our courses. At-scale implementation is achieved through each faculty member adhering to constant improvements in instructional and support strategies. Of course, once the philosophy of I-CAN has been comprehensively adopted, the next step is to share results and celebrate successes—in other words, leaders and teacher-leaders must lead by example.

Constantly adjusting instructional strategies is just as crucial as students adjusting study strategies to meet the objectives of a particular subject or assessment method. This is precisely why a key to success of a Kaizen approach like I-CAN is the self-motivation generated by constantly applying a positive, can-do growth mindset. The absolute best professional development faculty leaders can experience is to implement a new strategy in the classroom, then adapt and improvise this activity or strategy to achieve maximum effectiveness. As previously mentioned, committing to just one new activity each week will lead to about forty new activities each academic year.

Maximizing success of at-scale holistic approaches such as the I-CAN initiative relies on the ability to obtain participation by all faculty. Many times, this participation must precede buy-in, as waiting for complete buy-in from all faculty stands as a major obstacle for institutions attempting to apply more effective learning strategies, despite decades of research showing the significant value teachers bring to the learning process. Since buy-in is the last of six stages of change/resistance before ownership, the initial focus is on providing a consistently persistent level of TASE (training, accountability, support, and encouragement)—and logic—to facilitate movement out of the first stage of denial.

In the Kaizen environment, actions are expedited because they are based on using data and statistics to identify issues and problems. The human factor plays such an important role in instruction, it is imperative we minimize our emotional reactions (Q-TIP) by making decisions based on data; otherwise, changes and improvements would be limited by whether the instructor "felt" the need or desire to change.

Implementing new, active student-centered teaching strategies can be stressful for many instructors, creating a natural tendency for some to avoid change and simply continue with strategies they feel more comfortable with, even if these strategies have a negative impact on student learning. The encouragement and support from those further along the change spectrum can provide a much-needed incentive for others to venture outside their comfort zone.

Although accountability may need to originate at a different or higher level than an individual faculty member, the key to the other three areas mentioned earlier is regular collaborative meetings where the more progressive faculty members have an opportunity to lead by example. It is important to keep in mind how difficult it can be for teacher-leaders to inspire others toward buy-in—and ultimately ownership and extreme ownership—if they have not completely bought into the fact that it is all about learning.

When loosely applied, the concept of academic freedom seems to have given some instructors the leeway to teach as they see fit, although it was never intended to allow the continued use of ineffective strategies that discriminate against those who could benefit the most from postsecondary education: low-income, first-generation students. Teaching with strategies most effective for learning with the students you have takes precedence over many traditional strategies which one may be more comfortable using.

This is precisely why the AACC report, "Reclaiming the American Dream" (April 2012) stated a need to "courageously end ineffective teaching strategies." The words are clearly purposeful: implementing a new strategy does not take as much skill as it does courage to venture outside the confines of one's comfort zone and beyond self-perceived limitations. This is the same courage required of students to extend themselves and try new strategies. Just as with all other skills and behaviors, it is much easier to effectively teach that which is practiced by the instructor.

By employing the intentionality associated with coaching to every activity, every class period, and every assessment, teacher-leaders can constantly analyze their strategies for ways to improve learning. This intentional process relies on constant improvement, just as with the Kaizen concept and Six Sigma, and is much more about mindset than skillset. The ability to overcome a less developed skillset with mindset is one reason underdogs win in education, as well as in sports, business, and military. By developing a persistent and determined mindset of whatever-it-takes to increase student *learning* with a diverse population, results are achieved which are well beyond the norm. In other words, making an uncommon commitment to a common goal and purpose (*learning*) produces uncommon results.

Because over two-thirds of the jobs in this country require postsecondary credentials, the single greatest thing people can do today to increase opportunities in life for themselves and their children or future children is the pursuit of higher education. The country's enormous skill gap has created a crisis that can also be a wonderful opportunity for the community college system to enhance social justice and family-supporting wages for the most underserved. Understanding this situation can provide us a greater sense of empathy and purpose for our efforts. We must all redefine academic freedom to recognize the "freedom" afforded teachers comes with a sacred responsibility to strive for an environment of equitable opportunities for success for all.

As previously argued, even though teachers choose their instructional and support strategies, they do not typically suffer the immediate consequences of choosing and using ineffective strategies. Yet, they may suffer long-term consequences as enrollments decrease, and, taking a broader view, they may be adversely impacted by the effects of diminished skill sets and tax revenues for their communities. The students and taxpayers, along with the college, community, state, and nation, all pay the price for a poor choice of strategies which lead to reduced enrollment, retention, completion, and economic viability.

Just as the Japanese relied on the honor and integrity of workers to promote the concept of continuous improvement to increase the economic strength of their nation, so should this expectation extend to institutions of higher learning. It would be a breach of academic integrity to know a problem exists with student learning and yet do *nothing* to address the problem, just as it would be to know strategies proven to increase student learning/success and not implement them.

There is honor in providing a level of training, accountability, support, and encouragement that exceeds set standards. As mentioned previously, the minimum standard for the leadership mindset is the maximum—a standard that will never truly be met and a reason *constant* improvement can be so personally transformational. The prerequisite for these changes is a commitment to learning—for students, faculty, staff, and administration.

The reluctance to focus on learning may result from the paradigm where rigor is believed to be generated when students memorize an abundance of content. This knowledge-transmission approach had more value a few generations ago, but today, the overwhelming amount of information available literally at our fingertips has shifted educational rigor to quality learning associated with critical thinking and problem-solving skills. Critically analyzing to solve problems based on data and evidence is the ultimate objective of education in this century and is the very component of Kaizen that leads to lifelong learning and constant improvement in all areas of life, while also putting a premium on learning quality over quantity.

The cycle of Kaizen activity—Plan → DO → Check → ACT!—resembles that which institutions seek to employ in their strategic planning process, although large student achievement gaps reflect a much too common neglect at the level of instruction. Finding the root cause for a lack of effectiveness is crucial to the improvement process, as much of our time and energy can be wasted chasing multiple issues that could have been solved by addressing the root cause. The feeling of constantly "putting out fires" indicates a need for teachers/leaders to address root causes. In these situations, KISS is just another way of reminding us to stick to basics before specific details.

The reference to "putting out fires" reminds me of my first high school position where I taught chemistry and physics. Teachers designated specific duties in the lab to student lab partners. For instance, one pair was designated the fire extinguishers and was responsible for getting the fire extinguisher off the wall bracket and ready in case of a fire. One day in lab, as I was across the room working with another group, there was a slit in one group's gas hose and flames began to shoot out of it. By the time I saw the flames, the fire extinguisher group had already removed the fire extinguisher from the wall and had pulled the pin to extinguish the fire. I directed them to stop as I moved across the room and turned the gas supply handle off.

Although I had covered the details of their actions in case of a fire, I did not elaborate on the basics of firefighting. The first step of firefighting is removing air, or oxygen, from the fire and/or cutting off the supply of accelerant. After praising the extinguisher group for their prompt response to what they perceived as an emergency, we had a longer discussion about how to better address fire issues, whether in the lab or at home. As with many other issues in the classroom, this was one I had not anticipated—or maybe there was so much to cover that I just skipped over that part.

This was a teaching moment for me and a learning moment for my class: We were able to focus on the basics of firefighting (to essentially KISS it), and we discussed why some strategies work better in certain situations. Reflecting on this experience in the lab allowed us to discuss the advantages of remaining as calm as possible in the midst of chaos and confusion. Our discussion carried over to tests, and how overwhelming anxiety can only decrease the chances of success on tests. We then talked over techniques that could be used to reduce test anxiety, including more effective preparation.

Once again, it is much easier to adapt and improvise in any area of life if we understand the basics. This is particularly true for students: By connecting our discussion to a memorable event in the lab, students were able to use the experience as a tool with which they could relate other, more relevant examples from their lives. This is an example of maximizing learning by maximizing the connections made with other areas of the students' lives, thereby enhancing relevancy.

Kaizen can also be facilitated by implementing a leadership mentality throughout the organization (classroom, department, division, and institution), creating an environment where problems are solved at the lowest level possible. When the MVP of the college is clearly and consistently communicated (CC the MVP) by as many faculty and administrators as possible, and responsibility is comprehensively shared for finding institutionally appropriate solutions for all problems, solutions can be implemented at the lowest level possible, ultimately resulting in more control and empowerment for faculty. Think about it: Isn't it much easier for you to implement appropriate solutions when you fully understand and adopt your colleges' MVP?

ONLY NEW MISTAKES ALLOWED

A key component of Kaizen is that constant improvement is more important than maintaining an environment free of mistakes, hence the mental rule of "only *new* mistakes allowed." In other words, aggressively employing innovative strategies and solving problems at the lowest level, even though mistakes may occur, is more important than never committing mistakes but making only limited progress. Once a "mistake" is identified, students (or anyone affected) must be given the benefit of doubt, while intentional strategies are implemented to ensure the mistake does not reoccur. Using mistakes as opportunities to improve is a key to lifelong learning and constant improvement and therefore crucial to student and faculty success.

Nothing short of a professional educator and teacher-leader—someone committed to constant improvement in instructional and support strategies focused on learning—can effectively inspire and facilitate learning with a diverse and underserved population. The most effective teachers operate with a passion and purpose reserved for true professional educators by adopting the mantra that the *"only wrong answer in response to any variable impeding student learning is to simply do . . . nothing."* In other words, we can make progress or excuses but not at the same time!

In summary, the uncommon results obtained by WCCD, Indian River State College, and Miami Dade College (and many other colleges that have adopted a learning-centered approach) depend on the presence of a growth mindset (leadership mentality) throughout the institutions, and especially with faculty. This mindset fuels innovation and creativity, while creating an environment conducive to self-motivation and to taking proactive risks through well-defined boundaries and expectations. A paradigm focused on the positive aspects of a team effort must start at the very top and be constantly and courageously communicated with crystal-clarity and enthusiasm at every possible opportunity!

Although the challenges are immense, this is what professional educators do. There is simply no place in the community college of today or anytime in the future for anything less than a growth mindset committed to improvement, constant and never-ending (as in, I-CAN) in instructional and support strategies. What an incredibly honorable approach to serving our country by providing a truly equal opportunity for success through higher education!

CC THE MVP

When approximately a quarter of all community college students do not return for a second term and almost half do not return for a second year, we do not have an enrollment problem—we have a retention problem. The problem is spurred by a lack of MVP clarity. To CC the MVP—to courageously commit to MVP—provides the direction for a unified team approach to close socioeconomic achievement gaps and increases retention and completion. Just as explaining the "why" is most important in bringing relevance, meaning, and unity to students and faculty, it is also crucial to developing initiative to adapt and improvise without the requirement of direct oversight.

Terry O'Banion says, "The Completion Agenda is the most important and significant reform efforts in our lifetime! Never before has there been such overwhelming and overreaching agreement among ALL major stakeholders in this country. Never has there been so much sound research supporting these efforts. If we are to improve on our record of student success, the role of the teacher in creating learning must become the primary focus of the Completion Agenda." Realizing the challenges of inspiring all faculty to action, Dr. O'Banion continues, "To achieve even a modicum of success in reaching the goals of the Completion Agenda, will require leaders who will disturb the universe!"

The MVP provides unity of focus, as all faculty and staff are responsible for the mission of *inspiring and facilitating learning with a diverse group of students*. This cultural growth mentality seeks to meet the challenge of *"providing a high-quality education to millions of often underserved students"* (RTAD, 2012), something that cannot be accomplished with irrelevant instruction and low-quality support strategies. From a data standpoint, how effective we are with these "underserved students" can be determined by how well the most at-risk students are performing and how much student achievement gaps have closed.

This MVP must be constantly communicated and data shared throughout the organization at every opportunity by as many faculty and administrators as possible in order to avoid mission/vision slippage and maintain adherence to the Kaizen philosophy. The MVP is a constant reminder of the importance of our sacred responsibilities as community college faculty. Our responsibility is not to just convey information to students (we already know that telling is not teaching), but to *inspire and facilitate learning*.

Many teachers can identify the problems associated with student learning but do not feel it is their responsibility to change instructional and support strategies. However, there has never been so much sound research supporting a more active engagement in the learning process, nor has there been more for supportive relationships. This environment increases learning for all students, although substantially more for the least prepared. Neither the personal discomfort of change nor the inability to completely solve the problem is legitimate excuses for doing nothing to improve learning.

This mission of providing a truly equal opportunity for success through higher education is paramount to upward socioeconomic mobility and maintaining the values and principles that form the foundation of our American culture. In a time where work is learning and learning is work, we should constantly remind students of the dignity of work and value of education. Their pursuit of higher education is the single greatest thing they can do to increase opportunities in life for both themselves and their children or future children, and they should be reminded of this often and enthusiastically.

Courageous commitment to the MVP is needed for both focus and momentum, as the combined efforts of all surpass the sum of the individual parts. Although skill and talent can only take you so far, the positive can-do *mindset* of whatever-it-takes to increase student learning, especially for those first-generation college students from a life of generational poverty, will take you well beyond your self-perceived limitations and into that magical realm of growth outside your comfort zone—providing the experience needed to empower students with this same resilience.

The most common comment from faculty participating in constant improvement of instructional and support strategies is about how amazed they are that such small changes result in such profound and obvious improvements in student learning and motivation. Although we may not be able to directly control the number of faculty on our team who participate in constructive changes, we each directly control our own level of commitment to this process. By encouraging and sharing successful strategies, we can prompt small but impactful changes in our colleagues and others. The multiplying effect of these efforts become more profound as more faculty participate in strategies proven to enhance learning.

As an example, the average full-time community college instructor can teach as many as 10,000 or more students over a thirty-year career. If only one of every 100 students were inspired to become a teacher themselves, the average community college instructor would produce approximately 100 teachers over their career. If each of these 100 teachers also taught 10,000 students over their careers, there would be 1,000,000 students impacted! These exponential effects depend only on consistent but small efforts from all.

Carrying this concept to the classroom, if each course section/class had only one more successful student in that section that would not have statistically been successful prior, a college of 100 full-time and 100 adjunct faculty would result in as many as 700 more successful students. Since these were all previously at-risk students, the empowerment they experience will not only affect the students themselves but their family and friends as well.

The power of exponential growth should not be overlooked when planning for at-scale implementation. Using a financial example that illustrates the power of consistency, while also presenting the reality that results may not present themselves as quickly as we would like, can be a memorable learning experience. Using a calendar month with thirty-one days, how much money do you think you would accumulate in one month if you were given one penny the first day of the month and double that amount for the second day, and so on? The second day you would receive two pennies, the third day four pennies, the fourth day eight pennies, and so on.

Upon analysis, the end of the first week results in a grand total of $1.27 and the second week total is $162.56, resulting in accumulation of $163.83 for the first two weeks. Had you been given the same double amount every *other* day, this would be your total at the end of four weeks. However, continuing with this scenario results in tremendous increases (exponential growth). The third week produces $20,807.68, with the last day of the week alone paying over $10,000. At this point, the numbers become larger quickly, with the fourth week alone paying over $2,663,000—and there are still three days left in the month! On the thirty-first day you would receive over $10.7 million, bringing your monthly total to almost $21.5 million.

The benefits of exponential growth are achieved with efforts which are early—starting today is better than starting tomorrow—and consistent. Although it may take time to convert a cycle of despair and dependency into a cycle of prosperity and independence, it takes much longer when efforts are delayed and inconsistent. The sooner we can help our students develop growth mindsets the longer they will have to take advantage of the learning, growth, and confidence this mindset can produce.

Even as the degree of effort and improvement vary individually, results are magnified exponentially through total participation *toward a common MVP*. Buy-in is not a prerequisite to significant improvements, but participation is. For many, buy-in will come as student learning becomes evident. Obtaining buy-in for the mission and vision is one of the primary responsibilities of leadership. This total participation is a pathway to ensuring all instructors on campus have better prepared students. The question for each of us is how we can influence others through committed actions by constantly striving for excellence. Each of our actions will cause others to reflect on their own definition of excellence and commit to following your lead—after all, we must lead, follow, or get out of the way!

USING KAIZEN TO OVERCOME A
SENSE OF HOPELESSNESS

An international survey by the Brookings Institute several years ago found that over 30 percent of Americans did not feel their efforts controlled their success, and the percentages were even higher in European countries. We see this every day in community colleges. Many students do not see how their efforts control their success and instead exhibit a fixed mindset that sees success related to talent.

Of course, this may also apply to some faculty who may be stuck in the denial stage of change. Learning strategies proven to expand faculty control over classroom variables, variables we may have once considered out of our control, can be an empowering boost to overcoming a sense of hopelessness. We see this same thing in our students when they are taught more effective learning strategies. This potential empowerment is precisely why we must work to avoid blame, excuses, and a victim mentality, all of which give control to external variables and undermine efforts to meet our mission of providing a high-quality education.

The internal control of a leadership mindset comes from the all-important question for the Kaizen or I-CAN process—what are you doing about it? When you or your students realize there are things you can do to improve the situation, despair can be converted to hope for a better tomorrow.

A high-quality education is expected to help turn many of the perceived obstacles in life into stepping stones to success, as a more effective growth mindset and skillset leads to a more effective outlook on life and a realization by many that their previous mindset was amplifying their perceptions of obstacles and limitations. This is a reason why the advice given by people who have worked their way to success tends to be surprisingly similar—adopt a more positive, growth mindset that converts consistently small efforts into larger successes.

In Ruby Payne's book *Understanding the Framework of Poverty* (2005), she categorizes cultural paradigms from three different socioeconomic categories. She found that the group in the bottom third, those in poverty, tends to make decisions based on the present and on feelings, beliefs, and emotions. They may see education as abstract and not relevant to or even real in their life. This group was also prone to believing that destiny is based on fate and not on decisions and effort, supporting findings from other studies.

Generational poverty is more likely to foster survival instincts, which may lead to a sense of hopelessness and is further limited by a lack of encouragement and training. Of course, the fixed mindset that results from not seeing how efforts control success may also result from not knowing what can be done to improve. Herein lies the power of a high-quality education.

A Kansas State University study (Hart & Risley, 2003) reiterated what other studies have shown regarding the impact of income on a lack of stimulation during those crucial first four years of a child's life on a child's chances for equitable opportunity in life. To avoid skewed results, the study avoided households with obvious child neglect or abuse. Researchers found that in the households of higher-income college-educated parents (top third), children were exposed to over thirty million more words before even starting kindergarten than children from the households of lowest income (bottom third), least educated parents. Even middle-class children were exposed to over twelve million more words during this timeframe than the lowest income group. The importance of this study may not be in the actual number of words in the gap, but the fact there was such large gaps between different socioeconomic groups.

This study also found there were over 560,000 more encouraging than discouraging words spoken in the household of the top group, while over 125,000 more discouraging words were spoken in the lowest group. This means children were exposed to twice as many *discouraging* than encouraging words before even starting kindergarten. The middle-class group children heard twice as many encouraging than discouraging words.

What can we draw from these statistics? Clearly, the group needing encouragement the most tends to receive it the least. For faculty, internalizing these findings can provide the empathy and purpose needed to take our instruction and support to the next level because so many of our students come from environments that hinder their success. It is also through these findings that we can begin to see the importance of encouragement in all areas of life, and especially in the community college classroom.

These studies and results are shared to bring clarity and relevancy to the MVP while also providing the motivation needed to maximize learning and total student development. Our mission is designed to support the most underserved. A deeper understanding of this group helps solidify the purpose of our efforts in improving their quality of life, as well as the quality of life for their children or future children.

Although many community college students are underserved and underprepared, they are not incapable of learning. They may, however, require additional support, encouragement, and engagement in order to develop a growth mindset that realizes "I can't does not mean I'm incapable." The empowerment that comes with this mindset is truly transformative in the lives of students and faculty, as "I can't" is always followed by "YET!"

For underserved students to have a better chance at community college success, they need to feel more connected to the learning process. Indeed, the

Center for Community College Student Engagement (CCCSE) found that not "feeling connected" was cited as the number-one reason students left college. Data from WCCD (2015) showed that if a student failed or withdrew from one of their first five college courses, their chance of completion was cut in half, and these statistics have been mirrored by Valencia College in Orlando and in national statistics.

Withdrawal or failure from a second course and the chances of completion were cut in half again. By the third and fourth withdrawal or failure, the chances of completion were virtually null. These statistics reinforce the need to make the greatest improvements in those first-term, highest enrollment courses (gateway courses) so as to have the greatest impact on the greatest number of students.

We already know, usually through common sense, that students are far more likely to feel connected in an active, engaging, and supportive learning-centered environment. When administrators and faculty members commit to developing a culture of caring and appreciation for their students, they take a step toward helping students overcome their insecurities and low self-worth. Facilitating connections between your students, as well as with the subject matter, should be the primary concern of all first-day activities. These connections will set the stage for more effective collaborations and learning and are a key component of the constant improvements of Kaizen.

> If we are to improve on our record of student success the role of the teacher in creating learning must become the primary focus of the Completion Agenda. To achieve even a modicum of success in reaching the goals of the Completion Agenda, will require leaders who will disturb the universe!
>
> —Dr. Terry O'Banion

There are several points in this chapter worth revisiting:

- Kaizen is a daily process designed to be practiced by all employees which focuses on small ideas and improvements which can be immediately implemented.

- There has never been so much sound research supporting a more active engagement in the learning process, combined with supportive relationships.
- A learning environment where there is safety in taking risks can produce the most innovation, creativity, and inspiration for both students and faculty.
- Many colleges do not have as much of an enrollment or budget problem as they do a retention problem caused by a lack of at-scale implementation of more effective student-centered instructional, support, and assessment strategies.
- By combining your focus on improving positive student perceptions (affective domain) with implementation of proven instructional and support strategies, the synergetic effects produce results which are much greater than a sum of the parts.
- With over two-thirds of the jobs in this country requiring postsecondary credentials, the single greatest thing people can do today to increase opportunities in life for themselves and their children or future children is the pursuit of higher education.
- Making an uncommon commitment to a common goal and purpose (learning) produces uncommon results.
- It is a breach of academic integrity to know a problem exists and do nothing to solve it, just as it is to know strategies proven to increase student learning and success and not implement them.
- KISS is just another way of saying to stick to basics before specific details.
- Faculty should ensure they are assessing students on their ability to learn and not on their ability to compensate for ineffective instructional and support strategies.
- Although skill and talent can only take one so far, the positive can-do mindset of whatever-it-takes to increase student learning, especially for first-generation college students from a life of generational poverty, will take instructors well beyond their self-perceived limitations and into that magical realm of growth outside their comfort zone.
- A growth mindset fuels innovation and creativity, while creating an environment conducive to self-motivation and taking proactive risks through well-defined boundaries and expectations.

Chapter 5

Intentional Teaching

At this point in the book, you know that "leader" is interchangeable with "teacher": Great teachers lead and great leaders teach. Approaching our duties with a more intentional focus to promote a positive and encouraging learning environment allows us to lead students and colleagues from point A to point B. As with other concepts in teaching, intentionality is a process that requires frequent assessments, reflections, and adjustments. Intentionality is a purpose-driven, proactive—not reactive—process.

INTENTIONALLY TEACHING WHAT?

To better understand how classroom learning today differs from that of a few decades ago, we need only look at the dramatic changes in lifestyle and interactions with our environment that have occurred due to extraordinary advances in technology. Information and knowledge are the cheapest and most easily accessible than any other time in human history, although that cannot be said for the core competencies of communication and critical thinking. That access to information exploded further with the release of the iPhone in 2007.

In reflecting on where most educators learned to communicate and critically think, the result is that it naturally occurred in our upbringing as opposed to a classroom. Very limited technology forced us to apply effective means of communicating, critically thinking, and problem-solving to our everyday lives. Although these "soft skills" were plentiful, access to knowledge and information was limited mainly to books and experts in the subject matter. It is not a surprise that classrooms during this time focused on how much knowledge and information could be obtained through courses of study.

Fast-forward to today and the situation has reversed. A lack of basic soft skills and competencies for many students, combined with easily accessible information at their fingertips, has created the perfect storm whereby a passive learning environment focused on massive memorization for regurgitation on an exam is disconnected from the demands of the twenty-first-century workplace. This message could not be any clearer as employers have consistently voiced their concerns about graduates having limited soft skills.

A recent national survey indicated that 93 percent of employers cared more about critical thinking, communication, and problem-solving skills than an undergraduate's major field of study (HRA, 2013). Although there has never been so much overwhelming agreement among all the nation's stakeholders on the value of these life skills, as well as so much research supporting more effective learning strategies, it does require a courageous change in paradigm for many instructors and administrators.

The learning-college concept has been the most popular and effective reform model for postsecondary education since *The Learning College for the 21st Century* was written by Terry O'Banion in 1997. Anticipating that a paradigm shift needed to occur, O'Banion outlined a reform model that included both students and teachers as learners because when teachers stop learning, so do students. Unfortunately, efforts to implement programs and initiatives that do not involve a critical mass of faculty have mostly failed to meet the demands of the nation's Completion Agenda. The continued necessity to enact the Completion Agenda suggests that community colleges have still not fully shifted into the educational paradigm required for twenty-first-century success.

We now know that this paradigm should make use of breakthroughs in neurology indicating that maximum learning occurs in active learning environments. Active learning is not a fad, but a comprehensive shift toward teaching and learning strategies founded in research about how the brain naturally learns. To KISS this, we ask ourselves how learning could be maximized if not teaching the way the brain naturally learns. By maximizing learning, we would be maximizing the chances for success for our students in life and the workplace, a powerful step in achieving equity in opportunity in our communities.

Historically, formal education has been the site of a fundamental disconnect between how the brain naturally learns and classroom learning. This is one reason so many students say they love learning but hate school. The good news is that learning is a powerful motivator for future learning, and educators can take advantage of this by focusing on inspiring and facilitating learning. This also means that maximizing learning (and therefore motivation) must, in part, depend on a sense of relevancy to the student.

INTENTIONALLY ADDRESSING CONTENT TYRANNY

In many ways, technology has stifled critical thought and analysis. If these skills and competencies are not practiced in the classroom, students cannot be expected to practice them outside the classroom. This creates the modern-day dilemma for faculty: How to incorporate more active learning strategies when it takes the entire class period just to *cover the content*? Luckily, frustration that mounts when attempting to tweak an outdated and ineffective system can be relieved by implementing a new and more effective system.

An argument against content tyranny was published by the University of California Berkeley's Center for Teaching and Learning (2012). The study references the unproductive nature of content tyranny and identifies it as something affecting educational institutions all across the country. The article supports reducing content quantity to increase learning quality, as part of creating learning goals. As the article states, "Content Tyranny is a problem for most college instructors, that is, trying to cover too much material. The result is usually opposite—less material absorbed at a more superficial level—of what we hope for. Be harsh with yourself and cut the material that is not absolutely essential."

Accordingly, lectures should include the following kinds of material:

- Key points and general themes
- Particularly difficult material
- Material not covered elsewhere
- Examples and illustrations (images!)
- Material of high interest to students (relevancy)

By marking each topic from a lesson as either "essential" or "helpful," teachers can move those designated helpful to "suggested further reading." If this is too difficult or does not provide a release from content tyranny, teachers should seek a colleague's assistance to mark the topics, as well. In many cases, this can be a crucial first step to redesigning courses to maximize learning and performance. Overstuffed content leads to underexplained content and undermotivated students.

Although letting go of details in our subject matter can be a stressful process, the benefits of deeper learning, understanding, and motivation will surpass the stress. Trying to cover too many details leaves little or no time for learning concepts, leaving students and faculty frustrated. Reducing the quantity of content allows for an increase in the quality of learning. By reducing coverage of less relevant topics, teachers can spend more time on reflection, review, and application of crucial concepts and principles.

Recent research into American textbooks shows that every country that ranks above the United States in education features fewer topics and details in their curriculum, as well as in their textbooks. Their emphasis is more on constantly applying fundamental concepts in a variety of situations. In many cases, coverage in the United States school system is an inch deep and a mile wide (this is especially the case in mathematics).

Memorizing many details does not naturally lead to comprehension of concepts and principles: Instead, understanding concepts and principles allows students to learn details easier. The classroom must shift from quantity covered to the quality of the coverage. In addition, by giving students time to reflect on what was covered, teachers help them move more information from their limited short-term memory to their working and longer-term memory. The reflection, assessment, and adjusting of misconceptions allow students and faculty to maximize effectiveness.

As learning and applying concepts takes precedence over memorization of details, students become better equipped to adapt and improvise—in other words, they become more capable of critical thinking and problem-solving. This ability to adjust requires a clear understanding of the basic concepts and a training regime which takes the time for *repetition of the fundamentals*. It is this time required for true learning that leads to increased performance, making it essential to balancing quantity and quality—another one of the dichotomies of teaching/leading.

Core competencies will be discussed further in chapter 8, but it is argued here that it is through the intentional addressing of content tyranny that you will be able to find the time for activities which facilitate students' ability to think deeper and more critically. This enhanced thinking will be used to promote problem-solving skills in the classroom.

Critical problem-solving is an important skill, and not just for the classroom. On the basketball court, UCLA Bruins coach, John Wooden, prioritized developing players who were creative, confident problem-solvers. Sven Nater, a former player for Coach Wooden said, "He wanted us to be so automatic in our fundamentals and so versed in the concepts that we were ready to quickly devise our own solutions from the constantly changing problems our opponents posed. . . . Coach Wooden wanted to be as surprised as our opponent at what our team came up with when confronted with an unexpected challenge" (Nater & Gallimore, 2010). Coach Wooden knew it was much easier to adapt and improvise when there was a clear understanding of the basics.

In an active learning environment, life skills and competencies are naturally incorporated because communication, collaboration, teamwork, conflict resolution, critical thinking, and problem-solving are consistently practiced and coupled with the subject matter. These skills are not promoted in a passive learning environment where knowledge is simply transferred throughout the class session.

Redesigning those crucial first-term, first-year general academic gateway courses (often in accordance with the strategies in chapter 6) is a first step toward finding more time for inspiring and facilitating more relevant learning with a more diverse group of students. Instructor variation, as well as achievement gaps, can be significantly reduced with more standardized use of evidence-based practices grounded in the neurology of learning.

In a January 2009 *New York Times* article, S. Rimer illustrated the benefits of intentional, participatory learning. The article detailed MIT's decision to ditch the lecture format of two introductory physics classes and replace them with smaller lab-like classes to promote participation. The school made the move in part because professors conceded that the large lecture format was leading to student failure.

After years of experimentation and debate, as well as resistance from students—who initially petitioned against it—the department made the change permanent. The results of this change were astounding: an increase in atten-dance and a drop in the failure rate of more than 50 percent. These results not only illustrate the importance of an intentional release from content tyranny, but they also serve as evidence that buy-in—student buy-in in this case—is more likely to be achieved when participation reinforces the value of the change.

MIT is not alone in this pursuit of more active learning to promote the attainment of core competencies. "Other universities are also adapting, among them Rensselaer Polytechnic Institute, North Carolina State Uni-versity, the University of Maryland, the University of Colorado at Boulder and Harvard. In these institutions, physicists have been pioneering teaching methods drawn from research showing that most students learn fundamental concepts more successfully, and are better able to apply them, through inter-active, collaborative, student-centered learning." (S. Rimer, 2009)

GREAT TEACHERS LEAD AND GREAT LEADERS TEACH—WITH INTENTIONALITY

Once teachers release their students—and themselves—from content tyranny, it is time to teach with intention. Intentional teaching is the opposite of reac-tionary teaching. Reactionary teaching is not leading—it is frustrating and energy-draining. The stress of not knowing what problem or issue will be next, combined with a feeling of not being prepared, is enough to discourage many.

However, by incorporating intentional and foundational strategies designed to maximize learning, educators become better prepared to adapt and impro-vise with specific activities and techniques. As with all other aspects of life, it is crucial in teaching to develop and incorporate a system designed to con-stantly improve. This may start with the question, "What will I do tomorrow to move me one step closer to my goal and my students one step closer to their goals?"

As discussed earlier, many higher education instructors traditionally focused their efforts on covering all their course content through passive lectures and left the learning up to students. This approach did not require intentional adjustments to pedagogy, so it is unsurprising that it resulted in instructors who were caught unprepared as students showed up to classes with fewer and fewer of the skills crucial to succeed in academics, workplace, and life. Today, educators have been plunged into a learning environment, many of them without intentional training on how to teach specific skills that is much different than the environment of their previous college experiences.

One of the best illustrations of teachers' lack of intentionality came out of a survey of California college professors. Results indicated over 90 percent of respondents deemed critical thinking one of the most important skills students could have. However, less than 10 percent could even say how they intentionally taught critical-thinking skills on any given day (Bailey, Jaggers & Jenkins, 2015).

This disconnect between the skills students need and the design of the learning environment continues to put higher education further and further behind the curve. It is a reason for many educators' frustrations, as well as for the continued growth of achievement gaps. To fix this disconnect, we must answer two questions: First, how can educators foster intentional learning among their students? Second, how can institutions foster intentional teaching among their educators?

We already know that small, consistent changes (new strategies, activities, etc.) lead to cumulative effects that rapidly build momentum for larger changes. This principle can have transforming effects on both students and faculty (as well as on staff and administration). The key is that everyone, institution-wide, commits to consistent and persistent effort, no matter how small.

For example, if a total course redesign is our objective, and as with any process this requires a series of steps/stages, we ask the empowering question of what we can do each day to move us closer to the completion of each component of the course redesign. Intentional teaching requires intentional preparation with a specific purpose and goal. This leads to decreased stress and increased performance for both students and faculty.

Simple exercises can often be a first step toward integrating small, consistent change in the classroom. For example, faculty in the ILA consistently reference quotes and memes as "game changers" in their classes, with the biggest benefit being increased student engagement and communication. These very small, but highly relevant activities provide students with motivation for further learning and help promote educators' efforts to make course content relevant. Even a short discussion about a quote can be the first indication to teachers that very small changes have a powerful impact on what they once deemed out of their control—student engagement and motivation.

Other small steps might include just identifying obstacles that can impede performance. Teachers face no end of obstacles—there is always something when dealing with people, whether as a teacher, parent, or leader—accepting this fact helps begin lowering the stress associated with constantly dealing with the unpredictable. This has been referred to as "expecting the unexpected."

In our state's ILA, two words are used to drive action in response to this acceptance: adapt and improvise. These two words are combined with Q-TIP and KISS to set the stage for a more intentional approach to constant improvement. After all, if it is all about learning and growth then it is all about adapting and improvising to maximize learning and growth—for teachers, students, and administrators.

In addition to integrating small, simple classroom activities, adapting to and improvising with students in a classroom setting, whether virtual or physical, is crucial. As a chemistry instructor, I saw the astounding benefits of adaptation and improvisation. Our chemistry department at WCCD decided to adopt a nearby university's policy of dropping the lowest test grade, a reasonable grading strategy when your goal is augmenting student learning and when there is a comprehensive final exam.

After adopting this policy, an immediate impact was realized: A single mom who was back at school to become a nurse received a 36 on the first chemistry exam. Upon meeting with her after the test, it was obvious that her grade destroyed her confidence and made her question her ability to complete a nursing program. After asking her a few questions, I realized her main weakness was that she had not had enough practice with the word problems (a very common issue). She was reminded that she could drop her lowest test grade, but that she would need to commit to working on the homework problems each night.

A new rule was then improvised for her to follow: She must have something on paper for all of the homework problems, even for those questions she could not complete. I assured her that if she did this every day (Monday through Thursday), I would answer all her questions before she left for the day, and she would see her progress and confidence skyrocket before even getting to the second exam.

We continued to discuss her progress each day, and over time, there was a noticeable reduction in the number of questions she needed to ask. The more she understood the basics, which was reiterated with every question she asked, the more she was able to figure out the details on her own. The day after our second test, she came by my office before class and informed me she had not been able to sleep the night before due to her nerves. I agreed to go ahead and share her test with her if she promised not to cry. I then handed her the test with a 92 circled at the top. Her emotions overwhelmed her, and she broke down crying, apologizing for doing what I just asked her not to do! She could not wait to get home and tell her daughter!

All teachers have these moments. However, we are seldom taught how to intentionally create these opportunities. Without support, guided reflection, and structured collaboration, it is difficult to identify just what skills are responsible for such moments, much less what skills are required to recreate them for every student. It may be surprising to readers to learn that a low test grade can provide a wonderful opportunity to obtain a small commitment from a student that can then be applied every day. In fact, this is the very same strategy that was advocated for the aforementioned: Simply put, small, consistent changes are *guaranteed* to lead to improvements.

Frequent assessments can provide similar opportunities, enabling many problems to be addressed much earlier. Of course, when it comes to interventions, it bears remembering Maya Angelou's famous words: "Students may not remember what you said years after taking your class, but they will definitely remember how you made them feel!"

We must keep in mind the three very powerful Cs for student success: connection, collaboration, and celebration. You will notice that even interventions should make use of the three Cs for success—the initial meeting must first provide *connections*, a personal connection and a connection to the material through an agreed-upon commitment. This allows for more effective *collaborations* (through, for example, those daily question-and-answer sessions I held with my student) that can lead to substantial improvements in performance. Results are then *celebrated* to provide the motivation and encouragement for continued efforts.

INTENTIONAL STUDENT INTERVENTIONS

Another moment of memorable adaptation was experienced when an anxious student showed up at my office informing me that she had taken chemistry in high school and hated it. Here, integrated intentionality through the three

Cs in student interventions was used. The student said she had also failed the high-school course but was now in nursing and the course was required. She then wanted to know if I thought she would be okay in my class.

Considering how to handle her questions, I thought back to the old saying, "great teachers ask great questions." I asked her if she was willing to study chemistry every day. It must have been the way I said, "every day" that made her say, "You mean Saturday and Sunday too!?" I told her that I did not think she was ready for my class, but that she could come back to see me next semester and we would revisit our discussion.

At that point, she moved from what I sensed was initial denial into the bargaining phase of resistance to change, adamantly replying that, yes, in fact, she would absolutely be willing to do it every day. When I told her she would be fine then, she pointed out that I had not said how much time she should spend on chemistry each day. This is a crucial point in conversations where a direct change in behavior is required: When the student has moved through the denial and anger phases of change/resistance and has positioned themselves in the bargaining phase, you must frame a question in a way that ensures a "yes" in response.

As previously mentioned, obtaining a positive commitment is an important first step to students assuming responsibility for building a growth mindset of constant improvement, as well as engaging more in the learning process. This commitment is more likely to be obtained if the student senses the task is easy, fun, and/or enhances positive emotions.

Understanding this, the study habit of chunking was broached. Chunking, as many readers no doubt know, means breaking down a process into smaller steps until the process is no longer perceived as overwhelming. I asked if she had fifteen minutes a day, to which she replied, "Everyone has fifteen minutes. Sure, I can do that!" Then with a gleam of excitement on her face she exclaimed, "You mean fifteen minutes a day will be enough to get me through chemistry?" I replied, "Oh no. Fifteen minutes will not be near enough to get you through chemistry, but it will be enough to get you started on committing to a system of doing a little chemistry every day. The first week will not go by before you will probably voluntarily bump that time up to twenty-five to thirty minutes. I bet you will keep bumping up your time commitment, too, once you see how good it feels to make such progress."

Of course, I knew she would be given additional suggestions on how to more effectively use her study time, but the objective in this first intervention session was simply to get the rusty nut loose from the bolt. Obtaining a commitment to a seemingly easy study system is just the first step. To ensure compliance and persistence, teachers must monitor this commitment and provide encouragement. This approach, perhaps unsurprisingly, is more closely related to traditional coaching than traditional teaching: Effective coaches are leaders, and they do not simply tell players what to do; they work with them so each little success becomes a building block for future successes.

At this point in our conversation, the student had been introduced to the idea that there was power in her commitment to small, consistent efforts: Just fifteen minutes a day equated to over twenty-six hours of study time over the course of the semester. Now, if the conversation had started by telling her she needed to spend at least twenty-six hours (and probably a whole lot more) on chemistry, she very well may have been discouraged. She might have even decided she could not handle the course.

Instead, she was encouraged to make a smaller, much more doable commitment. After all, and as argued previously, developing a growth mindset is not a matter of making drastic changes—it is not about a switch flipping from the fixed to the growth mindset—it is a commitment to constant and never-ending improvement each day.

Intentional teaching like this cannot be distinguished from intentional parenting, coaching, counseling, advising, tutoring, and similar work. All of these situations provide teaching moments that can empower students (our colleagues, our family, and our friends) to move a little further beyond their comfort zone and into that magical realm of growth that exists beyond their self-perceived limitations. Small, continuous successes build the confidence needed to take on even greater challenges, while the greater the challenge, the greater the need for an intentional system to make the seemingly impossible more doable.

I would like to personally challenge you to find one area of your life you would like to improve and then commit to just one small task each day to generate action toward your wishes. If this involves something as important as health, there are many options related to dietary habits, physical activity, water intake, reducing stress, becoming more positive, and so on. By choosing just one small task, your brain perceives this as easier to accomplish with your current motivational level. The repetitiveness of this action leads to habit, much like muscle memory from repetitive movements. As the task becomes more instinctive and personally fulfilling, you begin to seek additional tasks to add as you realize "it wasn't really that difficult."

It is through this process that your brain becomes more motivated by the anticipation of additional dopamine bursts. Just as unhealthy habits in life can become addictive, so can healthy habits! All it takes is starting with one small commitment and then practicing the discipline required to stick to the plan. By making this a routine part of your daily schedule, the discipline required becomes less over time.

As one commitment/task leads to the adoption of another, and then another, the personal empowerment you feel will become evident to others. Building yourself first allows you to more effectively inspire others. Just as the goal of leaders is to develop more leaders, the ultimate goal of self-inspiration is to help others develop the inspiration needed to overcome life's obstacles and challenges. So, are you up to the challenge?

Of course, we all know that students benefit when we integrate accountability measures into these interventions. I ask my students to write down their commitment to improving their performance so they remember and are held accountable to their new responsibility. I vividly remember a student who taught me the importance of these measures. Years ago, in an intervention with a student from an earth science class after the first exam in which he made a 32, I acknowledged my surprise he had made such a low score. He replied that he was surprised too because he studied almost five hours for the test. After my question about when he spent this time, he replied, "the night before the exam."

Although putting all efforts in the night before the exam is a problem, I asked him to describe how he studied. I posed this reflection question to facilitate his thinking about his studying system. He replied that he had read the chapters twice and the notes three times. I then asked if all he did was read or if he ever got around to studying. "What do you mean?" was his reply.

When you inspire students to ask questions you know they are engaged and thinking about the topic at hand. Since these are student-generated questions they lead to more meaningful learning through more meaningful neurological connections with past learning. The intuitive and inquisitive nature of the brain seeks resolution to the cognitive dissonance which creates the student's self-generated question stimulated from your questioning—the Socratic method at its best!

The student was then asked if he knew he was coming into a test that would be completely made up of questions. He said "yes," replying that all tests were "nothing but questions." Recognizing the moment where logic meets reality can be impactful, as evidence by my response: "I know, but you said you studied and never once ask yourself a question. How could that possibly turn out good?" When the student asked what he could do to avoid this scenario in the future, he took the first step toward self-motivated empowerment.

We then discussed several examples of effective, meaning intentional, study strategies, and I helped explain that all of them require a thought process before answering questions, a key concept involved in Think-Pair-Share (T-P-S), one of the most commonly used active learning activities in the classroom among ILA participants. The key to this effective intervention was getting the student to realize that his efforts controlled his success and then inspiring him to desire further information by asking questions that focused on KISS.

The T-P-S activity is 1 of 289 interactive techniques described in the most recent update of a Kevin Yee's reference, *Interactive Techniques* (2020). Students first think about the question presented, then share and compare possible answers with a partner before addressing the larger class. The "thinking" part of the activity ensures each student has reflected on the answer(s) before then participating in collaboration with their partner(s), thereby enhancing the quality and diversity of input. The input is further enhanced as the entire class shares their results together. T-P-S is one of the most commonly implemented new strategies for ILA faculty, which speaks volumes for its effectiveness at stimulating thinking and collaboration.

The T-P-S activity, as well as the others mentioned throughout this book, is not required in an environment where "covering content and testing" are the only expectations. However, such activities are paramount for developing the skills and behaviors needed for students to flourish in the twenty-first-century workplace, as well as for providing the review and reflection needed for deeper learning. This is an example of a high-quality education designed intentionally for the demands of this century and with this century's students in mind.

Such exercises and activities can help motivate teachers and students to learn and to be more inspired to move beyond any prior self-perceived limitations. It can also help us be more willing to accept responsibility for our own growth, as well as that of our peers and colleagues—resulting in leadership throughout the class!

When winding down a meeting with my earth science student, we also discussed the advantages of using a system of 3 × 5 cards to assist with learning the new terminology associated with the course. To troubleshoot his behaviors, I asked him what he would normally do when he looked at the word on one side of the card and did not immediately know the definition. "I'd turn over the card and read the definition," he replied. I then pointed out that this reverted to his old system—essentially, reading over notes repeatedly. In fact, he already had a good flashcard system; he just blew it when he refused to force himself to come up with an answer before reading over notes.

We also discussed intentional strategies by which he could stoke his own motivation. I suggested that, when studying with the 3 × 5 cards and encountering something he did not know but, upon forcing an answer, found to be half-correct, he put it in a "half-correct" pile. This pile is visual evidence of progress, and hence ensures a major internal motivator. By putting this card in the "half-correct" stack, next to the "correct" and "incorrect" stacks, he sees the tangible evidence of his progress and picks up fewer and fewer cards from the "incorrect" stack.

To solidify our conversation through accountability, the student was asked to write down his commitment to looking up the objectives for each class session prior to class and to come up with a system for constant questioning.

TO-DO LIST INTENTIONALITY

To-do list-makers thrive on this system of self-motivation. By providing a means for focusing on one step at a time, to-do lists offer not just a critical tool for problem-solving but a sense of control. In fact, just the process of compiling a list and then reflecting on the order of the items can provide the brain with a sense of control. Such a sense may be especially important to students (or educators, or anyone) trapped in survival mode or in reactionary habits.

Importantly, list-making enables a brain to stay in the learning/growth mode and out of the survival mode of constantly reacting. With a plan in print providing a structured and more intentional approach, responsibilities are automatically chunked into smaller, more manageable tasks. Because these smaller tasks are perceived by the brain as easier to complete, they are therefore more likely to be completed. This is as much true for faculty and staff as it is for your students.

Many to-do list-makers find their motivation is further enhanced as they physically mark off each task: Research indicates that such actions provide a jolt of dopamine, and, for some, the jolt becomes associated with progress (Ryback, 2016). The euphoric feelings associated with the release of dopamine—a powerful neurotransmitter directly responsible for motivation and focus—by the brain makes us eager to repeat the behaviors, something neuroscientists refer to as "self-directed learning." The brain becomes acclimated to expecting the rewards of task completion, and this anticipation of a "better future" (more progress means closer to goal) subdues the negative emotional center of the brain.

This neuronal expectation of a better future is one reason to constantly use the impactful question to spur positive and productive thinking among your students and their life circumstances: What are you doing about it? Following this question with an intentional list of tasks and behaviors to ensure progress can generate motivation for action and even hope for a better future. More will be discussed on this topic of neurology and learning/growth in chapter 7.

Effective organizational and motivational systems such as to-do lists are an opportunity for educators to model intentionality. They also provide a reminder that progress and learning are processes that involve intentional steps to ensure completion. Introducing the concept of to-do lists—and completing them—can be very beneficial for students. For instance, if students were required to prepare a to-do list for their upcoming weekend, many may simply have only one thing on the list, such as "clean house." They may even have an additional task of "study for test."

Teachers can point out that these large tasks disregard the power of keeping the brain focused on each small task in anticipation of the reward of completion. Small tasks are typically perceived as easy, while the motivational action of completing each step allows for emotional fulfillment. The large tasks can quickly put the brain in the overwhelming mode of survival and lead to procrastination. If teachers help guide students in effective list-making and help students see this process as "fun," then all three requirements for increasing the chance of completion are present. By circulating around the room as students are completing their lists, teachers gain valuable information to correct misconceptions.

Even more impactful for your students could be requiring them to take on a large task they often procrastinate with by breaking it down into smaller, more doable tasks. Students can then reflect back on this process in a one-page summary. These written reflection exercises allow teachers to then choose the more impactful ones to share with the class. The point is to chunk tasks small enough to be perceived as easily doable, avoiding the overwhelmingness that leads to procrastination. Additionally, the more frequent completion of small tasks supplies the fuel and motivation for continued progress—and therefore continuous learning. This reflection activity prompts a deeper appreciation from the students on just how much these lists can help them.

While intentional activities like this prime students for learning, the activity itself does not always lead to learning—reflection does. Within the traditional educational paradigm, students have become accustomed to completing a task, getting a grade, and successfully completing a course. To ensure such activities lead to student learning, teachers must offer discussion and follow-up activities that students can use to break their to-do list into more specific tasks. The more steps on the list result in more frequent marking-off of these tasks, and this, in turn, provides more motivation.

By adding small rewards to themselves after each step, students can essentially train themselves to have a more resilient growth mindset which constantly seeks progress. This is also why one of the steps to critical thinking is to "put it on paper." Since logical action is opposite to emotionally reaction, moving the task list from an emotional human mind to an emotionless sheet of paper can be an empowering process (more on the topic of intentionality in fostering critical thinking in chapter 8).

Let us take a closer look at chunking. Just as chunking is important to deeper and more meaningful learning, it is also useful in everyday life. People remember more if information is chunked—just think about social security and phone numbers. The point of chunking is to minimize the *stacking* of material and concepts students do not know on top of more material and concepts they do not know, quickly creating frustration for both the student and the teacher.

In any environment where learning is paramount (military, sports, business world, etc.), a strategy of chunking is the way the brain naturally learns.

However, the review and reflection also necessary for learning takes time and is a reason why teacher-leaders should constantly look for ways to exchange less relevant class activities and assignments for ones more relevant to the expected outcomes.

Chunking and to-do lists were combined in an effort to relieve frustration for me in the late 1990s when I purchased a 100+ year-old two-story house in desperate need of renovating, which was only a few miles from the college where I was teaching. Dealing with some emotionally challenging times, I was determined to stay as busy and productive as possible as a means of self-therapy. Teaching both morning and evening classes allowed me to use each afternoon and weekend to work on the house, missing only four days the entire first year of the exterior renovations (before/after picture in Appendix E). Counterproductive to the self-therapy, each day I left frustrated at my inability to complete the to-do list for the day.

To my surprise, a simple solution of chunking solved this problem. After constructing my usual to-do list based on what I thought could be completed for the day, the list was then folded in half. The difference in my disposition was transformational! Instead of leaving frustrated each day I was now leaving satisfied with a feeling of accomplishment. On the days the "half-list" was completed early, a proactive start of the second half of the list was initiated. Many times, this would simply involve preparing for the work to be done the next day by laying out the tools and equipment needed.

Never underestimate the power of small but *daily* action toward your goals. If it is important enough to you—the biggest issue, urgent problem, health issues, underlying values, and so on—you should find time *daily* to make progress or improvement, no matter how small. However, if it is not important enough it will be easy to find excuses to avoid the daily actions. This daily process helps recondition the neurotransmitters to take the pathway to the areas of the brain responsible for reward and motivation. In essence, the brain becomes addicted to progress and your goal becomes part of your daily routine and not a separate task you must find time for.

Attempting to learn a new language is an example of the power of this process. Learning just one new word each day can result in almost a hundred new words in just three months. Combined with *constant* review and reflection on these words, learning/progress is quickly realized. It becomes easier to learn new words as you have more learned words to relate to; easier for neuronal growth to occur as new learning attaches to old learning. Find ways to inspire students to commit to this one principle of daily action toward a specific goal as a way to start the process toward progress-addiction and a growth mindset of constant improvement.

The perception (and reality) of daily progress was enough to let dopamine (and other endorphins) do its job by signaling the motivational prominence of task completion, thereby boosting the chance of future actions directed toward achieving the goal. This also serves as an example of why—in spite of the quote, "You can't want it more than they do"—teachers and parents must sometimes want something for their students and children more than they do until they are at a point where the motivational aspects of dopamine take over. Just as with the "go-getters" from the Vanderbilt study in chapter 1, the dopamine pathways are redirected to find personal satisfaction and happiness with achieving progress and productivity.

The 10/2 or "chunk and chew" strategy is a modification of chunking and is highly effective in supporting students' understanding of important concepts. It refers to the ratio of time spent learning and reflecting and helps ensure students do not become overwhelmed with teacher input without being given appropriate time to process information. The importance of two minutes of student processing time with every ten minutes of teacher-centered lecture is supported by research (Costa, 1981; Long, Swain & Cummins, 1996). Often, the two minutes supports student-directed review and reflection with someone the student understands—another student.

Adding 2-10-2 to "chunk and chew" reminds teachers to limit lectures of new material to no more than ten minutes before stopping and implementing a reflection or review activity. The timing is not the most important part of the phrase; rather it functions as a reminder to stop and provide an opportunity for students to engage. The first two minutes reminds teachers to start with an introduction to prepare students for learning, in part by building the relevancy and curiosity needed for deeper and more meaningful learning.

Of course, students should get most of the facts from their reading, while class time is generally devoted to more in-depth discussions and analysis. Turning each general topic into a question can lead to more focus and engagement on the part of the students. It is also a way to generate the curiosity needed to promote deeper thinking. What students actually do in class matters much more than what instructors do, which is why we must intentionally design class sessions to incorporate time for reflection and review about every ten to fifteen minutes. We must strive to always remember—the one doing the work is the one learning.

It is important to note that students cannot effectively learn when the brain is trying to memorize massive amounts of material, particularly if the material is seemingly unrelated and irrelevant to the student. The short-term memory is quickly overloaded, especially in today's society of quick and easy access to most of the world's knowledge. By stopping to reflect and review through the use of chunking techniques like those described earlier, information is moved from short-term to working or longer-term memory, building crucial momentum for further and deeper learning (scaffolding).

Most of us are familiar with the loss of motivation associated with a lack of reflection and review. How many times has a wonderfully motivating conference failed to lead to lasting changes? This is not because we do not want to change or see the need to change; it is because our return to our campus is met with relentless daily activities that sabotage attempts to implement a new strategy our daily lives do not seem to support.

But we do not have to wait for someone to tell us to reflect. We can take time to stop, review our notes, and prepare a specific plan of action that starts with a simple task. Research shows if we take action within forty-eight hours, the chances of success are enhanced. Avoiding procrastination from overwhelmingness is a learned skill and one that we, our students, and most everyone we know would benefit from practicing.

Dan Cable, a professor of organization behavior at London Business School, says that if employees (or students) feel like they will be judged for mistakes they make while learning, they may feel anxious, risk-averse, and less willing to persist through difficulty. Creating a supportive and encouraging environment can make this discomfort less daunting, an effective approach for both students and faculty.

INTENTIONALLY PREPARING EACH STEP OF THE LESSON

The three pillars of effective instruction include relevance, maximum engagement, and supportive relationships. If we want our students to thrive, we must integrate intentionality into each pillar. Relevance drives intellectual rigor, as students naturally think deeper and more critically about something they perceive as relevant. Educators must have an answer to one of the best questions students could ask, "*Why* do we need to learn this material or complete this assignment?" Explaining the why provides the relevance so crucial to deeper and more meaningful learning.

It is important to note that relevance can be achieved by simply making the presentation of material more interesting with stories, images, videos, analogies, and other methods of illustration. Although it would be great if we could make the topics themselves more relevant to each student's personal interests, education should be generally designed to expose students to a greater diversity of ideas. This is especially true for those students with limited experiences in life. Intentionally designed strategies that promote active learning and collaboration help create a greater degree of interests.

After establishing relevance, the key to maximum engagement is integrating intentionality in the organization of presentations or lessons. Although the class period may be an hour or more in length, chunking the lessons into smaller segments (what was introduced above as 2-10-2) helps facilitate learning, as students move more information and skills into working and longer-term memory. By conceptualizing the process of the lesson into four basic parts, student learning and neuronal growth can be intentionally nurtured. These parts are introduction, lesson body, reflection/guided practice, and assessment.

As with any endeavor, the first step is the most crucial. That is why the introduction is not the time to dive right into the lecture with new terms, acronyms, or details. It is the time to inspire and prepare students for the learning ahead. It is the time to provide a relevant and intellectually engaging experience that stimulates curiosity and a desire to learn more, an experience upon which reflection and review can be built. The more relevant and engaging the experience and the more senses it involves, the more impactful and memorable the experience will be, even if it is not directly tied to the specifics of the subject matter. The goal is to prepare students for the learning ahead.

We want students to think of this introduction as a magic trick; we want students to oooh and ahhhh and to ask, "How did he do that?" Chemistry demonstrations can have that effect, but so, too, can interesting facts, videos, quotes, stories, questions, and other examples. Our intent as educators should be to capture our students' attention, so they *want* to ask questions. Provoking students' inquisitive minds is so much more powerful than asking them to simply answer questions. A student (or any person) who asks questions is engaged, communicating, and critically thinking.

To foster maximum engagement, we must continue our focus on making connections. The introduction part of the lesson mimics the objective of the first day of class, which is all about making connections with students in preparation for the learning ahead. Making the important connection to the concepts in each segment of the class period enhances the next step of collaboration. In my career, I have often seen how instructors overlook the importance of making more intentional connections with students, and with students and the subject-matter concepts, and then wonder why students do not participate more in discussions (which are examples of those necessary collaborations).

Making connections is key to efficacy in all businesses. Businesses known for focusing on providing an extraordinary level of customer service always make the connection before moving on to the transaction. They do this for a reason—because it works! Chick-Fil-A employees always provide warm, positive requests to assist their fast-food customers, and always follow the customer's "thank you" with a response of, "My pleasure!"

CVS is another company known for exceptional customer service, the kind that makes lasting connections with customers. CVS has a Good Samaritan Van they use to serve stranded customers with car troubles. This service is free, with no catch, just a memorable experience that fortifies customer relationships and aligns with the company's values. In 2014, the company made another value-based decision to stop selling tobacco products despite losing $2 billion in revenue (Glazer, 2020). And in 2018, it began offering discount coupons to customers without insurance to buy medication to reverse opioid overdoses. When a company or organization makes daily decisions based on their MVP, a sustainable connection is made with its customers.

Years ago, when trying to determine how to interject "global insights" into chemistry courses, I decided to try something that would allow students to make quicker connections across cultural and language divides, connections that are ever more relevant in our global society. An assignment was created that allowed students to earn extra credit at the end of the course if they could verbally recite "hello" in twelve different languages. Students were given a list of about thirty-plus hellos in different languages to choose from. Now, this may not seem to have much to do with the topic of chemistry, but it has everything to do with learning and showing respect to other cultures. Every chemistry student that year chose to complete the assignment.

Little did I know how much this one little assignment would impact their motivation and excitement for learning. Of the many students encountered years after having them in my class, almost every one of them mentions learning those hellos (and not the wonderful lecture on atomic theory?!). Not only do they mention the hello lesson, they always do so in an enthusiastic manner, pointing out that they still remember some of the hellos.

Actually, knowing how to say hello in thirty different languages can help create instant personal connections outside the classroom, too. I learned this years ago, when my wife and I left a sushi bar. While paying at the counter, I noticed a little girl sitting behind the counter and reading a book—and knew her as the daughter of the Korean owners, so I waited to catch her eye before saying, "Annyeong Haseyo" ("hello" in Korean). Her eyes got as big as saucers as she came out of the chair speaking in Korean. I informed her that I was very limited in my ability to speak Korean, but the connection had been made!

This same approach has been used when traveling with my wife, and each time it has the same effect. As teachers—and as people—we can see it as our responsibility to make connections, modeling what it means to turn what appears to be large differences into a point of commonality. Once a connection has been made, it is amazing how natural conversations—even collaborations—can proceed.

Another unlikely connection occurred a few years ago when my wife and I went to a local, rural chilidog stand in southern Alabama to eat lunch. Upon walking in, we noticed the only two seats available at the bar were next to a grumpy-looking man who seemed to be having a terrible day, a bad year, or a disappointing life. He looked to be a hard eighty-plus years of age, and the scowl on his face said it all. I told my wife we could sit there, and I would sit next to him. As we sat down, I looked for something to say to make a connection. Noticing he was wearing a hat with an airplane on it, I told him that I liked his hat. He looked at me from head to toe and then back to head, taking in my overdressed outfit of a suit and tie.

After looking me over, he responded with a growl, "What do you know about this hat? Are you some kinda doctor?" After replying with a "No sir,

I'm not a doctor," he countered with, "Are you some kinda lawyer?" To that I replied, "No sir, but now you are starting to offend me." The very slight smirk on his face let me know that I might be getting through to him. He followed with the statement, "What would you know about this hat?" I proceeded to tell him that I did not know a lot about it, but it looked like one of those C-130 turboprop cargo planes. I ended with, "To be honest, that's about all I know about it because every time I was in one I was so excited about jumping out of it, I never learned any more."

His facial expression changed as he asked if I was "one of those para-troopers," to which I replied, "Back in the day I was, but now I work for the community college system." At this point his entire demeanor shifted as he began talking all about his life, his problems, how many times he had been arrested, shot at, and disowned by his family. I introduced him to my wife and although we only shared about twenty minutes of conversation, the connection and change in disposition by this Air-Force veteran was one of the most immediate and profound I have ever experienced. It did seem like life had been rough for him, but for our short time together none of that seemed to matter.

It is easy to see why making meaningful connections (with students, teacher, and subject matter) is the primary goal for the first day and is the primary purpose of every lesson's introduction. Commonly, after ILA faculty redesign their first-day activities to focus solely on making more effective connections, they report witnessing more student conversations the next class periods than ever before. These personal connections help student commitment, but they also help with conflict resolution and effective critical-thinking skills.

Once we have made a connection with someone by identifying common-alities, it is much easier to understand their point of view. Furthermore, once we understand other points of view, diversity of thought is accepted rather than perceived as a threat—an important step in conflict resolution. Whether through first-day activities, first steps to a lesson, or initial conversations dur-ing student interventions, the connections we facilitate pay big dividends in terms of our connections with students, their connections to each other, and students' connection to the content.

Ultimately, an intentionally prepared lesson looks like this: In the first part of the lesson, we establish the relevancy that is crucial to providing inspiration for students to connect to the content. If they perceive the content to be important in their lives, the connection is stronger and the motivation for learning becomes more natural. This is why using strategies and techniques which enhance curiosity can create more relevancy for the mind.

Once the students' curiosity has been stimulated with a relevant question, their minds are relentlessly determined to find an answer (intrinsic motivation), which leads directly to the second part of the lesson—the lesson body. We limit this part of the lesson to no more than ten to fifteen minutes, but not necessarily through a straight-lecture format. Instead, we incorporate questions to allow for more active participation and discussion. Great teachers ask great questions, but great teachers are not the answer key! Letting students flounder and figure it out on their own allows teachers to identify misconceptions, a key to maximizing neuronal growth as new learning must be connected to old learning for this growth to occur. Teachers can expect increased engagement (*collaboration*) in this portion of the lesson if the introduction adequately prepared (*connected*) students to learn.

In the third part of the lesson, which consists of reflection or guided practice, teachers help students transfer information into working and longer-term memory. Although reflection may occur throughout the lesson, the third part is student-driven and includes specific activities to facilitate the use of the material and concepts. Teachers should take the opportunity to incorporate life and study skills into these activities, while circulating around the room to check for understanding. This may also be a time to stop and address confusing points with the entire class.

There should never be a time when you, as an educator, and especially if you have an advanced degree, feel you do not know how to do something. Finding out can be as easy as a simple Internet search. A simple Internet search yields abundant resources to diversify teachers' toolboxes. A recent search for "active learning activities" resulted in the following:

- 17 Active Learning Activities for College Students
- 226 Active Learning Techniques—Iowa State University
- 101 Activities for Teaching Creativity and Problem-Solving
- Active Learning: 101 Strategies to Teach Any Subject
- 75 e-Learning Activities: Making Online Learning Interactive
- Interactive Techniques: 228 Activities/Strategies

To KISS this: Just Google it. At the very least, the search will provide a starting point for further learning. Adopting this lifelong-learning concept as an instructor allows one to intentionally incorporate this empowering concept into the learning environment.

The fourth part of the lesson, assessment, allows for a demonstration of learning and should take up no more than about five minutes. This part should be performed independently, as each student checks for understanding, and it may be in the form of a quiz or writing assignment. This formative assessment is not about the grade (although students may receive one for it), but about identifying individual misconceptions. In other words, it is assessment *for* learning. The assessment *of* learning will be the summative assessment on the first major exam. These assessments are a time to *celebrate* accomplishments and learning, while using mistakes as opportunities to further enhance learning.

Ultimately, by chunking each lesson into four parts, teachers ensure students do not have to stack information they do not know or understand on top of information they do not know or understand. Much like teaching a card game or software program, one bit of knowledge must be practiced and corrected before moving on to the next. As supported by neurological research, students are more likely to retain information for future use when using this method of learning progression which scaffolds a new step (new learning) on top of the previous step (old learning). The key for this connection is that the content was not just covered, but learned through intentional use of the four parts to a lesson.

More importantly, structuring lessons around these four parts allows for more intentional incorporation of active learning strategies, and in a more consistent manner. The benefits of what O'Banion calls a learning-college approach extend beyond just the students and into the realm of instructors, as they constantly practice the same communication and critical-thinking skills required of their students.

A high-quality education designed intentionally for the demands of this century with this century's students is one where both you and your students will be more motivated to learn, more inspired to move beyond prior self-perceived limitations, and more willing to accept responsibility for our own growth, as well as that of our peers and colleagues—leadership throughout the class!

***

This focus on learning (and not grades) was desperately needed years ago in a third-quarter general chemistry course. There was a particular student in the class I will call Don. Don was one of the hardest working students I have ever taught and used his discipline and work ethic to compensate for what did not come as naturally to him as it did for some of the other students.

After a relentless focus on word problems throughout the year in chemistry, the final exam, which consisted entirely of word problems, traditionally gave students one of their best test grades of the term, especially for those who worked through the review problems. Although Don had a high C average, there was no doubt the final exam would put him over the threshold for a B.

Little did I know that Don would score lower on this test than on any other! I knew something was not right by his unusual disposition upon leaving the exam, and should have known by the fact that he was the last student to turn in his paper. Don's exam grade actually dropped his overall average to just below a C, close enough that I could have easily justified giving him a C. However, the goal became to use this as a teaching/learning moment and try to help him regain the confidence I was sure he lost.

Luckily, I ran into Don on campus shortly after grading the exams. After asking him if he was sick the day of the exam, he said he was not. I repeated the question and added that he did not look well during the exam (which was the truth). He again said he was not sick, to which I replied that if he had been feeling ill, I would not feel right holding him accountable for a test taken under those conditions. Although I had not shared his test nor his grade with him, I could tell he knew he had not performed well on the exam. He then said, "Well, I did feel a little sick." I told him if he could be at my office at 8:00 a.m. the next morning, he could retake the test using a different version of the exam.

True to his past history, Don showed up with a look of confidence and proceeded to earn a 94 on the exam! Years later, his dad shared with me how much this meant to Don and his self-esteem. Don continued with his education, ultimately earning a PhD in molecular biology and obtaining a position performing environmental research for the US government. This is a reminder that when we as teachers say it is all about learning, we must be willing to back that statement up in our practices. The same holds true for our approach that mistakes are opportunities to learn.

Don is a prime example of a student who had earned the benefit of the doubt after taking over a year of chemistry, especially given his work ethic and commitment to following the one rule for all my classes—to show up prepared each and every day. Because we had that connection, I felt I knew him, and I felt better able to adapt and improvise without compromising the integrity of the classroom. As with any strategy or technique, the question remains the same—Did it enhance learning and growth? Is so, it is an effective strategy for that particular situation.

INTENTIONAL INSTITUTIONAL SUPPORT OF FACULTY

In order to achieve a greater degree of fulfillment by empowering a more diverse group of students with the skills needed for success in the twenty-first-century workplace, an institution needs to have an affirmative answer to two key questions. The first, *"Do you want to improve your teaching and support strategies in order to inspire more meaningful and relevant learning?"* A desire to constantly improve is a prerequisite to the self-discipline needed for the second question; *"Are you willing to work through the feelings of discomfort that accompany the area of profound growth outside the confines of your comfort zone?"* These two questions are just as relevant to administrators as they are for faculty and serve as a subtle reminder that change is a process that must be always recognized, encouraged, and managed.

The affirmative answers should lead institutions to prioritize course redesign for those crucial first-term, first-year general academic gateway courses. These courses not only involve the most faculty and students, but they are also part of the first experience students have at an institution and can therefore have the greatest impact on establishing a strong foundation for learning that leads to increased student retention. Course redesigns can also help significantly reduce instructor variation, as well as achievement gaps, through an institution-wide commitment to more standardized use of evidence-based practices grounded in the neurology of learning.

Often, first-term, first-year gateway courses are the ones usually staffed with an institution's most at-risk faculty—adjunct instructors. For many of these instructors, support is limited to a textbook and the publisher supplements associated with it. This system alone speaks volumes about the perceived lack of standards and accountability for learning and is also a major source of the instructor variation in course success rates.

When an institution or department provides a course built and designed on basic educational philosophies infused with proven high-impact strategies and incorporated into the learning management system (LMS), adjunct instructors are free to focus on incorporating more active and effective learning activities. These redesigned courses, complete with the five strategies discussed in the next chapter of this book, provide some of the most valuable "professional development" for adjunct and newly employed instructors. They send a message of the institution's prioritization of learning and student success.

The Alabama Community College System (ACCS), backed by a total commitment to student learning and success by the chancellor, Jimmy Baker, implemented a state-wide Instructional Leadership Academy (ILA) program to turn student success crises into an opportunity for unprecedented growth in instructional and support strategies.

The ILA reflects the system's priorities: It was designed to close the socio-economic achievement gap and increase retention and completion rates by creating a more active, student-centered learning environment that combines true equal opportunity with the "open access" of community colleges. This type of faculty-driven growth requires leadership (proactive problem-solvers) throughout the organization or institution, growth that in the ILA was monitored and supported through weekly online reflection posts and monthly collaborative sessions over the course of a year.

When 167 instructors participating in ILA were asked whether they thought all students should have access to high-impact strategies and resources that enhance learning, 100 percent of them responded in the affirmative. These instructors understood there must be compromises made to their comfort level in order to provide a more equitable opportunity for success for a more diverse group of students. To KISS this: If there is no evidence at the department, program, institution, or system level of standardization in instructional and support strategies, then there is no evidence of standards in instruction and support.

Without team-level standards, it is easy to see why there is so much instructor and section variance in student learning and success. A wide degree of instructor/section variance can turn registration into a roulette wheel where the chances of success for students depends more on which section they happen to register for. Starting with common goals for each course, faculty can then design a level of standardization to ensure a more level-playing field for students.

The added advantage to the institution of an environment where all faculty are participating in designing a more active and engaging approach to total student development is that students show up to subsequent classes better prepared and more confident. The skills they develop and the intellectual and emotional growth they experience are highly transferable to other courses and to life itself. Although the level of participation by faculty and choice of specific activities may vary, everyone is accountable to the mantra that "doing nothing is not an option."

Students, in turn, learn how to study and how to take advantage of the most important aspect of studying (which is also the least used, hence the increased frustration): advance preparation. With all courses providing unit objectives before starting a unit (discussed in more detail in chapter 6), students become very acclimated to a culture that expects them to show up having, at a minimum, already looked up these objectives in the textbook—a great start in helping students assume more responsibility for their learning while also empowering them with the mindset that their efforts *do* control their success.

Institutional support can come in other forms, too. While serving as interim instructional dean, and shortly after beginning our I-CAN instructional initiative, a division directors' meeting was held to discuss our plan of action in moving forward. Referencing a faculty survey from three years prior where "student writing" was listed as the number one concern of faculty, the directors were asked what they were doing in their divisions to address the issue. The room was silent, until someone looked over at the English director and asked what they were doing. We agreed this was a college-wide problem, just as our quality enhancement plan (QEP) involving the entire campus was focused on math skills.

Readers will not be surprised to hear that we also agreed that the only rule for our I-CAN initiative was that in response to any issue or problem impeding learning, doing nothing was not an option. This, of course, is simply another way to recommit to constant and never-ending improvement. We decided to take a positive, proactive approach focused on progress rather than excuses.

Consequently, our directors were challenged to come up with a possible solution that involved all faculty, and to do so in less than sixty seconds. Just to initiate quick and focused collaborations, I added that I thought we should have one writing assignment in every course each week (any topic in half to full page). Boy, did that get the conversation started, as the directors knew this would be a hard and stressful requirement to take back to their faculty.

Naturally, the concern was not in how many writing assignments should be required: I (and likely they) simply knew how much more palatable it would be to identify a possible solution instead of following someone else's requirement—in this case, mine. To my surprise, it took just over forty-five seconds for the directors to agree on three writing assignments in every course each semester. This is another example showing that education moves as slow or as fast as the leadership allows. Once each director took a leadership role in this meeting, the goal was quickly accomplished. Even though this requirement would not completely solve the writing problem, it was guaranteed to improve writing skills through an at-scale implementation across the institution.

Of course, you can probably imagine how well this went over with our math department, who already felt the pressure of our QEP. I was walking down the math hall one day and noticed that an entire class was engaged with an activity, with each student working at their desk (which was all too rare in this time of excessive lecture). As the instructor came to the door, I asked what his students were doing. He informed me they were doing "that damn writing assignment we are required to do. I do not know what this has to do with teaching math." Realizing his frustration, I responded that I did not know what it had to do with teaching math either, but that I hoped he would realize how much this has to do with teaching students.

It was a couple of months later when this teacher came to my office for a confession. He said that he had been teaching for over twenty years and had learned more and gained more insight into the lives of his students in one semester than he had in those entire twenty-plus years. What a powerful testimony to the impact writing assignments can have on making more personal connections with our students—especially coming from someone who already had a wonderful rapport with his students. The lesson here? Do not underestimate the power of making small adjustments in your classes which focus on the student and learning!

Institutional support for maximizing improvements in instruction is most effective when faculty are allowed time to participate in year-long training focused on *constant* learning, growth, and improvement with a diverse group of instructors from different departments and/or institutions. This provides the time for them to learn from multiple authors, try new strategies, adapt them to be more effective, share successes, gain valuable insights from a diverse group of faculty, and complete a total course redesign for their highest enrollment course. This is precisely why an ILA should be established for college faculty, a program that will be discussed in more detail in chapter 9.

The following serves as a chapter summary of the key points and concepts:

- Explaining the why provides the relevance so crucial to a deeper and more meaningful learning. This relevance, combined with maximum engagement and supportive relationships, forms the three pillars of effective instruction.
- 93 percent of employers indicated they cared more about critical thinking, communication, and problem-solving skills than an undergraduate's major field of study.
- Effective coaches/leaders do not simply tell players what to do, but they work with them so each little success becomes a building block for future successes.
- Frustration intensifies when attempting to tweak an outdated and ineffective system but relieved once a new and more effective system is implemented.
- The reflection, assessment, and adjusting of misconceptions are what maximizes the effectiveness of the experience.
- "What will I do tomorrow to move me one step closer to my goal and my students one step closer to their goals?"
- Students may not remember what you said years after taking your class, but they will definitely remember how you made them feel!
- Intentional teaching requires intentional preparation with a specific purpose and goal, leading to decreased stress and increased performance—for both students and faculty.
- The power of commitment to small, consistent efforts: Just fifteen minutes a day equates to over twenty-six hours of study time over the course of the semester!
- By stopping to reflect and review through the use of chunking techniques, we move information from short-term to working or longer-term memory,

building crucial momentum for further and deeper learning and activating the promise of scaffolding.

- Small, consistent changes are guaranteed to lead to improvements—for both students and faculty.
- When you inspire students to ask questions you know they are engaged and thinking about the topic at hand, a crucial prerequisite to a deeper and more meaningful learning process grounded in relevancy.
- To-do lists also provide a system which forces the mind to focus on one step at a time, something crucial to problem-solving.
- The point is to minimize the stacking of material/concepts students do not know on top of material they do not know, quickly creating frustration for both the student and the teacher.
- The added advantage to the institution of an environment where all faculty are participating in designing a more active and engaging approach to total student development is that students show up to subsequent classes better prepared and more confident.
- Great teachers ask great questions—and they are not the answer key! Give them time to think and respond. At least you will know their misconceptions (old learning) to connect with the new learning.
- By providing a course that is built and designed on basic educational philosophies and incorporated into the LMS, adjunct instructors are free to focus on incorporating more active and effective learning activities.

Chapter 6

Five Strategies for Course Redesigns

The necessity to change the education paradigm in American community colleges began with two landmark reports. The 1983 report, *A Nation at Risk*, initiated one of the largest K–12 educational reform movements in the history of the United States. *An American Imperative* (Wingspread Group on Higher Education, 1993) called for overhauling higher education in the United States in order to put students at the center of the educational enterprise. The "learning college" model was built on these two reports and became a popular and effective reform model for postsecondary education, particularly after the publication of *A Learning College for the 21st Century* by Terry O'Banion in 1997.

If implementing small-scale change can be a challenge, then transforming an entire system of education might be considered impossible. However, in his book, O'Banion suggests a framework for change that involves students, faculty, staff, administrators, and community members. Stressing the premier role of faculty in the process, O'Banion said, in his forum session at the Innovations Conference in 2015, "Substantial change in education will not occur unless the faculty are as deeply engaged as key stakeholders."

The importance of the faculty role has also been seen in highly successful boutique programs focused on helping a small cohort of students. Report-outs from these programs have provided valuable information about effective strategies for inspiring and facilitating learning. Unfortunately, efforts to scale these programs and initiatives often fail, particularly when they do not involve a critical mass of faculty.

This chapter offers insight into how five basic instructional strategies can lead to significant increases in student learning, retention, and completion, whether the aim is broad institutional transformation or improvement in a single class. These five strategies provide the guardrails needed to maximize the number of students benefiting from increases in learning, while minimizing the time it takes to achieve substantial improvements in student satisfaction, attendance, preparation for class, persistence, critical thinking, communication, teamwork, and problem-solving.

Although research has shown that any one of these strategies can improve test scores up to a letter grade or more, course redesigns can take advantage of the synergistic effects of incorporating all five strategies. Together, they form the basic structuring for courses; then, courses can be constantly adjusted through the use of activities and techniques chosen by individual instructors. Although these strategies increase learning for all students, increases are significantly greater for the most underserved students. These strategies have been shown to close achievement gaps and significantly increase retention and completion rates, which, in turn, lead to increases in enrollment. They are also strategies supported by extensive research, grounded in basic educational philosophy.

Each of these five strategies supports the three pillars of effective instruction: maximum engagement, relevancy, and supportive relationships. The combination of relevancy and relationships helps drive the intellectual rigor instructors desire from their courses. Reinforced by recent advances in cognitive science, a topic of discussion in chapter 7, the five strategies are general enough to provide guidance without impeding instructors' freedom to choose specific activities to develop an action plan for improvement. Of course, the freedom to choose also comes with a responsibility for the results of those choices.

Looking back just a few decades in higher education, we find plentiful examples of inefficiencies. First, if ten problems were identified as impeding learning for a diverse group of students, we would need to form a committee. Once a committee formed, the next order of business might be to vote on which *one* of the problems the committee would address. In contrast, in today's learning-centered environment, *every* problem impeding learning must be addressed because learning must be maximized for a maximum number of students.

Luckily, all of the five strategies for course design have been used in our state ILA to address most of the major issues impeding learning across all disciplines. Although problems in education are seldom completely solved, we, as professional educators, should always look for holistic ways to respond to problems associated with learning.

Dr. Eduardo Marti described this need in *America's Broken Promise* (2016): "[Community colleges] are the only postsecondary institutions that promise to educate and prepare all interested Americans for future degrees and professions. We must develop the strategies that will enable us to effectively educate all students. We must avoid the empty assurance of piecemeal approaches and partial solutions."

High-impact strategies like the ones in this chapter constitute a holistic approach to course redesign and can increase student learning in immediate and profound ways. For example, in introductory biology classes at WCCD, there was almost a letter-grade increase in test scores after using the data from course evaluation results to inform our efforts to increase positive student perceptions (see the following for more). After integrating frequent assessments, the number of students making below a seventy on the first exam in these same courses was reduced by more than half. When departmental data was shared institution-wide, these increases provided the momentum needed for at-scale implementation and educator buy-in.

The same effects can be realized when individual teachers share their student success data with other members of the department. Data must be constantly shared with a degree of transparency that inspires action. This was done at WCCD by providing the WDF rates for each course, as well as course evaluation results. All instructors, other than the instructor receiving the report, were designated "instructor A," "instructor B," and so on.

The transparency of the list stimulated departmental and divisional discussions about how to increase student success, as well as identifying at-risk courses for high WDF rates and large instructor variances within the same courses. The most common comment from faculty as they implemented these strategies was in regard to their surprise that such small changes could have such a big impact on their teaching and on their students' learning.

To KISS this: If we desire to have the best prepared students for the workforce or for higher education, then we must incorporate the best strategies designed to inspire and facilitate deeper and more meaningful learning. For those institutions or faculty who claim to have the "worst" students, it should not be an option to use anything less than the "best" strategies. We do not need more research to show us what works, but we may need more shared data to inspire a greater degree of participation throughout faculty ranks.

ASSESS STUDENT PERCEPTIONS

Accrediting agency standards are usually met through the assessment of student perceptions (e.g., course evaluations). Faculty can therefore use the results from these assessments to work toward creating a more positive learning environment. Doing so addresses the number one reason students leave college: They do not *feel* connected (Community College Center for Students Engagement, 2009). The strategy of using course evaluations to improve positive perceptions is an important checkpoint to gauge the level of commitment to closing student achievement gaps.

Since increasing positive perceptions of the learning environment has been shown to improve learning for all students, and up to five times more for low-income minority students (Berrett, 2013), this should be the first of the five strategies implemented by faculty to close socioeconomic achievement gaps. Currently, 93 percent of colleges and universities conduct these course evaluations at the end of each term, meaning institutions lose valuable input from students who withdraw. Combine this with an online response rate of approximately 29 percent (national average), and it becomes clear that we need to make more intentional efforts to gather student perception data—and earlier—to gain a better understanding of students' feelings/perceptions.

Many faculty have gained this insight on their own terms, practicing a proactive leadership mindset by, for example, adopting short surveys to give to students after the first major exam. These short surveys are often more effective when responses are anonymous and the students understand the benefit of providing honest answers. According to ILA participants who integrate these short surveys and then make simple adjustments based on the results, students respond very favorably.

Subsequent assessments and assignments were also found to result in noticeable improvements. Teachers can also use these surveys to include questions that require students to reflect on their own preparation, such as, "I prepared for each class by having already looked up each of the unit objectives in the textbook." Such questions work on the metacognitive aspects of student preparation by asking students to reflect on their learning and preparation.

Teachers can maximize the effectiveness of these kinds of early and short surveys by giving them to students early in the semester and by reading the results right away, making note of common responses, and developing an action plan. Upon return to the next class period, teachers can provide positive reinforcement to students' honest responses and inform students that they will be making adjustments accordingly. This in itself can be a powerful tool in conveying to students a teacher's genuine concern for student perceptions, as well as in creating the collaborative environment we know is more conducive to learning. It is also one of the best examples of how teacher participation in a proven strategy can lead to immediate and noticeable improvements in student motivation—an inspiration to implement additional proven strategies for success.

In fact, evaluations like these inform the first strategy for course redesign, which responds to the top reason students cite for leaving college: They do not feel connected (Community College Center for Student Engagement, 2009). In some ways, this should not come as a surprise because "connecting'" is the first of the three Cs for success. If they feel connected, students are more likely to persist through issues that might otherwise cause them to withdraw, mentally or physically.

By including a question on course evaluations regarding students' perceptions of whether the instructor cares for them as individual students, educators can gain valuable and quantifiable data as a baseline to monitor improvements in the percentage of "strongly agrees." According to a Gallup-Purdue University study of college graduates (Ray & Marken, 2015), only 27 percent of university graduates strongly agreed their "professors cared about me as a person," highlighting the need for more intentionality in this area. Another area of concern conveyed through this study was that 37 percent of graduates did *not* strongly agree that they "had *at least one* professor who made me excited about learning," which may have had an impact on the question regarding "caring."

At WCCD, instructors received 96 percent of agrees and strongly agrees for questions regarding positive perceptions on course evaluations, before even starting our I-CAN initiative to address unacceptably low course success rates, retention, and completion rates. Statistically, using a combination of these two responses would undermine improvement efforts because there was so little room (approximately 4 percent) for improvement. Making a data-informed decision, we chose to use only the "strongly agrees" when monitoring improvement for each of the survey questions because 71 percent was the baseline response for this response.

When asked by a faculty member why we were not including the "agree" answers in the analysis for improvement, the above statistical reasoning did not seem to satisfy. The question became, "Aren't 'agrees' good?" Our answer? They are absolutely *good*, but our mission statement clearly states we strive for *excellence*. Therefore, if "agrees" are good, then "strongly agrees" must be excellent. In fact, research has shown a general tendency for students to overinflate their positive responses unless they have a specific reason not to (Price, 2006). Regardless of actual responses, this data allows institutions and educators to set baselines, standards, and goals that they can then use to monitor improvements.

In the beginning of the I-CAN initiative, only about 28 percent of students at WCCD responded to online surveys such as these (consistent over a six-year period). After discussing the significance of these evaluations and the need for more valid data, WCCD placed a response rate on faculty performance dashboards, a report from the institution which includes not only course evaluation data but also course success data. This resulted in response rates immediately increasing to 67 percent. Faculty felt this response rate provided more valid data for analysis.

To help ensure faculty engagement, administrators agreed with faculty that survey results would not be used to evaluate faculty, as long as faculty used them to improve positive perceptions, as evidenced with their action plans for improvement. It was crucial to get faculty to focus on the goal of creating and implementing action plans for constant improvements rather than on the stress of being evaluated by their students. This was especially important considering faculty had never been required to use these evaluations to improve perceptions. Just as faculty tell students to focus on learning and the grades will improve, we must also focus on improving positive perceptions so that student performance can improve.

Once assessing student perceptions, teacher-leaders are better positioned to make improvements. Perhaps surprisingly, improving positive perceptions requires relatively low inputs for outsize outputs. For instance, positive perceptions often improve when teachers simply schedule office hours each week and designate them "student hours." Students also report more positive perceptions when teachers consciously integrate the frequent use of student names.

For many teacher-leaders, especially teachers who want to be leaders but are not yet on the leadership path, becoming aware of the power of student emotions and perceptions about their learning promotes a more intentional approach to each student interaction, helping foster a culture of caring and appreciation.

By obtaining total faculty participation in actions that can improve positive perceptions, institutions can achieve results that significantly impact student persistence and success. For example, during the early years of our I-CAN initiative and in an attempt to further enhance positive student perceptions, WCCD faculty agreed that in addition to the list of their expectations for students, they would also provide a list of what students could expect of them. This helped create a dynamic learning environment in which everyone's commitment to learning was clearly communicated. Although devising a list of what students can expect of faculty can initially be a little uncomfortable, most faculty quickly realize its benefits and are reminded through this process that relationships drive the intellectual rigor of the learning environment.

To address one of the most popular teaching maxims—*students do not care how much you know until they know how much you ca*re—survey questions should include a question regarding students' sense of the instructor's care. Developing a culture of caring and appreciation is crucial to overcoming the insecurity and low self-worth that may be felt by many community college students, as they are also attempting to develop the grit needed to persist to completion. Institutions can do their part by including a question regarding caring on the institutional course evaluations, and faculty can do the same by including it on the early, condensed evaluation questions given after the first exam.

At WCCD, in addition to a question on caring, division directors agreed on four other questions to be featured on faculty performance dashboards. By focusing on five basic questions, faculty were able to avoid the data-overload that can occur at the beginning of most major student success initiative. The other questions surveyed the students' perception of engagement, the enthusiasm of the instructor, the interest of the content (relevancy), and whether the student would recommend the instructor to fellow students.

The specific questions may require revisiting and revising to obtain more relevant answers regarding practices that have been proven to increase student satisfaction and learning.

A sampling of key questions include:

- I *felt* the instructor truly cared for me as a student.
- I *felt* engaged in the class sessions.
- I *felt* the material was interesting and applicable to my success.
- I *felt* the instructor maintained his/her enthusiasm for learning.
- I looked up the objectives in the textbook before each class session.
- I watched the lecture videos which accompany each objective before each class session.
- I would recommend this instructor to my fellow students.

Creating a dynamic learning environment begins with dynamic personal connections. The power of making meaningful connections with students is evident in research results from CCCSE: Students' chance of completion is doubled if they make a connection with just three folks on campus. But these connections must be intentionally created by instructor and students, as well as between students.

THE IMPORTANCE OF CLEAR LEARNING OBJECTIVES

The second strategy for course redesign requires providing clear learning objectives or expectations of what students should be able to do (explain, state, identify, etc.) for each summative assessment. These are sometimes referred to as "unit objectives" and are provided in advance of each unit of study, and they are distinct from course learning outcomes, which are to be achieved by completion of the course.

Just as daily goals are chunked into smaller tasks on a to-do list, these unit objectives result from chunking the course outcomes into smaller and more doable steps in order to achieve these outcomes by the end of the course. Unit objectives provide students with a specific focus on what they need to be able to do or know for each class period, as well as what they will be expected to do for each exam.

Because providing clear expectations is the first step to any process involving learning and/or performance, it is imperative that educators provide specific objectives in advance of content coverage. It promotes preparation and accountability for both the student and the teacher.

Providing these same types of expectations in the form of a study guide a few days before an exam, on the other hand, can retrospectively signal that preparing for class is not important or necessary. Students may simply wait to receive a study guide and then cram for an exam, which, as all instructors know, results in shallow memorization and less transferrable learning to carry over to other classes and situations. By converting each of the objectives to questions, students will already have the best study guide available at their fingertips.

One of the major obstacles to success for many low-income students (and for many families experiencing generational poverty) is the perception that efforts do not control success. Providing clear expectations is therefore the first step to empowering students with the control and confidence they need to improve. This strategy emphasizes to students that their efforts prior to a class session or prior to watching a lecture video *do* matter, and it provides them more control over their learning.

Students feel more in control over their performance and are energized by the structure and chunking the objectives provided. Ultimately, students are more likely to persist through challenges and hardships, while also increasing the chances their children will be inspired to do the same. The generational aspects of education highlight the meaning of the proverb, "Blessed are those who plant trees under whose shade they will never sit."

In addition, the process of creating objectives forces faculty to analyze course content for relevancy, which in turn helps faculty avoid content tyranny syndrome. Since increased quality of learning of concepts and principles can be more easily achieved by decreasing quantity of content, this constant evaluation of course content for relevancy is imperative.

Although career-oriented courses are constantly evaluating content for relevancy, this is rarely the case for general education courses. Faculty evaluation of courses to ensure current relevancy may involve substituting less relevant objectives with more relevant material, skills, or behaviors needed for success. Not many computer courses could survive if they continued teaching computer punch-cards over more relevant programs and processes, and other courses will die off, too, if they did not become more relevant to success in today's workplace. Constant evaluation and assessment of unit objectives by faculty, or better yet by departments, ensures current and maximum relevancy.

It is not always easy to engage in the process of building and then constantly assessing unit objectives. However, students (and faculty) experience a surge of motivation when objectives serve as a chunked to-do list. The feeling of progress helps raise everyone's confidence levels. This can only happen when crystal-clear expectations help students engage in the learning process, and when faculty help students hold themselves accountable for understanding the objectives and examining them in preparation for class.

Therefore, one of the first questions on student interventions, or even for students seeking assistance, should be some variation of the following: "Are you looking up the objectives in the textbook before coming to class?" This would hold true for any course, as long as all courses had unit objectives in place, and is just another way of asking what the student has done to prepare for class. A reminder that the only wrong answer is "nothing" helps focus students back on the first step to the study process. Learning objectives therefore signal the first shifting of responsibility for learning to the student.

Reiterating that help can only come after a student has completed the first step is another way to ensure the rusty nut is broken loose, although some students may need assistance on what is meant by "looking up" the objectives. Highlighting these in the textbook during class calls students' attention to the main points. Using supportive statements, tables, or pictures to clarify concepts is also helpful.

It is also important for students to know that, although they may understand the reading, they should read in order to create questions to be answered during class or on a lecture video. It is through understanding how unit objectives can enhance students' ability to prepare themselves for classroom lectures, activities, and discussions that allow faculty to maximize the effectiveness of these objectives.

Therefore, placing an emphasis on "being here prepared" covers the two most important aspects of learning and success for students: attendance and *prior* thought into the course content. Combining this with active engagement (through the plethora of classroom activities) in the class session addresses the top concerns of faculty and employers—ensuring students or employees show up, are prepared to work, and actually work while in class or on the job.

Unit objectives help to ensure more focused and "doable" preparation. They provide the brain with specific "questions" to be answered and are chunked to match each day's activities. In addition to knowing which chapter will be discussed, students know specifically which topics they need to review and exactly how they will be required to perform on the tests based on the verbs used for each objective.

Once students show up prepared, the responsibility shifts to the instructor to serve as the facilitator of learning. If students are abiding by their responsibility to show up prepared, the instructor is obligated to fulfill their responsibility to provide a course and lesson structured to maximize learning.

With an abundance of encouragement for their preparatory efforts, faculty can nurture a renewed sense of confidence among the more at-risk students, ensuring they accept even more responsibility for their learning. This is the process by which a growth mindset is developed through strategies that enhance students' feeling of control. Ideally, it helps students attain one of the ultimate goals of education—becoming a lifelong learner.

There was an opportunity to maximize learning early in my teaching career in the community college system. At the time, I was also coaching basketball. One of our ballplayers, I will call him Chris, had registered for my physical science class in order to fulfill his requirements for a teaching degree. After a talk about responsibilities on the first day of class, Chris stayed around until all the other students in the class had left.

Chris proceeded to inform me that science was not his thing, and he was only getting a teaching degree so he could coach. In a relaxed and casual manner, Chris says, "Hey coach. All I need is a C to get through this class, so I know you have my back!" Realizing this could serve as a profound learning moment, he was reminded that he was expressing what is called a "minimum mindset." A minimum mindset, I told him, is fixated on the minimum required to receive credit. Although he knew that a minimum mindset does not work on the basketball court, he needed a reminder that it does not work in life, nor will it work in our classroom.

I told Chris I would be pulling for him to be successful in the course, but added, "You will get the grade you earn. And just so we are clear, if you end up with a 69.4 average at the end of the term, you will receive a D. So, my suggestion is to use the *maximum* mindset you are accustomed to on the basketball court and carry that over to this class. That way, even if you fall short, you will pass the class."

Little did I know the effect this talk would have on Chris. In fact, the only reason I did know was that his English teacher shared with me an essay he wrote the following semester. The assignment required students to write about someone who impacted their life in a profound way. Chris wrote about how he was not accustomed to being challenged outside sports and how that one conversation the first day of physical science class changed his mindset and inspired him to become empowered with strategies that improved his academic performance and his motivation to learn. He finished his paper with a statement that he knows he will be a better teacher because of the impact that conversation had on his approach to academics and his life.

Reflecting on that conversation with Chris, I am reminded of a quote by teacher and speaker Todd Whitaker: "The best thing about being a teacher is that it matters. The hardest thing about being a teacher is that it matters every day!" We never know what words may inspire a specific individual, which is why we try so hard to show students we genuinely care about them and their success. Once they know this, it is much easier to help them move well beyond their own self-perceived limitations and into that magical realm of empowerment that exists outside their comfort zones.

Although Chris may have been overwhelmed by the entirety of the course, keeping him focused on one step/objective at a time allowed him to quickly—and through small successes—gain the confidence he needed to assume responsibility for his performance in the class.

UTILIZE LECTURE VIDEOS

Because lack of time stands as one of the primary reasons given by faculty for not implementing more active learning strategies, the third strategy concerns utilizing time-saving teaching techniques like lecture videos. Implementing active learning techniques and activities that increase engagement, relevancy, and general education outcomes is crucial as faculty work to limit less productive passive or teacher-centered efforts. Lecture videos help faculty spend classroom time in intentionally active learning.

When more information is available via smartphones than at libraries, students can easily become overwhelmed by the quantity of information. However, educators can take advantage of technology by creating short (five- to ten-minute) *instructor-made* lecture videos paired to each unit objective, effectively chunking an entire unit into smaller segments. While this frees valuable class time for the use of strategies that promote deeper learning and skills more essential to life success, such as critical thinking, problem-solving, teamwork, and communication, it also offers around-the-clock content availability. Such availability provides valuable support for all students, but especially the most underprepared.

Lecture videos allow the instructor to "flip" any part of the lesson, and they can be especially valuable when the physical class sessions must be canceled (due to weather or illness, for example). Videos also allow students more control over their learning because they have a way to compensate for their absence if they must miss a class session.

Although faculty can make any adjustments they deem appropriate when they miss classes, if students miss class they are at the mercy of the resources provided. Clarity on what they must specifically know or do (information conveyed by unit objectives), combined with lecture videos paired to each objective, make it easier for students to compensate for missed classes or a simple lack of comprehension. The 24/7 availability of these resources increases internal locus of control sensed by having allowed students to accept more responsibility for their learning.

Although videos from the Internet may provide wonderful supplemental information or visual enhancements, lecture videos should be *instructor-made and intentionally tied to the objectives.* Research from our own ILA supports students' preference for videos made by the instructor. More importantly, it is the teacher's class, the teacher's students, the teacher's content, and the teacher's tests.

Immediate personal connections between the instructor and the students are strengthened as the instructor, even when not on camera, plays a very real role and has a presence throughout the video. This also allows the instructor more control in tailoring to the specific needs of the class. The fact that the material originates with the instructor can also provide an increased sense of relevancy and control for students, thereby increasing the chance that students will watch the videos.

Although educators may be daunted by the task, they can use screen-capturing software to allow for fast and easy video production without having the videos dated with a physical image of the instructor. There are several options available online for producing these videos (such as Screencast-O-Matic) that do not require special equipment and also allow for video editing. The institution must support course redesigns complete with unit objective videos through relief-time, reduced class load, or special recognition of those completing these redesigns.

These videos are more effective if they follow the same strategies deemed successful in the classroom. Therefore, an introductory slide should ask a question in order to generate the viewer's curiosity before introducing the subject. Other methods, such as providing a fill-in-the-blank worksheet to complete as students watch the video, can help ensure engagement. Additionally, capabilities such as closed-captioning, which can be obtained through programs that automatically incorporate it, provide additional support for all students, not just those who are hearing-impaired.

The aforementioned worksheet keyed to particular slides can be helpful in a few ways: It allows students to maximize their focus on the video subject (as opposed to trying to copiously take notes). It also provides a kind of carrot and stick, as the worksheets can be turned in at the beginning of class for a partial daily grade and as evidence of students' preparation for class. Reflecting on questions emphasizing key concepts from the videos also helps establish a foundation for additional learning.

Of course, videos take time to make. Indeed, the number one reason WCCD and ILA faculty give for their reluctance in making these videos is lack of time. However, faculty must practice the same time management required of students in order to take a seemingly overwhelming problem and chunk it enough to create a seemingly easy solution. Although most people will fill any system they have to the point where they are busy, it is imperative to develop a new system that makes time for something as important as giving students access to course content 24/7. Furthermore, the beauty of making video lectures is that once the videos are produced, they are good to use for as long as each objective is used.

To effectively chunk this task, teachers might consider applying a small effort consistently over a period of time to produce significant improvements. Over the course of one semester, teachers could devote Friday mornings to producing these five- to ten-minute lecture videos. Such an effort could result in about fifteen videos each week. In just five weeks, they would have about seventy-five videos produced. This equates to approximately an entire course. Continuing such a system allows teachers to complete three courses in the span of just one semester and attests to the power of having an effective system where consistently applied small steps provide the chunking needed for completion.

It is important to keep in mind that the point of videos is not to have incredibly high-quality videos, but to have an audio and visual representation of material deemed relevant. Just as a lecture or activity rarely results in perfection, teachers should not be overly concerned if there are slight blips in presenting. For the student, the focus should be on looking up each of the objectives in the textbook *before* watching the video accompanying these objectives. Emphasis on following these directions should be the first response to any solicitation of assistance by the student.

Videos may seem simple, but they really work. San Jose State University (SJSU) implemented lecture videos in an engineering course with one of its highest rates of withdrawals (Finkelmeyer, 2012). When compared to performance in the traditional lecture section over the course of the semester, exam scores in the video lecture section resulted in improvements in excess of a letter grade, despite having more difficult exams covering more content. This prompted a call to action for implementing videos across all engineering courses at SJSU.

The science division at WCCD experienced these same types of increases in student learning, prompting every instructor in the division to make a complete set of videos for every course they taught. Having already committed to addressing all issues impeding learning, collaboration in this division was facilitated through the use of weekly newsletters from the division director and monthly meetings that allowed for collaboration and quick integration of effective strategies throughout the division. Establishing a complete set of these videos on the LMS of adjunct faculty ensured that every science student had access to the same resources as those students in full-time instructors' classes.

When WCCD began its I-CAN initiative, educators raised questions concerning online and traditional classrooms. Since traditional classes provide complete face-to-face lectures on all topics in the course, it was not clear that online courses were comparable to traditional courses because at that time most students in online courses did not have access to lectures. The solution to this problem? Requiring all online and hybrid courses to have a complete set of these lecture videos.

However, this resulted in another question from faculty. Just as with students, we know our colleagues are engaged and thinking when they ask the right questions. Faculty asked about the fact that online students can watch these videos as much as needed, while students in traditional course sections only have access one time—when they were present for the lecture. This prompted faculty to post their videos made for online/hybrid courses on the LMS for traditional classes, as well, which led to substantial closing of socio-economic student achievement gaps, especially for those first-year, highest enrollment courses and developmental courses.

Over 75 percent of the gap between higher- and lower-income students was closed in the top ten enrollment courses and completely closed in developmental courses, with lecture videos playing a major role in these closures. The closures led to several national awards, as well as considerable increases in retention and completion.

Extending this use of the LMS well beyond just online courses and full-time instructors has allowed WCCD maximum return on investment. In response to criticisms about the limited use of the LMS, many institutions claim they require all faculty to post their syllabus and/or grades on the LMS. However, the LMS is not just a document storage facility. It is a system to manage learning.

Administrators would do better to ask themselves more meaningful questions: Is there evidence the LMS facilitates *learning* through the use of *proven strategies, such as objectives, videos, frequent assessments, discussion boards, and so on.*? Is this resource provided for all students, or just those who happen to register for an instructor who provides such resources? Supporting course redesign efforts across the institution allows for maximum use of the LMS to facilitate learning while affecting a maximum number of students.

A big part of the value of these videos is that they promote problem-solving. Students can be instructed to pause the video while attempting to solve problems posed on it. They can be taught that only after they have something on paper and can no longer move forward in the problem should they return to the video to get them through their "stuck point." Such an approach to problem-solving is much more effective than having students read a problem only to immediately go to the solutions manual to see the entire problem worked out.

Although I have seen firsthand the results of video addition in my own chemistry courses, there are also several examples of amazing results achieved through other effective instructor-made videos. For example, when Hunter College in Manhattan, NY, used videos of no more than ten minutes for its general chemistry courses, teachers saw pass rates go from 60 percent to 85 percent almost immediately. Lehman College, also in NY, had an 80 percent minority student body and experienced improvements in general chemistry pass rates from 35 percent to 80 percent!

After witnessing the increased learning and preparation for class with the unit objectives and videos, every science instructor at WCCD committed to producing a complete set of videos for their unit objectives in each of their courses. This goal was realized by 2010 and paid additional dividends as these redesigned courses were also made available for all adjunct instructors for use in their classes. The strategy carried over to our college-wide I-CAN initiative a couple of years later and led to the production of over 7,000 instructor-made lecture/tutorial videos available on the LMS for students 24/7.

Although effective videos can stimulate a higher degree of preparation for class, as well as providing a powerful 24/7 support system for students, its added value is that it frees up time for activities that stimulate learning. Reflection and review activities promoting greater engagement, critical thinking, and communication can replace much of the class time spent on covering content through lecture. Requiring short worksheets with fill-in-the-blank questions from the videos help increase accountability and participation. As for the concern that class attendance would decrease with the videos, this notion was quickly dispelled with the addition of frequent assessments.

FREQUENT FORMATIVE ASSESSMENTS

The use of lecture videos also allows more time for another engaging activity and the fourth strategy for course redesign: frequent low-stakes assessments. Formative assessments provide valuable information and allow students and faculty to critically reflect on previously covered material and to quickly adjust learning strategies. By using short quizzes, essays, group work, discussions, and other assessment measures (rather than higher-stakes summative assessments) to increase learning, students (and teachers) gain immediate feedback, which is far more important than the actual grade value for these assessments.

These assessments are *for* learning; as such, they are not at all like summative assessments, which carry a greater weight and are assessments *of* learning. Combined with chunking and active learning activities, low-stakes assessments allow students to quickly gain the confidence associated with meaningful learning because they can make small adjustments before moving on to new material. For many students, failure to do this can quickly lead to frustration and a sense of overwhelm, pushing students out of the learning mode and into survival mode—a result of stacking information they have not yet learned on top of information they have not yet learned.

Since they are assessments *for* learning, multiple types may be used. Many teachers incorporate daily grades into one grade at the end of the term that is approximately the weight of any given summative (unit) assessment. These grades cannot be made up, except for rare exceptions (such as multiple missed days due to an illness or special situation). Having a couple of extra daily grades allows students to miss no more than one or two class days and still maintain a perfect score. As with all other activities, however, it is imperative students are crystal-clear on requirements at the beginning of the course to avoid future misunderstandings.

Although traditional pop quizzes may come to many readers' minds as examples of low-stakes assessments, such activities are not always the most effective at assessing for learning. Students often perceive quizzes as just another extension of exams, especially when turned in and graded by the instructor. Instead, teachers can try using more innovative approaches to stimulate the use of the skills crucial to success in the workplace and in life. A simple Google search will yield a myriad of examples teachers can incorporate into classes. The purpose is to increase attendance, preparation for class, and engagement in the learning process, all of which leads to higher-quality learning.

The institution and instructional leaders can support these efforts and expedite at-scale use of more effective activities through regular brainstorming meetings to share successful strategies; such meetings take advantage of the diversity of innovations by including faculty from as many departments as possible. Providing faculty with the opportunity to participate in the ILA (as discussed in chapter 9) is a great way to expedite innovation and leadership development in the instructional division.

It is important to point out that, initially, students frequently resist the requirement to be more engaged in their learning (in part because it takes much less energy to sit and listen passively). One instructor informed me she had tried group discussions, but students did not like them. When asked what she was doing about it, she replied, "Well, I won't be doing those anymore!" Understanding that resistance is a natural reaction to change, teachers are less likely to take the resistance personally (Q-TIP) and make hasty decisions to eliminate activities that enhance learning.

After all, if we polled our students, I bet we would see that they do not particularly like homework or final exams, either, but we do not eliminate these activities. As leaders and as teachers, it is our responsibility to inspire students to do that which they need to do but may not want to do—and to do it long enough that they then want to do it. For parents, this is the same approach we must use in raising children.

A recent article, *"The Dangers of Fluent Lectures"* (Flaherty, 2019), summarized a new study in *Proceedings of the National Academy of Sciences*. The study concluded, "Students who engage in active learning learn more— but feel like they learn less—than peers in more lecture-oriented classrooms. That is in part because active learning is harder than more passive learning." This is also true of many instructors who typically perceive students learn more when instructors cover more.

The reality is that students objectively learn considerably more when "actively engaged in building knowledge about key concepts." So, although there may be initial (and potentially widespread) resistance to all kinds of course changes, course ratings from students often increase significantly once they realize the value of these activities toward learning. Not only do their test scores increase, but they many times find themselves carrying over relevant learning and skills training to other courses—and to life in general.

EMPLOY EARLY AND INTRUSIVE INTERVENTIONS

The fifth strategy—early and intrusive interventions—also works in synergy with course evaluation results to improve positive student perceptions. This strategy is also focused on developing more supportive relationships and making connections. As we have seen in the material on course evaluations, faculty-student interactions (interactions that lead to and deepen connections) are crucial to student persistence, retention, and completion rates. These interactions are especially crucial for the most at-risk students.

Skepticism upon hearing about data out of Valencia College in Florida that showed students' chances of completion are cut in half upon withdrawal or failure from one of their first five courses and cut in half again upon their second failure or withdrawal, quickly dissipated upon analysis of our own data at WCCD. Our findings were almost identical. Even more disturbing was that the data showed by the fourth withdrawal a student's chance of completion was less than 1 percent at WCCD.

Although our intervention strategies included frequent, early, and intrusive interventions, this data provided additional motivation for enhanced intentionality focused on increasing learning and supportive relationships in those high-enrollment, first-term/year courses. These courses can provide the highest return on intervention efforts, leading to increased retention and completion rates.

For example, we know that first-day or first-week interventions for students retaking a course are critical for developing an individual plan of action to improve performance. Consequently, faculty should plan to meet with all students scoring below a 70 percent on the first exam, an effective intervention strategy for making necessary adjustments while inspiring corrective action.

When the science division at WCCD adopted frequent assessments, they experience a 50-plus percent decrease in the number of students making below a 70 on the first exam, thereby considerably reducing the number of these particular interventions. Early interventions like these allow for small corrections, which, in turn, help give students motivation and confidence for future corrections. All interventions should identify and clarify misconceptions about what is required to successfully complete the course. Then, and as discussed in previous chapters, interventions should focus on obtaining the student's commitment by making a list on paper for their plan of action.

Recently, similar material was presented to an area community college. A teacher responded with, "I heard what you were saying about interventions, but I would never email a student just because they missed a class." Sound familiar? The teacher followed up with another familiar claim, "Because this is college, and there are some things they just need to figure out themselves."

These statements remind us of other statements faculty often make in response to change, many of which are discussed in chapter 3. It also reminded me of more than one interviewee for a faculty position at my own college, in which the interviewee referenced how much it meant to them in graduate school when they received an email from the instructor acknowledging their absence and offering their assistance if needed. If an intervention as simple as an email can make such a lasting impression on advanced degree-seeking students, we can only imagine the impact on our most at-risk students, especially those who are low-income and first-generation.

When the instructor was asked if she would say anything to her own child in her class who had missed two days in a row, she immediately replied, "Of course I would." I questioned why it mattered who the parent was when deciding who would receive intervention. She said she would not be intervening as a teacher but as a parent. After being reminded that a parent who uses school data to intervene with a child could be considered in violation of FERPA guidelines, the teacher acknowledged she might need to reevaluate her strategies.

The point that needed to be made was—and is—this: It is not that we *must* treat our students as if they were our own children, but that we *can*. If we treated our students the way we would want to treat our own children, we would make incredible progress in closing achievement gaps.

There was also a math teacher who pushed back against suggestions for more interventions by saying, "This is college and students just need to figure it out." Would he have had the same response if he had found his own daughter in her room crying out of frustration and overwhelm from a math class? Would he open the door to her room and just tell her, "This is college and you just need to figure it out?" Probably not.

Many times, interventions are short and impromptu opportunities. Our resistance is typically more mental, and perhaps emotional, than a reflection of limitations of time or ability. I am reminded of a baseball player I will call Jim. Jim majored in pre-med and took my first-semester organic chemistry course back in the mid-1990s. Most of the students had taken my general chemistry courses prior to organic chemistry, and we had established a rapport. However, because success in general chemistry courses does not naturally lead to success in organic chemistry courses, the first test can be a wake-up call. Of course, it was reiterated that although we would like to do as well as possible on the first exam, our ability to learn from our mistakes and use them as opportunities to improve is much more important.

While handing back the first test papers I noticed that Jim had received a D on this test (he later shared with me this was the lowest test grade he had ever made). Knowing he had attended the most prestigious private school in our area, where the focus was on preparing for college, I laid the paper on his desk while speaking softly, "We are no longer in Little League, Jim. It's time to step it up." If there was any doubt about how this short conversation would affect Jim, it was quickly dispelled: He never earned less than an A on any other subsequent tests. For Jim, it was not as much about him not knowing how to study as it was underestimating the effort it would take to be successful in this course.

Fast-forward ten years: I saw Jim's parents in the grocery store. Although I had completely forgotten about that day in organic chemistry class, his dad began to talk about what a profound impact my words had on Jim and how he continues to talk about it to this day. Just as with Chris, my former basketball player who wanted to be a coach, I would have never known about this impact had someone not shared it with me.

It is exactly the same with all our students. We simply may never know how much we have affected them. This means we must never underestimate the power of short, personal, and sincere interventions. Sometimes these interventions are just a pat on the back or a foot in the rear (so to speak), and this is why it is so important to connect with students as much as possible and to realize that encouragement and appreciation are a universal language.

Whitaker's words can be a stark reminder of the impact small gestures can have on students: The best thing about teaching is that it matters, and the toughest thing about teaching is that it matters every day, with every intervention, every activity, and every encouraging word! The strategies we choose to implement make a difference.

SYNERGETIC STRATEGIES

It is clear that teachers must take on a variety of new responsibilities in order to effectively redesign their course for maximum effectiveness. But it is equally clear that they cannot do this alone. Institutional leaders can offer a variety of support mechanisms to ensure faculty are as engaged in the learning process as their students. Chapter 9 provides examples of how institutions and administrators can not only support faculty efforts, but can help develop a leadership mentality throughout the faculty ranks that inspires continuous improvements in instructional and support strategies.

The synergetic effects of these five strategies combine for more improvement than the sum of their parts. When we implemented all five strategies across an introductory biology course at WCCD and tracked our data, we found that over *1,200 more students* showed up prepared for class than the year prior to implementation. Furthermore, overall withdrawal rates for the top ten enrollment courses on campus were cut in half the year after implementation.

Although these five strategies increase learning for all courses, implementation is particularly imperative in course redesigns for first-year, general academic, gateway courses. When almost half of community college students do not show up for their second year (according to data from the American Association of Community Colleges from 2012), retention is a significant problem and major contributor to lower enrollment and lower graduation rates. It is a problem for institutions, but it's a bigger problem for students.

> As leaders and as teachers, it is our responsibility to inspire students to do that which they need to do but may not want to do—and to do it long enough that they then want to do it.

To ensure all students have equitable opportunities for success, all students must have access to the same high-quality practices to enhance learning. This means adjunct faculty members should have a completely developed course on their LMS. This allows adjunct faculty to focus on facilitating a more active and engaging learning environment rather than developing a course that has been taught at the institution for decades.

We received numerous comments from adjunct instructors at WCCD, as well as from their students, indicating the profound effect this system has on learning. A ready-built course sends a clear message to new instructors about the mission, values, and purpose of our institution, a message that clearly communicates standards and expectations.

The five strategies in this chapter provide the instructional foundation for building a learning college, but a college-wide initiative is not a prerequisite for their use. Individuals or departments can use these strategies and the many effective engagement and active learning techniques they encompass. A quick Google search of active learning strategies yields dozens of specific activities related to these five core strategies. A powerful environment for transformation results from combining this information with positive, constructive collaboration and the courage to change.

Implementing these five proven strategies for enhancing student learning, persistence, and completion empowers faculty to achieve results previously unattainable with less effective instructional strategies. By integrating them into our teaching practices, we also help facilitate success for the diverse students who access community colleges. Ultimately, these strategies form a foundation for more effective learning and enhance the effectiveness of all activities chosen by the instructor.

Integrating these instructional strategies into the curriculum requires courage on the part of our teacher-leaders. It requires the courage to try something new and a willingness and adaptability to adjust and fine-tune each strategy for maximum learning and effectiveness. Luckily, the result of empowering a more diverse group of students to advance toward their higher education goals and build more productive and rewarding lives is a powerful incentive for drawing on that courage.

Several key points in this chapter are worth revisiting:

- The combination of relevancy and relationships drives the intellectual rigor.
- Data must be constantly shared with a degree of transparency that inspires action.
- If the desire is to have the best prepared students for the workforce or higher education, then we must incorporate the best strategies designed to inspire and facilitate a deeper and more meaningful learning.
- Each of these five strategies supports the three pillars of effective instruction: maximum engagement, relevancy, and supportive relationships.
- Substantial change in education will not occur unless the faculty is as deeply engaged as key stakeholders—Dr. O'Banion

- Creating a dynamic learning environment begins with dynamic personal connections. The power of these interactions and their impact on learning cannot be overstated, especially for the most underserved students.
- Just as faculty tell students to focus on learning and the grades will improve, we must also focus on improving positive perceptions so student performance can improve.
- Providing crystal-clear expectations is the first step to the learning process, and failure to do so results in many students being behind before we even start the lecture.
- Placing emphasis on "being here prepared" covers the two most important aspects of learning: attendance and prior thought into the course content.
- Developing a culture of caring and appreciation is crucial to overcoming the insecurity and low self-worth that may be felt by many community college students.
- Although effective videos can stimulate a higher degree of preparation for class, as well as providing a powerful 24/7 support system for students—the time newly available in class for stimulating activities is a bonus.
- Once students show up prepared, the responsibility shifts to the instructor to serve as the facilitator of learning.
- By integrating lecture videos, we saw an over 75 percent closure of the gap between higher- and lower-income students in the top ten enrollment courses and complete closure in developmental courses.
- Frequent assessments are for learning, as opposed to summative assessments which carry a greater weight and are assessments of learning.
- Do not be surprised if many of your students resist the requirement to be more engaged in their learning, as it takes much less energy to just sit and listen passively.

Chapter 7

Neurology of Learning

Recent advancements in neurology and the physiology of learning have provided the groundwork to understand how the brain naturally learns, something it has evolved over millions of years to do very well. Faculty frequently focus on differences among their subject matter, students, location, and institution, but the basic neurological needs of the students' brains are strikingly similar. These commonalities mean learning can be enhanced and achievement gaps closed through strategies designed to take advantage of how the brain naturally learns.

The neurology of learning provides the "why" behind the effectiveness of the five high-impact strategies presented in the previous chapter. Using this knowledge of neurology, teachers can redesign courses to maximize learning while also providing the motivation for future learning. Creating lifelong learners is one of the primary goals of education, and it is a much easier goal to reach when all college employees are also committed to it.

As we discovered at WCCD, when faculty adopt a more proactive approach to inspiring and facilitating learning, others at the college are moved to do so, as well. The saying that "a rising tide lifts all boats" is especially true when it comes to the efforts of faculty. Chapter 9 offers compelling evidence for the effectiveness of a program designed to ensure this "rising tide."

In his book, *The Art of Changing the Brain* (2002), James Zull offers a better understanding of brain functions and how to use these functions to promote more flexibility and variation to learning strategies. The book's insights provide the motivation for educators to reevaluate their pedagogical approaches to enhance learning for a greater diversity of students. Ultimately, by incorporating a greater degree of relevancy/rigor in intellectual processes, educators can inspire and facilitate deeper and more meaningful learning for a greater number of students.

It is important to note that although Zull references extensive neurological research regarding learning, he still refers to the "art" of changing the brain. Once teaching becomes grounded in fundamental principles supported by neurology, the continuous adapting and improvising may seem more like an art—the beauty of a profession ripe with hundreds of variables related to human nature and emotions.

Educators may find it helpful to understand the way the brain works. The four-phase learning cycle described by David Kolb in *Experiential Learning* (1984) extended earlier work by John Dewey and Kurt Levin about how we acquire information. According to Kolb, this learning cycle is "the process whereby knowledge is created through the transformation of experience." Kolb identifies the four phases of the learning cycle as concrete experiences, reflective observations, abstract hypotheses, and active testing.

Kolb suggests that for basic experiences to lead to learning, the brain must connect experiences to prior knowledge and past experiences through review and reflection activities. In other words, the brain must make new experiences relevant to old experiences. This relevancy is how the brain determines how new information may be useful, by developing a hypothesis, which then leads to active testing of the hypothesis. As a cyclic process, the final phase of testing becomes the start of a new first phase, as the observations we make during testing allow for additional experiences and enable us to use mistakes as opportunities to improve through further adjustments.

This learning cycle simply reflects the steps of logical thinking, and is part of the scientific method of observing, forming a hypothesis, experimenting, recording data, and formulating conclusions. This learning cycle, as outlined by Zull, is how the brain naturally learns. From an educator's perspective, the cyclical—or "process" part—matters. Learning clearly involves much more than simple short-term memorization of seemingly irrelevant material through the use of only the back cortex. It is a process that seeks to maximize engagement of the sensory cortex, back and front integrative cortexes, and the motor cortex. When we more extensively and intentionally facilitate the use of all areas of our students' brains, we create a more meaningful and memorable learning experience.

In the article *"Better Teaching Through Brain Biology"* (2002), Pierce Howard uses Johannes Gutenberg's invention of the printing press as a compelling analogy. Howard states, "Gutenberg is said to have encountered a grape press (Phase 1; concrete experience), then connected it to his memory of a coin stamp (Phase 2; reflective observation), with the resulting mental construction of a combination of the two (Phase 3; abstract hypothesis), which he then built into what we know today as the printing press (Phase 4; active testing)—see, connect, construct, test."

Almost a century ago, Graham Wallas developed a four-phase model of creativity in his 1926 book, *The Art of Thought*. In many ways, Wallas' research provides the groundwork for Kolb's description of the learning cycle. In this book, Wallas identifies the four phases of creativity as preparation (concrete experience), incubation (reflective observations), inspiration (abstract hypothesis), and evaluation (active testing).

The work of Wallas and Kolb, as well as many others, provides a clear explanation of the importance of reflection and review in order to move information from short-term memorization to working or longer-term memory, something that has been verified by recent developments in neuronal mapping. However, these steps are too often omitted in the instructional process. Too often, students are required to complete these steps outside the confines of the classroom, and this often proves an overwhelming task for those lacking the skills or knowledge needed for success.

As educators, we can help students engage in more meaningful learning processes. For example, to help direct your own intentional efforts toward promoting more relevant student learning, ask yourself what skills your students need to enter and be successful in college. Then, ask yourself if the majority of your students enroll with these skills in place. Many times, especially early in the term, we may find that we grade students on skills they have not yet learned, regardless of how common we may think these skills should be.

Identifying these skills, and then devoting time very early in the course to teaching (not just telling) these skills, provides valuable dividends as the course progresses. Encouraging all gateway course instructors to participate in this process ensures that students receive the repetition they need for transformative and transferrable learning, something that requires intentional institutional support and encouragement for at-scale implementation.

In essence, due to the physical changes in the brain promoted by learning, the art of teaching must be the art of changing the brain. Zull calls it "applied science of the brain" (p. 4). This phrase, along with educator sayings like, "telling is not teaching" and "explain, don't blame," serves as reminders that although we talk about facts, their meaning depends on students' individual experiences. Many times, and due to Zull's applied science, the explanation part is more effective when students make these discoveries on their own through intentionally designed activities that promote active engagement.

Higher education has always been diligent in covering content (concrete experience phase, although many times with limited use of diverse sensory stimulation) and testing. As has been pointed out, information today is cheap, fast, and easily accessible. This means there is a deep need for teachers to focus more on the quality of learning than on quantity. With all we now know about the brain, we have a valuable opportunity to evaluate and use information to help students create new ideas while helping them develop skills needed for life success.

WHY DO WE NEED TO CHANGE?

Just a couple of generations ago the skills of communication and critical thinking were more readily abundant because we needed them to survive. What was not readily abundant? Vast stores of information, something we typically obtained through formal education. We know that today this situation has flipped. Although information is readily abundant, critical thinking and communication skills are more of a rare commodity.

Data has shown for decades the need for adjustments in teaching strategies to better conform to the changes in society and technology. The rapid acceleration of changes has necessitated the need for more aggressive changes in pedagogy, as stated by the 2012 report, *Reclaiming the American Dream (RTAD)*: "Transformation in instructional strategies" with a directive to "courageously end ineffective teaching practices" are now required.

In fact, data shows that continued use of ineffective teaching strategies that do not support the natural neurological learning cycle could be one of the most destructively discriminatory practices today because it inhibits upward economic mobility for those needing it the most. For this reason, the RTAD report called for a "dramatic redesign of educational experiences" because of "unacceptably low student attainment gaps." This report even added the statement, "To remain open access, virtually everything else must change."

Like the focus on the science of the brain, this focus on learning may seem like a new concept. But the *Chronicle* of *Higher Education* (CHE) alluded to it over seventy-five years ago, as is referenced in Dan Barrett's 2015 article in CHE:

> Big changes in the classroom were on the way, according to an authoritative report by the federal government. Experts were realizing that disciplinary expertise and research prowess were no guarantee that a professor could teach. Some colleges were devising alternatives to rote learning, helping students integrate knowledge from different subjects, or challenging them with courses on contemporary problems. Teaching was finally going to matter.

Just as with proven high-impact strategies described in the previous chapter, instructors who have redesigned their courses to incorporate strategies supporting the natural neurological functioning of the brain commonly say they never knew how much of a difference small changes could make in terms of student learning and success. For instance, Kelly Hogan, a biology professor at UNC Chapel Hill, gained a newfound understanding of recent advances in neurology of learning in response to a call for gateway course redesigns. Upon reflecting on her own teaching, Hogan said, "Nothing I'm doing here is in line with how learning works" (Supiano, 2018). This realization can provide the forcing function to inspire individual and institution-wide change.

In the book, *Creating Significant Learning Experiences: An Integrated Approach to Designing College Courses* (2003), L. Dee Fink acknowledged that faculty may want more active and engaging learning experiences but may not know how to create or integrate them. Fink writes, "Although faculty members want their students to achieve higher kinds of learning, they continue to use a form of teaching that is not effective at promoting such learning."

Knowledge transmission through lectures are generally, as Fink stated, "less effective in helping students to retain information after a course is finished, developing problem-solving and critical-thinking skills, and developing ability to transfer knowledge to other situations, as well as diminishing student motivation to continue learning."

In other words, the passive learning environment used by many instructors does little to promote the building of crucial life skills and a motivation for lifelong learning. Although there is a place for limited lecture during classroom time, the majority of the time should be spent actively engaged with the content, other students, and the instructor. It is this environment that greatly enhances both the communication and critical-thinking skills so necessary in life beyond community college.

We already know employers value these core competencies. Just recently, Baird, A. and Parayitam, S. (2019) surveyed fifty organizations employing over fifty people and identified the top twenty-one skills employers felt were most important. All of the top-ranked skills are directly related to just two competencies: communication and critical thinking.

Core competencies are enriched and learning of course concepts improved when our courses are intentionally designed to promote these skills and values. If we think of the classroom as our home, then the three pillars of instruction—engagement, relevancy, support— form the foundation to our home, and the five high-impact strategies discussed in the previous chapter make up the "dried-in" portion of the new home construction as required by building codes (which are, in this metaphor, our course standards).

The remainder of the house is the most visible, and this is the everyday learning activities chosen by the instructor. Thinking about the classroom in this way can help us visualize a classroom that supports the way the brain naturally works, as well as developing core skills transferable to other courses and life itself.

Students learn best when they see clear connections between phases of progress. Similarly, each phase of progress is more effective when the previous phase is in place. We can activate this knowledge with the pedagogical technique known as scaffolding. To refine our house metaphor: Specific active-learning activities are more effective when supported by the five strategies, and these strategies are more effective when they support the three pillars of instruction.

Taken together, these efforts toward intentional education support our students' natural neurological functioning (learning). As we consider this, we must always keep in mind that maximizing effectiveness requires constant change and adjustments. We must also recognize that change is much easier, and details more relevant, when the basic concepts and principles are in place.

Since the fear of change can undermine growth, educators require the encouragement and positive, can-do approach of colleagues and their administration. This can also help educators as they work to overcome the challenges of finding the balance between quantity and quality, or the amount they want to cover versus the amount their students learn and understand, while also providing their students more control over their own learning.

Encouragement can help educators make major improvements with these challenges, especially because an institutional can-do attitude can help educators take the first step to try something new. Through increased positive and constructive collaborations, educators have an opportunity to provide leadership and inspiration for their colleagues to overcome these two biggest challenges.

It becomes more natural to offer encouragement to those yet to reach the buy-in phase of change if leaders can relate to their own frustrations when they might not have had the level of buy-in or ownership they currently have. Many times, when the teacher and/or leader has internalized the "why" to the point where they now have buy-in (or especially ownership), they tend to lose patience with those who have not yet achieved that level of buy-in.

Just as the teacher must allow students time for reflection in order to obtain a deeper learning and growth (change), so must the instructional leader allow time for faculty to reflect. By constantly communicating the MVP at every opportunity and using every resource at your disposal, to include articles, reports, brainstorming sessions, departmental meetings, and so on, meaningful change can occur.

This brings us back to the point that we can only do what we know, but when we know better we must do better. In order to know better, institutional support should be provided by constantly sharing proven strategies that support how the brain naturally learns, while also supporting and recognizing innovation in the classroom. Providing a high level of training ensures institutions are not evaluating faculty on that which they have never been taught, no matter how common the skill or knowledge is assumed to be.

This concept holds just as true for students in our courses, as one of the biggest underestimates students and faculty make is in regard to the amount of time and repetition required for mastery—which is precisely why education requires a team effort where core competencies are taught and applied in every course. After all, how limited would learning be if reading was only practiced in reading classes, writing only practiced in writing classes, and math (quantitative reasoning) only practiced in math classes? The same holds true for all core competencies, behaviors, and values.

Back in 2013, teacher Chris Mercogliano wrote, "May we live to see the day when our dominant educational model sheds its scaly dragon skin and is reborn as a dolphin swimming in an ocean of possibilities" (Life Learning Magazine, November/December 2013). I believe his words were prophetic. In my work at WCCD and ILA, I have never heard of an instructor who has redesigned their course, become familiar with brain-based learning, and committed to more active, engaging, and relevant class sessions, and has decided they would like to go back to the "old way of teaching." The increases in learning are so obvious they provide continuous motivation—for both teachers and students.

THE BRAIN-BASED LEARNING CYCLE AND LESSON PLANS

Phase one of the learning cycle is provoked by concrete experiences and starts in the sensory cortex of the brain. In this area, we receive input from our environment and then process it through our senses. Therefore, activities promoting a diversity of sensory stimulation lead to increased learning for a more diverse group of students.

Lab activities in the sciences, for example, take advantage of the visual, auditory, tactile, and olfactory senses to immerse students in an environment which promotes more detailed observations, communication, and critical thinking. In fact, these experiences can often help compensate for the limited life experiences of many of our students.

It is important to note that educators in any course can (and should) provide "lab time" (active learning through reflection, review, assessment) throughout the class period in order to stimulate usage of maximum parts of the brain. The active environment provides concrete experiences that are easier for the brain to remember, making it easier to move to phase two of the learning cycle. This dovetails with the four parts of a lesson described in chapter 5, where active learning is intentionally incorporated after the introduction and main lesson body (lecture), and prior to assessment.

It is important to acknowledge that anything a teacher does can provide students with a concrete experience. Although students may not always understand what we hoped they would understand from that concrete experience, every student will learn *something* because their brain did something with that experience. Although teachers can use this information to their benefit, it can work against teachers, too. Zull states:

> A student in history class may not learn much history but may learn the teacher thinks history is interesting; or that teacher dislikes students; or that he is just overwhelmed. These give an experience of some sort that his brain processes and ultimately acts on in some way—may close the book and look out window; or look at phone texts. (p. 20)

This is why, to obtain a higher quality of learning, teachers must intentionally enter phase two of the brain-based learning cycle. Phase two activates the *back integrative cortex* through reflective observations. By providing reflection activities that intentionally require students to reflect on concrete experiences, teachers help students make necessary neuronal connections between new learning to old learning.

It is in the back integrative cortex that sensory images from phase one connect to prior experience, or learning in existing neural networks of the brain, creating meaning. These connections are crucial: New neuronal growth cannot occur in mid-air but must be connected to existing neuronal networks (old learning). Without these connections, no one can understand or contextualize anything.

Of course, prior knowledge means that none of our students begins with a clean slate. Prior knowledge, even when incorrect, can be very strong and very persistent. It does not disappear with a dismissive comment or red mark. Because wrong ideas cannot be banished by simply stating they are wrong, teachers must work to present the logic, facts, and evidence in a way that allows students time for their brains to make the necessary connections.

This is the same work required when we work with colleagues skeptical of new strategies. We typically find encouragement—in both colleagues and students—when we see someone searching for connections by asking questions. Questions are often an attempt to clarify and create a more relevant connection to old learning.

In terms of the lesson structure, educators should use the introduction and lesson body to start students in the first phase of the learning cycle. This is done by introducing those concrete experiences. Phase two of the learning cycle, making connections, takes more time. Therefore, this time must be intentionally scheduled into part three of the lesson, the reflection portion of the lesson, as well as constantly intertwined throughout the lecture.

As Zull states, "Even the quickest learner needs time for reflection. She must let her integrative cortex do its thing. If she doesn't, her ideas and memories will be disconnected and shallow. They may be adequate for the moment (to pass a test, for example) but still transitory and ultimately unfulfilling." Without connections, memorizing without understanding is the only possibility.

The time spent in reflection is where the majority of the transferal of knowledge into working or longer-term memory occurs. This is especially the case when learning activities maximize the use of senses. Without this part of the lesson, information is left in short-term memory where capacity is limited. If teachers move on to new material without taking time for reflection and review through active engagement, students are forced to stack information on top of information they do not know, quickly reaching maximum capacity of their short-term memories.

It can be a challenge keeping students engaged and attentive. Using the neurological power of humor to reduce anxiety can provide a window of opportunity for quality learning. Even if the humor itself is not directly related to the subject matter, it can help to make students more receptive and attentive to that which is relevant to the course content. Neurologically, humor and depression are incompatible and the highest-performing teams take advantage of this fact to relieve stress, maintain a more relaxed focus, and help make the unbearable more bearable.

I was recently reminded of this when, upon pumping gas at a local gas station, I heard someone yell my name. Although I did not immediately recognize her, she told me her name and proceeded to convey how much she enjoyed my class from many years prior. Speaking with excitement about her young daughter in the car, she proceeded to talk about how much the class discussions of using humor to revitalize focus and stay positive meant to her as she recently went through some of the worst times of her life. Although the topic of humor was introduced and discussed in one of our weekly quotes, using humor to reduce stress was a daily practice used to overcome the stresses of a chemistry class—a good case of leading by example.

The enthusiasm and appreciation in her voice was enough to convey her sincerity, as this simple past lesson on humor allowed her to "live a better life" in spite of the overwhelming stresses in her life at the time and serves as evidence of how basic life skills can become more relevant as one matures through life's challenges.

The value of humor was also evident one day in a particular chemistry class that had a classroom mood in need of revitalizing. Although chemical demonstrations were always a great plan B for these situations, this particular day a video clip from one of the prank television shows was shown. Three minutes later the laughter allowed for a much-needed mental break before solving another word problem.

The art instructor, and my golf buddy at the time, told me at lunch that he was walking past my classroom and was wondering what the video had to do with chemistry. Although it may not have had much to do with the topic of chemistry, it had everything to do with preparing *students* to *learn* more chemistry—as well as a reminder to relish in the small mental breaks that life can provide when we don't take ourselves too serious. This simple method of chunking lessons with humor can help sustain longer and more strenuous mental activity.

Phase three of the learning cycle ignites the *front integrative cortex* through plans of action and *abstract hypothesizing*. Phase three is the transformational part of the cycle, during which a learner can create something new from present and past knowledge. The front integrative cortex is, as the name suggests, the area of the brain that integrates information to make decisions, develop strategies, and solve problems. We should note that this is not only necessary for students, but it is crucial to our continued growth as professional educators. During this phase, learners evaluate the connections made in phase two for relevancy in creation, explanation, or improvement.

We can help the students enter phase three during our interventions with students. For instance, we can help students commit to a new plan of action. This is necessary because their current approach is a sure way for them to continue getting the same substandard results. It is also necessary because a new plan of action helps brains continue to learn. This is another reason there should be continued emphasis that students must put their commitment on paper to solidify their commitment to change and increase the odds of change. As in all other phases, encouragement is very important for this phase. For many students (and all learners), the fear of failure can stop the learning cycle from doing its work.

Although the power of putting commitments and plans on paper has been stated in previous chapters and is well-known in the business world, let us look at what the data shows. A psychology professor at Dominican University in California, Dr. Gail Matthews, recently studied the science and art of goal-setting with 267 participants from all over the world. She found that you are 42 percent more likely to achieve your goals just by writing them down. However, it has been reported that less than 20 percent of people describe their goals in written form.

Since the human brain can process visuals 60,000 times faster than having to imagine things, writing down goals allows us to visually see them, which in turn affects how we act. Essentially, we are more likely to be productive if we can visualize what we need to do, instead of just thinking about it.

Phase four of the learning cycle consists of *active testing*, which occurs through the *motor cortex*, an area of the brain responsible for movement, speech, writing, and other similar actions. The fourth part to a lesson supports this phase of the learning cycle by providing assessments. In active testing, we practice applying our new knowledge, and we learn to recognize previously undetected misconceptions.

This is where the value of frequent assessments is realized as both student and teacher can identify and correct misconceptions before more summative, high-stakes assessments. Such testing may even lead a learner to have more concrete experiences (observations), which then begins another cycle. To facilitate this part of the learning cycle, teachers can and should incorporate more frequent (daily) low-stakes assessments into classroom activities to quickly correct misconceptions and facilitate sounder connections between new information and old information through established neural networks.

Ultimately, a balanced use of all parts of the brain is essential for deep and meaningful learning, and this is why students need to both *receive* knowledge and *use* knowledge. The traditional knowledge transmission approach favors the back cortex and results in more information than can be used (drowning in information) because such information typically comes too fast for learners to integrate and comprehend (starving for knowle. Although they may end up with information, it does not produce knowledge because not enough time was spent on reflection.

THE FOUR PARTS TO A LESSON

This review of the four phases of learning as they relate to brain processes allows us to better understand the value of the four basic lesson parts introduced in chapter 4: the introduction, the body, reflection, and assessment. These lesson parts are constructed by the teacher and should be designed to support the four phases of the learning cycle. The *introduction* prepares the brain for learning through questions that provoke curiosity. This communicates and supports relevancy, which then allows for a more effective *lesson body.* The lesson body should consist of concrete experiences, as well as reflections and observations through which students can accumulate additional observations. Images can be an effective addition to these first two parts of a lesson.

The *reflection* part of the lesson explicitly facilitates connections between new information in the lesson body and old learning through activities that promote active engagement. It is imperative that teachers make time for this part of the lesson so students are able to make meaning and integrate the information they have received. Although all parts of the lesson are important, reflection is most crucial to deeper, more meaningful learning. It is during the reflective part of the lesson that reflective observations and abstract hypotheses can be made. Ending the lesson with an *assessment* activity allows teachers to immediately correct misconceptions, which is crucial to improving student learning and success. A variety of assessment strategies allows for a more accurate determination of overall learning, as well.

As Pierce Howard (2002) stated in his article:

> The teacher can assume that students share certain common experiences that can be used as a foundation when presenting new information. If the students do not share a necessary experience, then the teacher needs to provide it. When a teacher simply assumes that all students can relate to a new concept or experience, he takes the risk that some will be unable to learn the new material deeply. If all they do is Phase 1 and Phase 4 of the learning process, they are just taking notes and taking tests—short-term success, long-term failure. This is myopic teaching.

Howard's words illustrate how teachers can be powerful student allies. By creating common experiences, teachers create the relevance that helps students become lifelong learners. The more emotionally stimulating these experiences, the easier it is to foster relevancy, which drives the intellectual rigor of deeper thinking. Relevancy is the glue that connects old learning to new learning—and that supports the bridge to further learning. We must continually remind ourselves that if the information covered cannot be made relevant, then the information covered *is not relevant*. If that is the case, we must ask ourselves why we are taking the trouble to cover it.

The following is a summary of key concepts in this chapter:

- The neurology of learning provides the "why" behind the effectiveness of the five high-impact strategies.
- Many times, especially early in the term, we may find that we grade students on skills they have not yet learned, regardless of how common we may think these skills should be.
- By removing the word "fault" from our vocabulary, the focus is on our responsibility to teach the students we have and not the ones we wish we had.
- Data shows that continued use of ineffective teaching strategies that do not support the natural neurological learning cycle could be one of the most destructively discriminatory practices today since it inhibits upward economic mobility for those needing it the most.
- Although learning is increased for all students in a more actively engaged environment, it is the students who need education the most that benefit the most from maximum engagement, relevancy, and supportive relationships.
- Activities promoting a diversity of sensory stimulation lead to increased learning for a more diverse group of students.
- No one can understand anything if it is not connected in some way to what they already know (prior learning).
- The time spent in reflection is where the majority of the transferal of knowledge into working or longer-term memory occurs.
- A balanced use of all parts of the brain is essential for deep and meaningful learning, hence the need to balance receiving knowledge and using knowledge.
- Using a variety of assessment strategies allows for a more accurate determination of overall learning, as well.

Chapter 8

Problem-Solving Using Data

The first step is the first step for a reason, but it can be hard to take, even if we know "you can't steal second with your foot on first." Sometimes, however, the first step provides the confidence and motivation to continue with the second step, which then builds momentum to proceed to completion. This is something faculty find much easier to teach to students when faculty have already practiced it. Because it requires courage to take the first step in an environment of uncertainty, this behavior is often referred to by leaders as "using initiative."

WHERE TO START?

There are many variables which can affect the ability to use initiative, which is one reason for the saying, "Never, ever ask permission to lead—you will know when it is time!" Although courage is crucial in taking the first step, so is an understanding that problems will not solve themselves and require leaders to make things happen with intentional efforts and not wait for things to happen. As mentioned previously, when mistakes do occur—acknowledge them and then take ownership by making the adjustments needed for improvement.

When this positive and proactive behavior is modeled, a greater degree of purpose and passion are promoted throughout the organization, creating an environment conducive for building leadership throughout the team.

155

Sometimes motivation for these efforts can be found in the saying, "If it is important enough to you, you will find a way. If not, you will find an excuse."

It is this aggressive approach to problem-solving that is one of the leader's greatest assets. This aggression is not an anger or aggression toward your students or colleagues, but a proactive and positive approach to problems by addressing the performance or behavior and not the person. The dichotomy?—not so aggressive that you overlook key observations that a pause could have produced.

When purpose and passion exceed internal fears, it becomes more natural to move beyond self-perceived limitations and into the realm of profound growth that occurs outside our comfort zones. However, when personal comfort and fears take precedence over purpose, it can be difficult for faculty and for students to muster up the courage to take that first step—hence, the power of encouragement! It is crucial we work to help each other and our students identify the first step and then encourage them to take it because otherwise overwhelm can take over. This process is also a reminder of the MLK quote, *"You don't have to see the whole staircase, just take the first step."*

My grandson's thirteenth birthday challenge serves as a reminder of the power of chunking into smaller steps, as well as the power of consistency. Since he was becoming more active in sports, he was challenged to do 10,000 pushups over the course of the next year for $100 if he documented and completed the challenge. With a less than enthusiastic reply, he proceeded to inform me that this was an "impossible" task and for "just $100." Reminding him that he was "just thirteen years old," I followed with, "Is it really impossible, or are you not able to mathematically break down the impossible in order to make it possible?" Knowing how much he enjoyed a mathematical challenge, this question stirred his curiosity.

Now is the time to interject chunking with the question, "Can you do ten pushups?" His reply was, "Anyone can do ten pushups. I can do twenty for you right now." I told him he did not need to show me, I just wanted to know if ten was "easy"—which he emphatically confirmed. "So you could do ten when you get up in the morning and ten when you get home from school, then end the day with ten pushups before you go to bed?" After he replied with, "Of course," he was reminded that would be 30 pushups a day and there are 365 days in a year.

When it comes to larger problems, we naturally tend to get caught up in the details, and our focus spreads to multiple steps, all of which seem necessary to complete *right now*. We might become paralyzed by a sense of impossible immediacy. This is the reason it should be constantly reiterated to students that a problem should never be more difficult than one step—as this is all we should focus on at one time. To extend the MLK quote mentioned earlier, after taking that first step on the staircase you simply need to see the next step, and then the next.

The effectiveness and efficiency of to-do lists serve as evidence of the benefits of this problem-solving process, turning overwhelming problems into small, more doable steps. After doing the mental math, his eyes widened as he said, "That's over 10,000 pushups a year!" What an empowered feeling to realize an "impossible" problem can be immediately perceived as "easy" when applying chunking—which is the reason for this strategy.

Since the task has now been perceived as easy, it is time to obtain a commitment. I then followed with, "Since you have now determined how easy it is, are you willing to commit to doing 10,000 pushups over the next year for $100 or not?" Without hesitation he replied that he would be willing to take on this challenge, to which I replied, "Good, because if you don't complete the challenge you owe me $100." After informing me that I was changing the rules, he was reminded that he was asked if he was willing to "commit"—a willingness to do whatever it takes—and that this should not be a problem since he just confirmed how "easy" it would be using the system of just thirty pushups a day. The only rule was that his progress must be documented.

This documentation of results is the same approach used when implementing strategies in the classroom, as the data will provide the motivation for continued progress and future improvements. I must admit how impressed I was when his calendar showed "30" written on each day of the week. However, I thought he might be slipping when I noticed a "0" on Saturday and Sunday, until I saw a "60" written for Monday and another "60" for Tuesday. This is a potent lesson that we had not discussed in our prior conversations.

To reference an old quote from sports that also applies to life—"You do not need to have the lead if you have the heart to come from behind." His deficiencies on the weekend were compensated for by doubling up on the next two days. As in life, our success is determined by how well we can compensate for deficiencies, mistakes, or poor past decisions.

During my busy road schedule over the next several months I made the mistake of not maintaining oversight and support. The next time I checked his calendar, I noticed several weeks of no documentation. His initial enthusiasm had diminished in my absence and was a strong reminder of the need to maintain oversight and support long enough for habit and self-motivation to dominate. As mentioned earlier—we must sometimes want it more than them until they can get to a point where they realize they want it also.

We were discussing this story with my dad, who was 82 years old at the time, and he quickly calculated that he was doing over 9,000 pushups a year and informed us that he was adding two more each day so he could surpass the 10,000 goal. Using this as additional motivation, my grandson and I agreed to restart our commitment. The only difference was that I would be doing them with him. Many teachers use an approach similar to this by assigning "accountability partners" in their classes to provide mutual support to each other.

Although I was working over 100 miles from home at the time, this approach realized immediate improvement as I would text him on my way to work and inform him that I had completed my 30, finishing with—"What about you?" After several minutes of delay, he would respond with, "I have now!" My grandson quickly flipped the script on me as he would text me early in the morning to let me know he had completed his 30, ending with, "What about you?"

Working together, teamwork made the dream work as we were able to finish our 10,000 before the end of the year. The weekly communication with my dad also provided additional motivation for my grandson—and me! Just as it was with my grandson, establishing early connections with students allows teachers to harness their influence and establish a learning environment conducive to self-motivation. In this environment, coaching and training takes precedence over telling.

To summarize, solving seemingly overwhelming problems starts with chunking the process into small enough steps to be perceived as "easy." The second step is to obtain a commitment, preferably in writing, as data is then used to monitor progress and provide continuous motivation. This motivation is further enhanced when the commitment is mutual among colleagues and/or departments. However, do not underestimate the power of continuous collaboration and sharing of data.

Turning seemingly "impossible" problems or tasks into smaller, more doable steps (chunking) applies to any situation where there is a feeling of overwhelm. The smaller steps help minimize distractions and facilitate taking initial action, both of which lead to increased chances of success—especially when combined with frequent *collaboration* with team members and *celebrations* of progress.

The benefits of taking initial action and minimizing distractions are evident in everyday life. Years ago, I was impressed with the ability of my five-year-old daughter to complete jigsaw puzzles that seemed well above her skill level. One day I dumped a jigsaw puzzle on the floor for her to complete and then left the room. Standing behind a door I watched as she meticulously sorted out all the pieces with a straight edge. Then, she took out the four with a corner. She proceeded to move all the other miscellaneous pieces to the side and out of the way. Using the image on the box as a guide, she was able to construct the entire perimeter of the puzzle before sifting through the remaining internal pieces.

Her work on this puzzle illustrates how to avoid the overwhelmingness associated with the big picture. This is especially necessary in education, where so many variables and options affect not just the students, but the staff, the faculty, and even the institution. We can begin to effectively problem-solve by identifying internal pieces as distractions and moving them to the side. Then, we can focus our attention on the first step: simply identifying the corners of the puzzle. Once the corners (basics) are situated, we can begin to look at the limited number of pieces that connect to the corners, making up the remainder of the puzzle's perimeter. Only with this foundation in place, can we efficiently handle the details.

When purpose and passion exceed internal fears, it becomes more natural to move beyond self-perceived limitations and into that realm of profound growth, which occurs outside our comfort zones.

So it is with problems we encounter in life. In the first chapter, it was pointed out that for community college students, focusing on the details without a clear understanding of the foundational basics quickly leads to frustration and overwhelm. The same holds true for us: By putting energy into just the first, foundational step, we are better situated to figure out the rest. Of course, my daughter's work on the puzzle also offers an excellent metaphor for internal motivation rooted in progress: With each successful piece we put into place, we see our progress, and this provides the motivation we need to find the next piece.

This motivation can be deterred if too much emphasis is placed on the final goal, answer, or solution. Just as with the puzzle, the final result will become clearer the closer we get to the end. By creating smaller steps there are more frequent accomplishments which re-energize continued effort. We do not need to know the final answer, only the next step, and then the next, and so on. The small successes of each step provide the confidence and motivation to continue. Where the pessimist may complain about how far they are from the goal or answer, the optimist is celebrating attainment of each step—the proof they *are* making progress!

One of the best examples of this is from a scene in the movie, *Facing the Giants*, where the coach challenges a high-school football player (Brock) to crawl the entire football field—with a player on his back! To help the player focus on one step at a time and not necessarily the final goal of crossing into the end zone, the coach blindfolded the player. If you have seen this movie, you probably would have noticed that encouragement was not provided at the end of task as that was time for celebration. The encouragement was provided continuously along every step of the 100 yards. It was not until the blindfold was removed that the player realized his attainment of the goal. He was too focused on each step of progress to be deterred by a final goal that seemed too far out of his reach.

To expound on this movie scene, the coach tells Brock that he is the most influential player on the team and that if he walks around defeated, so will the rest of team. It is that moment that the rusty nut becomes loose from the bolt! Brock commits to taking a leadership role and lead by example and the rest is movie history. As the teacher you are the leader in the classroom, although we relish in those moments where a student takes the leadership role and inspires their classmates, and sometimes us. If educators allow the challenges and distractions of today to defeat them mentally, so will the rest of the class—especially the most at-risk students.

At WCCD, an example of the power of taking the first step was reiterated shortly after beginning our I-CAN instructional initiative. By this time, the power of helping students feel connected was evident. As dean, I wanted students to feel this connection from administration as well as faculty. My plan of action to solve a long-standing problem of disconnection focused on the courses where the majority of students registered—those top ten enrollment courses. Having already committed to meeting with every orientation section, it seemed like a natural addition to also meet with these top enrollment course sections.

Upon notifying my secretary of my intentions and requesting a schedule that would allow a visit to all sections, she informed me that there were 117 different sections spread over day, night, weekend, and satellite campuses. This was a daunting task, but the purpose of these visits seemed too impactful to avoid. Scheduling about eight of these five-minute motivational meetings each day allowed me to visit all sections within four weeks—once again, the power of chunking in action. The overwhelming student response to these initial visits over the first two days, as well as the personal inspiration I gained from them, was enough to continue with the commitment and was a stark reminder that to experience the rainbows we must be willing to put up with a little rain (and sometimes a few storms)!

As part of a follow-up reflection activity to these visits, instructors required students to write down and discuss the parts of my talk they found most beneficial. Not only did this activity provide professional development for the instructors, as they were provided valuable information from students on what they found most relevant, it also gave me insights that reinforced the need to provide students with more discussion about successful life behaviors and habits. However, it was the inspirational and personal stories of persistence and resilience that were shared which seemed to resonate with students the most. As research has shown, students indicate a desire to be taught these crucial, but often overlooked, aspects of becoming more resilient and purpose-driven in their quest for success.

Because of its importance to student learning, faculty should do whatever it takes to generate the courage required to take the first step in implementing more effective instructional and support strategies. Pairing with a colleague to simultaneously implement a new strategy can provide the support needed to get that "rusty nut loose from the bolt." Meeting to reflect on these newly implemented activities and share results can create the motivation for continued innovation.

A newly hired instructor could also provide leadership by prompting collaboration among department members to share their highest-impact strategies, techniques, or activities. Once collaborations begin, departments must continue them on a regular basis in order to practice effective critical thinking and problem-solving that builds a culture of inquiry focused on maximizing learning—for both students and faculty.

For those teacher-leaders who may have already loosened the nut from the bolt, providing encouragement for those yet to do so is a wonderful way to interject leadership—just as my grandson did by taking the first step and jumping off the cliff and into the water. Your purpose as a teacher-leader can override others' fears. But you can also override your own. If your fear is strong, consider that implementing more effective instructional and support strategies proven to close achievement gaps might not be as painful if the student impacted is your own child, a child that might be subjected to a life of poverty and neglect if they do not obtain a postsecondary credential and skills more conducive for success in the workplace.

CULTURE OF EVIDENCE

The process of integrating instructional leadership involves addressing issues with faculty, the very members who have the greatest impact on student learning, success, retention, completion, and enrollment. It will be necessary for teacher-leaders and administration to encourage a cultural transformation that abhors socioeconomic achievement gaps. This becomes possible once we know where we are and where we are going, so providing current performance data for the entire institution and combining this with standards and/or goals based on this data is a great start.

At the same time, we cannot underestimate the power of the "why"—everything we do, and everything we change, must be all about learning. Just as with problem-solving any subject, and in life itself, we must identify where we are and where we want to be in quantitative terms. Rather than taking on the responsibility of convincing more reluctant faculty to implement more effective strategies through dialogue, we can let the data and the logic do the motivating.

By using data to define our parameters, we commit to a culture of evidence, making decisions based on data as opposed to feelings and emotions. In other words, we would rather act critically and logically than react emotionally. This can be important: Even though we may sometimes "feel" our strategies are effective, the data may show otherwise. The real question regarding effectiveness is whether there are *more* effective strategies for learning with a diverse group of students—and this is the question we must ask ourselves to ensure constant improvement.

Indeed, one of the most common results from initiatives such as I-CAN and the ILA, in which the focus is on complete course redesigns and more active, engaging, and relevant instruction, is that W/D/F rates are cut in half. This leads us to the prerequisite step absolutely essential to maximizing participation and development of faculty: accountability for data/results. This means accountability for evidence of constant improvements based on data—the primary requirement of all accrediting agencies.

Faculty action plans should therefore be created in response to reflections on performance data for their classes. The plans should also provide documented evidence of faculty's willingness to constantly improve. By integrating the evidence into the plan, a sense of positive restlessness eventually becomes part of the culture of accountability—accountability to ourselves, our students, our community's taxpayers, and our institution.

Each term or year, the loop is closed on accountability as faculty provide evidence of their implementation and the results experienced. Their reflection on their new data and experiences allows them to develop a new plan of action for the upcoming term or year, thereby completing the learning cycle and starting a new cycle based on results.

Institutions often express concern that despite abundant and amazing professional development activities, there is little improvement in student performance outcomes. More often than not, the lack of success is a consequence of skipping the critical step of implementing a system of accountability for data/results. This accountability can be as subtle as having each instructional department share their newly implemented successful strategies, as well as evidences of increased learning and engagement.

In our ILA, each month provides additional professional development on a topic. To ensure something is actually developed from these monthly activities, faculty share new strategies they implemented since the prior month's session that enhanced learning. As a participating faculty member, your accountability in this case is to the cohort/team and is a chance for you to interject your leadership by inspiring your colleagues with the results of your efforts. After all, gaining insights into successful approaches from twenty or more of my colleagues without providing at least one of my own successful strategies in turn would not be upholding my responsibilities as an ILA teammate.

Determining where each faculty member is in terms of student engagement and success involves displaying course success data in a way that clearly identifies both stronger and weaker areas. Although a departmental average success rate may not be "any worse than anyone else in the state," expanding this data down to the individual instructors may show an unacceptable level of variance. Socioeconomic achievement gaps tend to be much smaller in courses employing more active learning strategies and much larger in courses that do not. Instructor and section variance contribute to these gaps.

Converting problem-solving from an experience in which faculty assume a defensive posture into a more offensive, proactive posture is much easier if a leader understands the denial stage of change. Blame and excuses often make up the defensiveness and require an abundance of logic and data, along with encouragement and a reminder to Q-TIP, to move into the more productive stages. For teacher-leaders, this is a reminder of their responsibility to convert negatives into positives, crises into opportunities, and complacency into action. Sometimes all it takes is asking the right questions to generate reflection—after all, great teacher-leaders ask great questions!

In one of our first division director meetings at WCCD after implementing I-CAN, data—with a keen emphasis on the top ten enrollment courses—was shared with all divisions. At least one of these courses was taught in each of our general academic divisions. Upon discussion of our lowest success rate course in this group (math), many offered an emotionally reactive response of, "Well, our success rates are no worse than anyone else in the state."

Although this statement may or may not have been true, we all agreed it would not help the image of the college to advertise this on our marquee in front of campus. It was (and is) not as much about what we are doing wrong as it is about what we can do to improve. But because we cannot do better until we know better, analyzing course success data for the first time provides a start to "knowing better."

Providing more detailed analysis of achievement gap data can also serve as motivation for change. Although this data can be broken down by race, our data at WCCD resembled national data which showed that the largest gaps were the socioeconomic gaps—low- versus higher-income students. Kelly Hogan, hired as a teaching-oriented professor at the University of North Carolina at Chapel Hill to improve undergraduate education, was receiving wonderful success and satisfaction ratings from students. However, when a colleague shared performance data broken down by race and gender in an introductory biology course, a different story came out. About one in fourteen white students earned a D or F. For Latina students it was about one in seven, and blacks, one in three (Supiano, May 2018).

This example shows that high course success rates do not necessarily mean there is *not* a problem. While low success rates definitely indicate a problem, so, too, do wide variations based on instructor, section, format, and other variables. For example, since student achievement gaps can arise from large instructor variances, it is important to standardize basic strategies for each course.

When WCCD analyzed a history course with three different instructors, all three courses required five major tests, although each had vastly different points assigned to different forms of other assessments. Thus, despite using the exact same score on the five tests, a student could have earned a B, C, or D depending on which instructor they had. Situations like this turn registration into a roulette wheel where chances of success depend more on which instructor's class the student happens to register for.

This same scenario of success variance occurs in many cases where it also depends on when the student takes the course, whether at night or during the day, with full-time or adjunct instructor, with first-year or seasoned teacher, and especially whether the teacher uses ineffective passive, teacher-centered strategies or effective active, learning-centered strategies that promote a higher quality learning experience.

In addition, overall averages can sometimes hide more relevant data that would allow us to develop action plans more intentionally focused on implementing strategies proven to close achievement gaps. The action plans we create in response to this kind of data serve as evidence of our commitment to constant improvement, although it must be noted that initial action plans tend to be more defensive in language as it takes time to be reminded to Q-TIP it.

To avoid emotional responses, educators need to take time to reflect after analyzing course success data or course evaluation results and then follow up with a second analysis in which they respond with a proactive plan to improve learning and positive perceptions. Action plans developed through departmental collaborations can provide a more equitable degree of standardization.

Advisors are often asked to recommend an instructor. When this happens, the ideal reply is that it just comes down to different personalities and approaches, and not that basic resources supporting learning may be excluded in a given section. A culture of evidence, which allows for a more detailed analysis of data, leads to a more intentional plan of action for providing a more equitable learning environment. It comes back to relating the question to our own hypothetical child. Would we recommend an instructor at our own institution for our son or daughter? Without evidence of instructional standardization in a department, division, or college, where is evidence of instructional effectiveness?

USING DATA EFFECTIVELY

Problems can be solved and a culture of evidence created through transparency by listing all individual instructor W/D/F rates in order of high to low (showing names only to the instructor receiving the data). This allows for a more accurate and comparative definition of effectiveness, while serving as a powerful motivator for collaboration and innovation. As with any crisis, the cream often rises to the top.

When challenged, teacher-leaders frequently take courageous steps to create a learning environment more beneficial to meeting the challenges of higher education this century. This is much easier to do when the evidence is transparently rooted in data. Many times, teacher-leaders able to productively respond to data are further along the phases of change—they understand the need for change, even if they may not feel they have the freedom or support they need to make the necessary changes.

The goal for the institution and/or departments is to create valuable and specific data and to make it available in an easily readable form on a regular basis to more easily promote faculty action. Identifying benchmarks and baselines, as well as standards and goals, is an integral part of the data analysis process. Departmental, divisional, college, state, and national averages all provide insight into what the next level of performance may look like. Just as teacher-leaders do in class, the institution and its administration must encourage, recognize, and appreciate all efforts in the right direction since the focus is on constant improvement and not on the final goal. This goes for faculty colleagues, as well.

Results from the use of new strategies should be shared and celebrated so they can be a fuse igniting further innovation and inspiring some of the more reluctant faculty to take the first step and loosen the rusty nut from the bolt. This was done shortly after beginning our I-CAN initiative at WCCD through the idea of a "Faculty Spotlight" shared by another dean at the college. Each week a faculty member from a different division was "spotlighted" to highlight successful strategies.

These "spotlights" required a summary response from the faculty member about the strategies they use to "inspire and facilitate learning with their diverse group of students." The summary was followed by a statement from their division director about why the faculty member was valuable to the division and to students. The associate dean and the dean of instruction also added a statement. The spotlighted faculty member was presented with a Certificate of Appreciation in front of their class and had their photo taken with their dean or associate dean.

Summaries and photos were featured on a one-page newsletter emailed institution-wide. Although these were sent weekly in the beginning to build momentum (and CC the MVP!), they were later moved to a monthly email. Not only did this recognize and support successful and innovative strategies, it also provided a wonderfully encouraging and consistent form of professional development. Faculty were able to see the many consistencies among these most effective instructors, as well as gain ideas for new strategies in their own classes.

The spotlight also helped to initiate a departure from departmental siloes, as faculty began to see the value of strategies that could be used effectively across all departments and divisions. This institutional recognition or award has also been termed a "risk-taker" or "innovation" award to convey the appreciation for moving out of one's comfort zone in an attempt to expand learning.

In addition to the qualitative aspects of the spotlight, we used quantitative student success data to clearly identify current levels of performances. This made it much easier to then set quantitative standards and goals (expectations). This process—identifying the level at which we currently operate, and then setting appropriate, reachable expectations—is the same process we use in the classroom. Using this process to identify standards reinforces an institutional commitment to a culture of evidence. Making data-driven and informed decisions, and using strategies like faculty spotlight, gives faculty the encouragement and insights they need to continue to innovate.

When the institution or department provides this quantitative information on a graph after each term or academic year, it tends to have a much more visible impact and stimulates a stronger desire and motivation to improve. The intent of such a graph is to obtain maximum visual impact so as to obtain maximum incentive from faculty to seek more effective instructional and support strategies—to get more rusty nuts loose from the bolt. In other words, let the data do the talking. For example, to further expand this graphical and visual impact, differences should be maximized by eliminating unused or redundant areas of the graph. This means if the range of success rates is from 40 to 80 percent, then the graph should start at 30 to 35 percent and end at 80 percent.

An example of the impact data can have on decision-making comes from an institution much like many others in the country, where instructor variance in success rates is vast. Prior to beginning our ILA and in an attempt to provide data to inspire action, course success data from all top-nine enrollment courses in the state was analyzed to identify variances and the impact of variance on students.

This analysis of course success data showed an art appreciation course (one of the highest enrollment first-year courses) at one institution had one full-time instructor with a 57 percent success rate (43 percent W/D/F rate), and another instructor for this course at the same institution had a 72 percent success rate (28 percent W/D/F rate). In this case, the first instructor had over 40 students each year who were not successful in their course (translating to 400/decade or 1,200 over a typical teaching career). These students, statistically speaking, would have been successful in the second instructor's course.

Given national statistics showing the chances of completion are cut in half upon withdrawal or failure, and then cut in half again upon the second withdrawal or failure, negative impacts are substantially amplified. On the other hand, each student who successfully completes a course due to the use of more effective learning strategies (who, statistically speaking, would not have successfully completed it previously) would have their chance of completion doubled!

It can be an empowering moment when we realize that every additional student who is successful in a course in which they would not have been successful prior to the implementation of more effective learning strategies is from the most at-risk group. In other words, each of these students benefit the most from the confidence they develop as they realize they are not incapable of learning.

Now, back to that art appreciation course. If this *one* course at this *one* institution had achieved the state average success rate for this course, over 200 more students would have successfully completed the course each year (2000/decade). We can expand the effects of this success to the immediate family and see that successfully finishing a first-term gateway course and increasing a student's chance for completion makes a difference in the student's life and in the life of their family.

We can expand the effects further to see the impact of successful completion on the community: the total cost to the taxpayer for those students to retake the art appreciation course is in excess of $100,000. In summary, wide instructional effectiveness gaps such as this are costly for the student, the institution, and the taxpayers and are all too common for many other courses across the country. Solving this problem requires adherence to a culture of inquiry and evidence by using data—data that can sometimes be more compelling when using the number of students affected as opposed to just percentages.

Whether the motivation for the institution is increasing student success or increasing revenue, this data helps clearly define the value of adopting more effective instructional and support strategies, as course success rates are the most important leading indicator for retention and completion (other than individual assessments in class). In addition to identifying problem areas and providing incentive to improve, data can also be used to celebrate accomplishments and market successes.

As one of the most educationally researched countries on the planet, it is not a matter of knowing what strategies are most effective in facilitating learning and solving problems of inequity in education, but in implementing these strategies at-scale. Once implemented holistically and at-scale, these data-driven strategies are guaranteed to increase student learning, course success, retention, and completion. Required high-impact strategies used in response to issues, obstacles, and problems associated with student learning form the guardrails for our uphill and wavering climb to effective learning.

Monitoring improvements from baseline data can be a powerful motivator for building the positive and persistent resilience needed to overcome the challenges in higher education, as well as using this data to inspire action in other faculty and institutions. This is why the ACCS incorporates active classroom research components into its state faculty development program (ILA). Faculty approach each of their proposed changes as a research project, allowing for adherence to data that answers the question, "How do you know it improved learning?" This research component will be used to establish a cultural commitment to constant improvement in those instructional and support strategies so vital to student success, as well as providing the data and evidence needed to inspire others to action.

Although collecting baseline data, implementing chosen strategies, and obtaining the results from this implementation can show the impact on student learning, it is the synergy effects of implementing multiple high-impact strategies that can produce the most profound and significant increases in student learning. This increase in learning is what helps students realize their efforts can control their success, thereby effectively solving one of the biggest problems hindering success for our most at-risk students—their feelings of inadequacy. Students who once believed things happen *to* them now believe *they can make things happen*—an empowering realization that will help them live a better life and make a better living!

> The advantage of using data to improve critical thinking and problem-solving skills with faculty is that they then become much more effective at teaching these essential skills to students!

In summary, for problems to be solved at the lowest level possible, it is imperative leaders model effective problem solving. Team meetings (department, division, college, etc.) are a great place for this modeling/training to occur. By following the basic guidelines below, leaders become more proficient problem-solvers in their quest to build additional problem-solvers throughout the team.

These meetings are also the time to *ask the right questions* to the team and allow time for silence and thought—you are not the answer key! Recognize the positive aspects of suggestions and provide follow-up questions to more deeply engage team members in the logical thought process. You are not there to solve problems for them but to inspire them to make better observations and formulate better educated guesses (hypothesis) in order to have the greatest chance of success when it comes time for action (experiment).

You are challenged to implement the following steps in your next departmental meeting by identifying the number one problem impeding student learning and then following with the question regarding the top three things that can be done to improve the issue.

- Identify the problem, issue, or mistake—*What do you think is the problem or issue?*
- Take ownership by identifying possible solutions—*What can you/we do to improve?*
- Identify resources needed for implementation—*What do you/we need to accomplish the goal?*
- Decide on what will be done, who will do it, and when will it be completed; schedule next meeting for follow-up to share data and successes.
- Move on to next problem!

Do not be discouraged if the first meeting generates more excuses and negativity from those less experienced in the art and science of problem-solving when it comes to students and learning. Keeping a positive and focused tone on what can be done to improve by responding with, "What can(are) you do(ing) about it?", is one of the best ways leaders and team members can facilitate action from colleagues. After all, teamwork is what will make the dream work if each member is adapting, improvising, and communicating! This allows for maximum team growth where they begin to believe in *themselves.*

Although there are variables outside the control of the teacher-leader, one of their greatest assets is the ability to focus on that which they can control and control it. Through this process, small successes pave the way for larger successes as confidence builds and more and more variables once perceived as outside the control are addressed. You may recognize this process as training for a growth mindset of constant improvement, self-motivation, and team accountability. As always, once the *connection* is made with team members and the mission and effective *collaborations* have begun, don't forget to *celebrate* successes!

The following points from this chapter are worth reviewing:

- A problem should never be more difficult than one step, since that is all we should be focused on at a time.
- Pairing with a colleague to simultaneously implement a new strategy can provide the support needed to get the "rusty nut loose from the bolt."
- By using data to define parameters, we commit to a culture of evidence and make decisions based on data as opposed to feelings and emotions.
- Although a departmental average success rate may not be "any worse than anyone else in the state," expanding this data down to the individual instructors may show an unacceptable level of instructor variance.
- To avoid emotional responses, educators need to take time to reflect after analyzing course success data or course evaluation results and then follow up with a second analysis in which they respond with a proactive plan to improve learning and positive perceptions.
- While low success rates definitely indicate a problem, so, too, do wide variations based on instructor, section, format, and other variables.
- The goal is to have valuable and specific data available in an easily readable form. Identifying benchmarks and baselines, as well as standards and goals, is an integral part of the data analysis process.

Chapter 9

Achieving Faculty Buy-In for Transformation

According to a 2017 study of over 1,500 college presidents by the American Council on Education (ACE), presidents' top concern (next to finances) was "faculty resistance to change." Because constant improvement based on data is the foundational requirement of every college accrediting agency in the country, presidents' concern over faculty resistance to change is also a concern for resistance to constant improvement. Those refusing to participate in this culture of constant improvement are a threat to the accreditation of the institution, as well as to the mission of the community college.

In many cases, institutions fail to provide clarity as to specifically what change is needed and why. Without knowing what they should be changing and why they should be changing, it would be difficult for faculty to come close to the magnitude of change necessary to transform higher education. This takes us back to the need to CC the MVP—we must constantly communicate with crystal clarity and courageous commitment to the MVP of higher education.

The overwhelming concern over the lack of faculty buy-in reveals a lack of buy-in from those in instructional leadership positions. Building leadership throughout an organization can build a culture of learning and inquiry founded on the principles of equity and social justice through enhanced learning for those students who may need it the most. This culture abhors incrementalism and fosters innovation and positive, constructive collaboration. A prerequisite to obtaining buy-in from faculty is therefore a culture built through relentless commitment by instructional leaders. After all, one of the primary responsibilities of leadership is to obtain buy-in and acceptance for the MVP of the institution.

Before attempting to facilitate these changes, leaders, administrators, and teacher-leaders must ask themselves, "What is it we specifically want faculty to change?" If presidents and instructional leaders cannot clarify this to themselves, how will they stand a chance inspiring needed change in faculty? Once the goal and mission have been made crystal-clear, it is crucial to explain why the change is needed. This makes the changes relevant. It is unrealistic to think faculty will simply adopt strategies that some believe go against traditional paradigms in higher education simply because someone told them they should. Leaders must provide data, surveys, reports, articles, and comments from businesses to facilitate action with a laser focus on learning.

If the mission statement itself does not convey a direction which can be merged with a culture of evidence and accountability, then the institutional mission statement may need to be revised to better reflect the mission of the community college system. Too many times institutional mission statements are written more to impress than to practically inspire a culture of constant improvement.

In a learning-college environment, every employee—not just administrators and faculty—understands their contributions to inspiring and facilitating learning. This includes groundskeepers, security, and maintenance workers who ensure the safe, clean, comfortable, and structured learning environment needed to maximize learning. Every employee or department should be able to *connect* their efforts and responsibilities to this sacred mission of total student development. After all, *connecting* is the first of the three Cs to success, and in this case, it is the means by which more employees of the college can become purpose-driven and mission-focused!

The lack of references to learning in community college mission statements across the nation raises a concern indirectly addressed by the Lumina Foundation in a quote referenced earlier in the book: "It is not that learning matters, but that it matters most of all. It is about the learning, stupid!" The AACC reiterated the mission of the community college in the 2012 RTAD report; "to provide a high-quality education to millions of often underserved students." To meet this mission, every employee at the college, and especially faculty, must take on the responsibility of inspiring and facilitating learning for a more diverse group of students.

Understanding the "why," the focal point, and the common mission that supersedes the details, creates an institutional purpose greater than one's self. Some of you may recall a popular legend about the time, during a tour of NASA headquarters in 1961, John F. Kennedy encountered a janitor mopping the floors. "Why are you working so late?" Kennedy asked. "Mr. President," the janitor responded, "I'm helping put a man on the moon."

This worker understood there was a greater purpose to his efforts than simply "mopping the floor," and so it is with all employees at an institution. They must not only know but internalize the common goal of expanding learning—or ultimately, improving the quality of life for their communities—and how their personal efforts contribute to this goal.

Additional reflection should occur as each department or division constructs their own mission statement (examples in Appendix B). At WCCD, we wanted to ensure contributions by the students, as well, so the WCCD Student Diplomats were challenged to develop a creed for students. Working in conjunction with the English division director, this group completed the challenge and made signs of the student creed to post in buildings around campus (Appendix C). In addition, each department designed inspirational quotes and pictures for the hallways.

In marketing, the Rule of 7 states that a prospect needs to "hear" the advertiser's message at least seven times before they will take action to buy that product or service. If the goal is for a positive cultural change, action must be intentionally directed toward CCing the MVP at every opportunity—constantly communicate with crystal-clarity and courageous commitment to the MVP. The sense of hope and inspiration should permeate through every aspect of the institution and be evident to newcomers. Many times, an empty wall is a missed opportunity to send a powerful and uplifting message!

Creating a learning-college culture requires making constant improvement a central part of everyday activities, and this should be the focus of every meeting. Each committee or departmental meeting starts with a discussion of what has been newly implemented that increased student learning and motivation. This can be followed by comments about what teachers are planning in an attempt to increase student persistence and completion.

When these conversations started in a newly formed retention committee at WCCD, those outside the instructional area were reluctant to contribute. An employee from the business office expressed concern that they were at a disadvantage since their only direct dealings with students was when collecting tuition payments. However, another committee member suggested placing a stamp or sticker on students' receipts to promote persistence. Examples given included: "See you at graduation!"; "WCC— where persistence leads to success!"; and "We are all here to support your success!"

This is a testimony to the power of focusing on learning: Even though some committee members expressed reluctance, each suggestion prompted additional innovative suggestions until all committee members were engaged. The approach led to additional initiatives at WCCD, such as the "Get the Tassle" initiative previously discussed, and a student services initiative called "WE CARE."

Whereas a negative or fixed state of mind tends to focus on negative aspects and excuses, a positive growth state of mind tends to focus on the positive aspects of what can be done to improve. Both mindsets perpetuate a cycle—the key for leaders is to ensure positive and constructive collaborations by constantly working to shift conversations into a more positive direction. Engraining this into the culture of a team is a common denominator among all the *highest*-performing teams.

What *specifically* do we want faculty to change? If presidents and instructional leaders cannot clarify this to themselves, how will they stand a chance inspiring needed change in faculty?

Under the old paradigm, where covering content and testing are the instructor's only responsibilities, there is little room for effective change. After all, students are assumed to be responsible for their own learning whether they know how to learn and study or not. Shifting to a focus on learning opens up unlimited options for facilitating and inspiring learning. This is why instructional leaders should advocate for each department to submit the successful strategies they have implemented over the previous term, as well as the strategies they plan to implement in the upcoming term. This helps stimulate the team approach to learning and can lead to additional interdepartmental innovations, as in the retention committee example mentioned earlier.

The underlying accountability to the team serves as a forcing function that occurs as faculty who previously may have been least likely to contribute, and seek to be part of something productive. Helen Keller conveyed the power of teamwork in her quote, "Alone we can do so little; together we can do so much!"

After clarifying specifically what and why faculty are expected to change, leaders must determine a system of reward and recognition for compliance to the desired action and changes. And, of course, they must decide on a system of consequences for noncompliance. Without either of these systems in place, it cannot be surprising that faculty participation, and ultimately buy-in, is lacking.

In addition to such systems, leaders must determine whether there are any standards for instructional practices. If not, are there any written expectations for effective instructional practices? Ultimately, the natural progression to buy-in can be best achieved if there is a culture of standards and expectations backed by a system of recognition and reward for those complying and consequences for those who do not. Internal organizational motivation for innovation thrives in a culture where there are clear expectations for constant improvement. This is just another way of repeating that doing nothing is not an option.

In general, the narrow scope for many quality-enhancement programs has hindered at-scale buy-in and improvements in performance indicators for a larger number of students. That is why institutions should advocate so strongly for using initiatives that stand a better chance of reaching a larger number of faculty and students—it is much more likely to lead to meaningful change.

When instructors do buy in and activate the instructional leadership initiative, they can then take on the work of incorporating the five highest impact strategies into course redesigns for first-term highest enrollment courses. Their effort often results in students' acceptance of more responsibility for their learning, which, in turn, reinforces the faculty's ability to provide a more active and engaging learning environment where learning is more relevant and transferrable to other courses and the workplace.

LESSONS FROM AN ILA

There are two types of colleges today: those that prepare students for the future by focusing on relevant and engaging learning and those that allow faculty and administrators to live comfortably in the past. To put this another way—either the focus is on learning, which provides a higher quality of education and total student development to a more diverse group of students, or the focus is on maintaining and enlarging achievement gaps by continuing with the archaic approach of simply covering content and testing. Because the latter leaves learning entirely up to the students, undermines social justice, and condemns millions of underserved students to a life of dependence and limited opportunities, our choice is clear.

Expecting significant changes without a mission and system of accountability laser-focused on enhancing learning for both faculty and students is an unrealistic expectation. Instilling a leadership mentality throughout the organization is needed to achieve meaningful and lasting change. Leadership, and not just on the part of administrators or "management" alone, is required to inspire others to do that which they need to do but may not want to do.

In the scaling-up of effective instructional strategies from classroom to department to division and then from college-wide to system-wide, the most common denominators in each of these areas was that when faculty became more excited about learning their students became more excited about learning—and achievement gaps narrowed!

Building a leadership mentality throughout the organization requires much more than a professional development session. Instead, what is required is extensive training and collaboration in a positive environment characterized by high expectations. This training should move faculty well beyond their self-perceived limitations and into the realm of profound growth. This can be accomplished by incorporating leadership principles throughout a year-long program intentionally designed for maximum growth in a minimum amount of time.

The power of a positive growth environment is a reason that the remainder of this chapter focuses on lessons learned from an Instructional Leadership Academy (ILA) implemented across the Alabama Community College System (ACCS). The ILA is designed to considerably shorten the learning curve for institutional change, while facilitating quicker movement through the phases of denial, resistance, and grief associated with that change.

Prior to establishing effective collaborations, common ground among all instructors was identified and constantly reiterated. The first commonality was the fact that we all teach students first, content next. It is this mindset that establishes our priorities as instructors to develop the total student—to provide them a better opportunity to make better decisions, live a better life, and make a better living.

Our next common ground was established by identifying two core competencies that every course in the state should be intentionally incorporating into their curriculum—communication and critical thinking. This small but impactful addition provided a common focus and goal of all courses while also dismantling individual silos for the sake of effective team collaboration designed to develop both emotional and cognitive aspects of intelligence. Although only listed as two competencies, communication includes all forms of effective communication to include conflict resolution, while critical thinking also serves as a prerequisite to effective problem solving.

Our statewide ILA was started in 2018 with 152 participants in seven different cohorts from five colleges. The origins of this program go all the way back to the science division at WCCD, where we converted our training approach to an institution-wide Instructional Leadership Challenge. The lessons we learned from these earlier programs allowed us to develop this intensive year-long training ILA program for faculty from all instructional divisions throughout the state. Analysis of course success data from the top enrollment courses across the system provided the incentive for more intentional efforts to address student success issues at the classroom level where new strategies would directly impact students.

The key to our successes with this program started with a state chancellor laser-focused on the student experience. His willingness to do what others were not, such as developing a common system for collecting and analyzing performance data across the state and extensively focusing on addressing student learning at the level that can produce the largest improvements—the classroom, is the primary reason this approach was so effective.

Accountability for data-driven decisions and constant improvement in instructional and support strategies by faculty also served as a focal point.

As a testimony to the effectiveness of a chancellor providing statewide leadership laser-focused on student success, ACCS was recently recognized by Complete College America for increasing degree completion rates. The 150 percent-time graduation rate (three-year) for first-time, full-time community college students increased 39 percent from 2015 to 2019 in Alabama. Although there is much room for improvement, this data serves as evidence that teamwork is essential to achieving the dream, while strong leadership and buy-in from the top are crucial to developing the "team!"

Based on this experience, it was learned that establishing a successful instructional leadership program starts with identifying lead facilitators with extensive classroom experiences and a passion for equity of opportunity through education - warriors for student success. It is not usually feasible to expect someone such as a dean to have the time to devote to leading a program that attempts to maximize transformation in instructional and support strategies. Administrative duties tend to overshadow academy responsibilities for both deans and associate deans.

Creating a position(s) dedicated to obtaining maximum results from a maximum number of faculty, in order to maximally impact student learning in the minimum amount of time, is an important part of an effective program, and was evidence of the commitment of our chancellor to student learning and success. The goal of this position should be a total focus on inspiring innovation, collaboration, and celebration throughout the faculty ranks.

However, these types of improvements require an investment in human capital. Too often, and many times based on past experiences, administrators see expenditures as a cost instead of an investment. When this view is combined with a lack of understanding of the impact that successful students can have on the marketing and advertising aspects of an institution, there is more of a reluctance to invest in programs targeting instructional and support strategies in the classroom.

Positive advertising is even more impactful when at-risk and underserved students experience newfound success with formal education, which in turn inspires their friends and families to seek increased opportunities through higher education. As mentioned previously, it is difficult to obtain faculty buy-in for transformation if the higher levels of leadership have not committed to the process. Just as we have experienced across our system, investing in proven learning strategies leads to exceptional returns on investment!

The need for more participation and buy-in from the faculty ranks on developing a learning-college approach is one of the reasons programs such as the CCLP at KSU was developed. Although leadership positions require administrative and managerial skills crucial to maintaining an organization's order and structure, the degree of transformation in instruction required of today's community colleges cannot be accomplished with administrative skills alone.

The crucial need for enhanced change (transformation) management through positive encouragement and accountability is a reason why leadership principles, behaviors, and mindsets must be incorporated into professional development of all faculty in order to develop the leadership throughout the organization that is needed to meet the demands of twenty-first-century class-rooms and solve problems at the lowest level possible.

This training should challenge all faculty to seek the next level of effective-ness. The growth mindset expectation is needed to effectively inspire growth in students, as well. With faculty on the front lines of increasing learning and core competency development, they do not have the luxury of pawning off this responsibility to others in the organization. Because they have direct contact with students each day, faculty will be either a part of the solution or a part of the problem. The purpose of an ILA is to ensure faculty become part of the solution by developing a lead-by-example approach designed to model lifelong-learning for students and colleagues.

This leadership expectation is clearly conveyed through documents such as the Professional Educator Commitment Statement (Appendix A) and Leader-ship Oath (Appendix B). The Commitment Statement is similar to the one used at WCCD in each faculty interview process before hiring. Interviewees were asked to explain how their personal attributes would fit into a system with these sets of standards. Divisional directors and department chairs also have a Leadership Oath to which they commit. Putting these expectations in print allows for quick future reference when needed, as well as explicitly outlining the sacred responsibilities bestowed upon us as professional leaders and teachers—just another way to CC the MVP!

In addition to "leadership," ILA includes the keyword "instructional." Because great teachers lead and great leaders teach, this word just adds to

the program's uniqueness by addressing the most important aspect of learning—the instructor. Every article, activity, and discussion is focused on how
to adjust strategies, approaches, classroom activities, and support strategies in
order to achieve a greater degree of intellectual rigor and diversity of completion among students. By addressing the number one variable affecting learning—the instructor—educators are able to make maximum and sustainable
improvements in a minimum amount of time.

Our first ILA cohorts serve as examples of how important mindset is to
teaching, learning, and leading. The seven cohorts were homogenous in the
sense that they each contained faculty from the same college. Although far
from ideal for a leadership academy, very few of the over 150 participants
volunteered for the program.

Upon analysis of the average success rates for the top nine enrollment
courses at each college for this first-year group, a direct correlation was found
with the degree of participation in ILA activities and assignments halfway
through the academy for each cohort. Colleges with higher levels of course
successes in their top enrollment courses prior to ILA also had higher levels
of assignment completion and vice versa. This data seem to mimic classroom
data which tends to show that the students who need extra-credit/learning the
most tend to take advantage of additional opportunities the least.

As might be expected for a first-year program, it took the entire year to
achieve noticeable buy-in for participants. However, each subsequent year
resulted in a substantial decrease in the length of time to achieve buy-in
across the entire group. This data serves as evidence of the power of participation in proven high-impact strategies which can provide immediate and
substantial increases in engagement and motivation to learn and is, many
times, a prerequisite to buy-in for constant improvement in instructional and
support strategies.

These experiences serve to reaffirm that faculty buy-in for instructional
transformation is maximized when institutions provide the TASE in an environment of high expectations and continuous research, both literally and in
practice. The combined effects of this TASE are as important in a learning
environment for faculty as they are for students.

Many institutions will go to great lengths to avoid the resistance associated
with addressing faculty and classroom instruction across the entire college.
This is partly what leads to an abundance of boutique programs, which work

with a limited number of students, usually through small initiatives in the student services division. Due to the lack of at-scale implementation, as well as the avoidance of addressing basic instructional philosophy, it is no surprise these boutique programs have yet to yield substantial changes in performance indicators.

Many times, issues addressed at the student services level are meant to compensate for what may not be going on in the classrooms. Although these approaches may benefit the small number of students they serve, an equitable environment for success depends on all students having access to strategies supporting learning. Although academic freedom is commonly used as a reason for not addressing instructional issues, academic freedom has never meant that instructors can use whatever strategies they want regardless of destructively discriminatory effect on students.

In fact, addressing the need for instructional improvements often diminishes the divide that many times exists between student services and instructional divisions. Faculty and staff begin to see their roles as much more synergetic, stimulating much-needed collaboration into effective and meaningful change across the entire campus, and for all students.

Staff tend to hear more about students' challenges, both in and out of the classroom, because this is where students usually go when confronted with obstacles or frustrations. The frustration on the part of student services staff over a perceived lack of more effective instructional strategies, as well as more accountability in addressing student learning, leaves many staff feeling like they are alone in their efforts.

By bringing faculty and staff together to discuss instructional improvements, with the common ground of "inspiring and facilitating learning," real change can begin to happen. This is one reason why every committee or departmental meeting should begin with discussions about how learning has been facilitated and inspired through small changes in each area of the college. This environment helps develop a bolder and more proactive leadership approach where each employee, regardless of division, is given time and space to focus on their own role in inspiring learning.

The expectation for all participants in an ILA cohort is to provide inspiration to each other for action, support each other for efforts, and celebration to each other for accomplishments. This positive environment catapults growth and development among even the most reluctant, skeptical, or resistant faculty.

Every meeting begins with discussions about how learning has been facilitated and inspired through small changes in each area of the college.

Institutions can develop a group of future ILA trainers by identifying a cohort of faculty to participate in an ILA. Whether an entire cohort is comprised of faculty from one institution or whether a group of faculty from an institution are part of a cohort from multiple colleges and universities, taking this first step to achieving a quicker path to leadership throughout faculty ranks speaks volumes for institutional commitment to student learning. In a positive and proactive growth environment even the more resistant faculty look at issues from a perspective that many may have never considered.

The first three years of our state ILA provides a wonderful example of the power that a year-long ILA can have in obtaining not only buy-in but ownership in the process of constant improvement in instructional and support strategies. Although only 36 percent of the 167 participants in the 2019–2020 ILA cohort (second year of the state academy) indicated that they volunteered for the program, evidence of buy-in for continuous improvements in instructional strategies was unanimous by the end of the year. It was evident, however, that the majority of participants achieved buy-in within the first few months of ILA. For the following year, buy-in was realized sooner as over two-thirds of the faculty indicated they had volunteered for the program.

Using faculty from as many disciplines as possible also helps to create the diversity of thought needed to stimulate innovation. What is innovative for some may be common practice for others. Leaders are often able to turn differences into commonalities and can help establish common ground with an understanding that all faculty are engaged in the work of teaching students. In a collaborative and engaging learning environment like the ILA, the qualities, values, and enthusiasm of the more effective teacher-leaders tend to rub off on other faculty members over the course of their work together and create additional common ground for effective collaborations.

The common ground that is desired is also a benefit in the classroom. Although our students may come with different specific challenges, all students have basic needs and basic neurological functions in common that can be used to promote learning. In addition, faculty are expected to also incorporate common core competencies crucial to academic, workplace, and life success.

By identifying commonalities, faculty members are encouraged to abandon traditional silos for the sake of the larger mission of learning. Although these silos can be a very comforting place for faculty, the comfort is partly due to the fact that siloes have traditionally allowed faculty to do what they want, when they want, and how they want without accountability for results. Dismantling these silos can be a very stressful process; it is imperative it occurs in an encouraging and supportive environment of high expectations and an understanding by leadership of the natural phases of change. It is in this type of environment where innovation can thrive.

Our ILA at the ACCS has the advantage of using faculty from different institutions to promote an even greater degree of diversity. This program is an eleven-month academy, with the first meeting being crucial to establishing expectations and guidelines for both the online portion of the program and all-day workshops. The monthly workshops have been conducted online via ZOOM since spring 2020. The remainder of the program is used for online work and course redesigns. The purpose of the online work is to combine a large amount and diversity of knowledge through multiple topics, authors, and approaches while also challenging archaic paradigms in the comfort of one's own home.

This schedule allows for coverage of the basic concepts in the ILA workshops in time for faculty to begin implementation of their newly redesigned course for the fall term, although they may only have the first unit of their course ready to implement. As fall term begins, faculty can continue preparing each unit in advance of its coverage in class by using lessons learned from the previous unit. The redesign is for the highest traditional enrollment course they teach and serves as an end-product for their work in ILA, as well as evidence of intentionality in course structure and effective learning strategies. The core structure of these redesigns uses all five of the highest impact strategies designed to enhance learning.

Many aspects of these redesigns are already required by standardization of online course offerings through Quality Matters, a nonprofit, quality assurance organization that certifies online courses with their stamp of approval if the courses meet certain standards. This intentional attention to online courses may raise questions about why there is not more attention paid to the quality of traditional courses, as well.

Because faculty are hired to teach courses in their major field of study and not necessarily to remain abreast of the issues and problems in higher education, most are poorly informed about these issues, and this also can make it difficult to achieve buy-in. Buy-in requires an understanding that there *is* a problem in order to initiate a move from the first phase of change, which we know is denial, although completing this transition out of the first phase also requires a realization that what has traditionally been used as a reason to not focus on learning is no longer valid.

Although academic freedom is commonly used as an excuse for not addressing more instructional issues, it has never meant that we can use whatever strategies we want regardless of the destructively discriminatory effect on students.

Faculty read two articles each week and provide a reflection post on the LMS. These articles have had key points highlighted and include comments and questions to stimulate discussion. The one requirement for these posts is that they must be positive and constructive, which curtails the natural tendency to focus on more negative aspects. Although workshops are the venue for open collaboration, the article posts do not need to turn into a blog site where volleys of disagreements are not likely to be efficiently addressed.

Effective leaders have a way of turning negatives into positives, something that requires practice, especially in an educational environment where transformation is required. As stated previously, a culture is not determined by what is preached or expected but by what is tolerated by the team. It usually only takes a reminder to those who may venture into more negative comments for them to realize that in an academy designed to promote leadership, it is imperative that rules of engagement are respected. For ILA participants, being positive in a negative situation is not naïve; it is leadership!

Leaders would rather be annoyingly positive and optimistic than destructively negative and pessimistic. As for any large group of people, perceptions of the group tend to reflect the most vocal people in that group. If the most vocal faculty also tend to be the most negative, then this becomes the perception of those outside the group. Creating a more positive and proactive environment in an ILA where disagreements and mistakes are opportunities to learn and improve will produce results which elude the less committed.

In the 1860s, Henry Wells, a founding member of Wells Fargo Bank, was asked what it takes to succeed in business. He said, "There is one very powerful business rule. It is concentrated in the word—courtesy. This statement is posted on the walls of every Wells Fargo branch in our market." Dan Cathy of Chick-Fil-A has incorporated this philosophy into the training of their employees, as well. In our ILA, the one word that provides a focal point to all we do is "respect." This word allows us to address issues as they arise by constantly referring back to the concept of respect.

As a leadership academy, it is imperative to make the distinction between "being respectful" and "not being disrespectful." Being respectful is an intentional act that shows self-discipline and a concern for others, attributes that lead to success in the workplace. Because it is the responsibility of higher education to prepare students for the culture of the workplace, cultural behaviors expected there must be taught and required by faculty who also practice these behaviors. After all, with the many disadvantages our students have it is imperative we provide them with as many advantages for success as possible.

It is also important to note that disagreeing is not necessarily the same as being negative; identifying problems is also not the same as being negative. However, presenting problems without a possible solution is not respectful of others. If a possible solution cannot be identified, a request for assistance signals a willingness to find successful solutions. Putting a problem in someone else's lap to solve without having the professional courtesy to have thought about it long enough to provide some assistance is not respectful.

In this day of advanced Internet technology there is too much information available to simply "not know." This takes us back to one of the most powerful questions for building leadership throughout the organization, asking ourselves again and again, "What am I doing about it?"

Rudyard Kipling once said, "The strength of the wolf is the pack, and the strength of the pack is the wolf." This is one of the first quotes used in ILA to provide the team accountability needed to ensure maximum innovation. Effective professional development is not always about what can be provided for you, but also what you can provide for others. No one instructor can change education for an entire institution or state, but this goal can be accomplished by the combined efforts of all.

Accordingly, in the workshop sessions, each participant is responsible for sharing new strategies and activities they have implemented during the previous month that have enhanced learning, a crucial component of ILA. This shift to focusing on others is a great way to develop leadership behaviors across an entire organization, and it shows the power of breaking down silos for more effective collaborations.

Each cohort has an assigned online facilitator. This group of facilitators are past participants of ILA and are responsible for monitoring approximately 12,000 online posts each year in response to approximately 75 different articles and reports and keeping track of submitted assignments by participants. An updated progress report is submitted each month online to ensure accurate documentation of completed assignments.

One of the ways participants show their respect to their colleagues in the cohort is by showing up prepared, the very same rule we have for our students. Having their own paradigms challenged at home by reading the articles, participants can more effectively contribute to productive collaborations in the workshops.

Expansive knowledge of instructional, motivational, and support strategies is essential for facilitators, as "street cred" can be vital to success when working with large groups of faculty to instigate the transformational change expected from participation in an ILA. There is nothing more valuable than having facilitators who can connect with faculty and work to obtain maximum results in a minimum amount of time in order to impact a maximum number of students from these instructors' courses. Investments in training key faculty members to be leaders in this movement will provide the momentum for future in-house training and continued improvements.

Each workshop session requires faculty to talk about new strategies they have implemented over the past month(s) and how it has enhanced learning. Our coordinator for the facilitators refers to these as "data digs" which remind faculty to indicate how they knew that the newly implemented strategy enhanced learning by following the data—data that at first may not be inherently obvious.

As mentioned earlier, it would not be respectful to the other faculty in the cohort for one to show up without a new strategy or activity to share, as he/she would be there to gain knowledge and encouragement through the action of others without bringing something to share themselves. The same holds true for all assignments, as the success of the program depends on the combined efforts of all. As each participant begins to see themselves more as a leader, they become more responsible for their own training, as well as contributing to the training of others.

The data digs are designed to focus faculty on following data when implementing a new activity or strategy, meeting the basic requirement of all accrediting agencies for constant improvement based on data. The group asks if each new activity inspires and facilitates learning; a follow-up discussion focuses on the data and evidence of improvement: "How do you know it enhanced learning?"

Although summative test scores can provide data on students' knowledge at that moment, the lack of transferability of that knowledge into future courses and situations leads to questions of how much learning actually occurred. The data digs prompt faculty to ensure they have evidence, whether qualitative or quantitative, of enhanced learning. This data can provide powerful encouragement and incentive that inspires others to action.

Faculty work in the ILA concludes with a final presentation where each faculty shares the changes they have made over the previous year and the results of these changes. This activity is an extension of the classroom research each participant has been performing over the course of the year. Serving as an inspiration for other faculty, these past presentations were some of the most enthusiastic and inspiring that I have ever heard from faculty— much less from this many at one session.

These presentations provided the best professional development faculty could attend and is a reason the decision was made to record each of the presentations the next year. Of the over 300 completers for the past two years of ILA, every one of them indicated they used multiple strategies and activities which enhanced learning and engagement!

ILA facilitators often share their most surprising aspect of serving as a facilitator—their realization that what they once thought of as "student problems" are constitutive of any large group, even faculty. Issues such as misreading information, allowing biases to affect perceptions, not turning in assignments on time, approaching assignments as tasks to be completed instead of lessons to be learned, along with others are incredibly common.

Faculty and facilitators are often reminded that there are seldom issues which are only student problems; most are just people problems.

When our responsibilities require us to deal with larger groups of people, these issues seem more pronounced. Human nature makes it easier for students or faculty to justify not following procedures when these procedures are not perceived as relevant to their current concerns. Once again, it is the responsibility of leadership to obtain buy-in through CC-MVP so that the relevancy or "why" is clear.

It is important for institutions to remember that not all faculty pose problems, just as not all students do—in fact, the vast majority desire to be part of the solution. In fact, although most people actually desire to be part of something special, most do not know how to go about developing this "special" something. Nonetheless, we tend to focus more on those who do not do what is required of them than we do on those who do.

There is a saying that "students do not do optional," but once again this issue is a people problem and is not specifically reserved for students. The only group for which this cannot hold true is leaders because leaders must lead by example. Maybe this is why it is said that, although we all benefit from encouragement and appreciation, if the leader *needs* to be motivated by others, then he/she is not the leader! A leader's crystallized understanding of the importance the community college mission has on achieving equity in opportunity and sustained economic growth should provide an internal motivation which exceeds that of the average person.

"Chancellor Challenges" offer another important opportunity in the ILA. These monthly challenges serve to walk faculty through a complete course redesign by the time they complete the academy (see Appendix D). The challenges provide faculty with the checkpoints they need to be accountable to such a comprehensive task. This is a clear example of how chunking works for students and faculty in gaining more participation.

If a process seems too overwhelming for most to get started, then it is usually a sign the process has not been chunked into small enough steps. The entire ILA program works on chunking through small but consistent efforts over the course of a year and then working through one step at a time. The cumulative effects of these small steps results in a transformation in mindset as well as skillset.

DATA AND TESTIMONIALS

A word of warning to those who may not have participated in initiatives using multiple proven strategies focused directly on the classroom and student learning: The results well surpass typical increases from programs outside the instructional division and without significant faculty input. One of the most common comments made by ILA participants in reference to new activities implemented is, "I never realized how something so small could make such a big difference!" Yet the true power lies in collective contribution, which combines results into a sum much greater than the individual parts.

Our state was inspired to develop an ILA program after results were shared from three Alabama community colleges that began to focus on data analytics to spur innovation and collaboration in top-ten enrollment courses beginning in 2012. By focusing on top enrollment courses, there is an opportunity to impact a maximum number of students early in their college career. These colleges and their resulting performance data increases were shared in the preface.

Reflecting back on this data, these three colleges experienced an average increase in fall-to-fall retention rates of 15 percentage points just four years after implementation. One college had over 500 more successful students per year in seven of their top enrollment courses, while another one had over 500 more successful students per year in eight of these courses. After four years, these three colleges had the highest success rates in those top-ten enrollment courses of all the community colleges in the state, as well as the highest increases in fall-to-fall retention rates during that time.

The graduation rate increases for these colleges was even more dramatic, with an average 15-percentage point increase, although, because each school's graduation rate started so low, there was over an 80 percent increase. One of the colleges, which began with a 13 percent graduation rate saw a 27 percent rate six years later—a rate that more than doubled (~108 percent increase). Another of the colleges began with a 20 percent graduation rate and jumped to a 37 percent graduation rate (an 85 percent increase), while the third college saw a 65 percent increase in graduation rates.

The power of ILA-led course redesigns can be seen in these numbers. When fifty faculty members execute a course redesign for their highest enrollment course, over 10,000 students in these courses *each year* are directly affected. If this strategy only produced an average of one additional successful student in each instructor's section, over 600 more students a year would be successful in those courses. Furthermore, by allowing students from other instructors' classes (especially adjunct instructors) to have access to the redesign, the number of students impacted can substantially increase.

Data from sixteen of the most active participants from two colleges during our first year of ILA (2018) showed over 440 students were successful in their courses who, statistically speaking, would not have been successful just two years prior. This averages out to approximately two students per section. Those faculty who previously had course success rates of less than 70 percent saw their W/D/F rate cut in half (a 52 percent decrease), while those who had previously shown greater than 70 percent success rates averaged a 24 percent decrease in W/D/F rates.

The question for any new activity is, "Does it inspire and facilitate learning?" The second question focuses on the data and evidence of this improvement, "How do you know it enhanced learning?" The third question is for relevancy, "How will this learning help them live a better life and make a better living?"

Driven in part by this data, the next two years of ILA produced over 320 faculty completers in sixteen cohorts from 19 colleges across the state. From these, 163 instructors voluntarily completed a total course redesign that was vetted by facilitators and included all five of the highest impact strategies discussed in chapter 6 for their highest enrollment course. These redesigns directly impact over 15,000 students each year, and substantially more if incorporated into the course LMS for adjunct instructors' students. This number of students does not include those affected by the remainder of ILA participants who began work on their redesigns but did not complete them for formal submission, as well as those working to redesign their other courses.

Although over 60 percent of the 167 participants in the second year of ILA (2019) did not volunteer for this experience, 158 completed the program.

Of those, 69 percent who included data in their final presentations showed decreases in W/D/F rates between pre- and post-ILA fall terms. Half of the faculty averaged an over 32 percent reduction in W/D/F rates, and thirty of the faculty showed average W/D/F rates had been cut in half! Of the seventy-seven instructors starting with less than 70 percent success rates (meaning, W/D/F rates greater than 30 percent), only ten had no decreases in W/D/F rates.

The real power of these numbers is communicated in combination: There were 1,190 additional successful students based on the decreases in W/D/F rates and class enrollments. This averages out to about one more successful student per section for these faculty. Expanding these 1,190 students/year out over a decade, and 11,900 students are affected. This is the number of students whose chance of completion has been doubled thanks to faculty efforts inspired by their participation in the ILA.

Furthermore, we expect these successes to multiply as students are empowered with effective learning strategies and the confidence to persist, attributes that research shows carry over to their children and future children, as education affects sustainable generational success. In addition, many friends of these students may become encouraged by their success, resulting in additional enrollment benefits.

Socioeconomic achievement gaps were also analyzed for 2019 ILA participants using Pell-eligible versus non-Pell-eligible students as an indicator for lower and higher income. Of the 153 faculty with data included in their final presentation, 89 experienced decreases in socioeconomic achievement gaps for their classes from fall 2017 or 2018 to fall 2019. The average decrease for these faculty was in favor of the lower-income students by 64 percent! Fifty-five of these faculty saw the gap for Pell-eligible students cut at least in half.

Although research shows there tends to be slight decreases in student success when implementing new strategies, the multi-strategy approach of ILA offset these initial decreases. This data speaks volumes for the tenacity and determination of dedicated faculty to challenge old paradigms and constantly seek ways to inspire learning. In addition, their lead-by-example approach inspires other faculty. Constantly sharing data can be a very powerful motivator for continued innovation and improvements and gives us a reason for the third C of success—celebrate!

These increases also show the power of addressing lagging indicators like retention and graduation rates with more leading indicators such as W/D/F rates in top enrollment first-year courses. Improvements in performance indicators are the direct result of providing a learning environment more conducive to building core competencies and skills transferrable to other courses. Celebrating these successes as an institution is vital for continued motivation for improvements.

Frequent assessments and test scores also provide leading indicators and are the direct result of more intentional teaching and courses designed to increase student responsibility for learning. Although the third year of ILA was challenged with comparing data from the first year of COVID-inspired changes to pre-COVID baseline data, the vast majority of ILA faculty experienced either no decreases in success rates or increases in success rates.

Below are a few excerpts from testimonials of the ILA participants in the first two years of this program. The subject area of the instructor has been included for each. The intent is to show how empowering a program can be when high expectations are combined with high levels of encouragement and training, and when connection is followed by collaboration and celebration. Although the following is just a sample of these testimonials, there are over a hundred more that convey the same degree of appreciation and excitement for the future. Each has been transcribed verbatim from the original testimonial.

- *Emergency Medical Services*—From the beginning it was stressed we were not to be negative. As ILA progressed, I came to realize why that was important to stress. What I did not realize was how negative a person I had become. ILA was the first to call me out on it. So, between the second and third meetings I took time to think and reevaluate life. It has made a huge difference in life, and I think my students sense it. What I now see is just how jaded many of my coworkers are, and how much we need ILA to not just give us new teaching tools (although that is AWESOME) but how much we need to check our attitudes and always strive for what is right and good.
- *Math*—ILA has been a transformational experience that has completely changed my professional life and my attitude toward teaching. During the last few years we have been looking at data more closely than ever before, and it had become clear that I had to get better at teaching the courses that

were not "preaching to the choir." However, I did not know what to do. It was very fortuitous that ILA came along when it did. My mindset has completely changed about teaching, and I would strongly urge any faculty to take part in ILA if given the opportunity. My favorite thing about the program is that it is 100 percent common sense. Most of what we learned; I'm thinking "Why have I not been doing this for years?"

- *Math*—ILA has been an eye-opener! It is exciting to see what is going on not just in our neighborhood, but across the state with these classes. Running into previous cohort members at conferences where they are showing some of the changes that they have implemented not only energizes me as an instructor but really gives me hope for the future of our profession.

- *Nursing*—I have been in nursing education for twenty-five years, but with no formal training in education. I learned to teach by "how I was taught" and "by watching other instructors." The ILA has been the missing link for me in many ways. Since I have been in ILA, I prepare for class with a completely different mindset and strategy that I know can offer success to my students. ILA has brought excitement and a new vision for my role as a nursing instructor, and I am eager to share this information with my nursing colleagues.

- *English*—The ILA has been one of the most rewarding experiences I have had as a professional since my time in graduate school. It is rare to be in an environment where I am reading and learning again with others. This has created a rich opportunity for discussion, reflection, and dedication. I highly recommend ILA to others because I can see the difference it has made in my classroom and in the relationships I have developed with my students and colleagues. We are laughing and enjoying learning in ways that I never thought could happen in higher education.

- *Art*—It has been my pleasure to take part in the ILA. Initially, I thought that taking part in ILA would *not* be beneficial. However, at the completion of the academy, I can say that it is just the opposite. I have read a lot of interesting articles and taken part in a lot of discussions that have been invigorating and inspired me to try new ideas and teaching methods in the classroom. While in ILA, I have developed some active learning strategies that I am currently using in my classes. Class attendance and student success have improved. The strategies that I have learned in ILA will definitely continue to be used in the future.

- *English*—My involvement with the ILA has enabled me to shift more into a concept-based approach to teaching my courses. This is something I had been trying to accomplish previously, but this program has given me more of the tools and insights to make this change. This change has led to improvements in student learning even more in my other courses rather than in the class I'm specifically redesigning for ILA. For example, in my 200-level literature course, over 50 percent of my students made a B or higher on the midterm exam.

  This is a much higher average than in previous semesters. While I taught the same content, my focus was much more on concepts relevant to the literature. Students also remark that they're better able to see the connections between this course and other classes. They also remark that they better understand why they need these courses for their degrees even if they're not English majors. Students are seeing the relevance of the course and succeeding in both critical thinking and communication.

- *Art*—ILA gave me five strategies that have proven results. These strategies help increase student learning, success, and completion. If that was all I had gotten from this experience it would have been worth it. It was more (MUCH MORE). ILA has been an eye-opening experience for me. What I didn't expect was how much I didn't know. Even if you think you are an amazing teacher you can benefit from the information and strategies we have been learning.

  When it is about learning (true learning) your attitudes, your teaching, and your focus all start to change. The conversation becomes about Challenge, Discovery, Ideas, Questions, and Problem Solving. The moment I saw the spark in my students eyes and the days I walked into class thirty minutes early and half my class was already there eager and ready to learn, and the day I watched them battle it out over controversial ideas, I knew I had found the sweet spot. Thank you ILA for giving me the knowledge to get my students THINKING and really LEARNING. Aren't we in the business of creating lifelong learners? Model it people. ILA is a GAME CHANGER!

- *English*—ILA has been an eye-opening and invigorating experience that has shown me how essential it is that I be an intentional, positive force in the classroom. I can say without a doubt that ILA has given me the tools I needed to slough off my antiquated modes of thinking and, in turn, to become an instructor who is better suited to transform the ways my own students think, communicate, and learn.

- *English*—The ILA has been beneficial for me in at least three ways: I have gathered ideas from the readings related to activities I can incorporate into my classes to increase relevance; posting responses helped me to create a file for each reading, and it is in these files that I have summarized the ideas I plan to implement, thus creating a to-do list to which I can refer as I go. In short, I have gained a better understanding of objectives and a more focused class organization.

  Although the ILA has required time in reading, posting, and attending sessions, I am grateful that I was included in the group because to complete this academy, I had to set aside time to read the articles, to figure out the applications for my classes, and to begin implementing some of what I've learned. Had I not been in the academy, I would not have taken the time to research and find the variety of articles and to create a list of ideas to implement. As a full-time teacher since 1990 and online teacher since 1998, I've had plenty of time to get into a few ruts; the ILA has helped me to begin digging my way out by providing some new perspectives and ideas. I appreciate the opportunity!

- *Psychology*—I have had many great experiences in my life journey; a few were life-changing. The ILA was a life-changer! ILA has exposed me to other instructors who love their discipline and are motivated to go the extra mile to make the information they are teaching relevant, and to invest in relationships with their students. ILA has been a comfort to me, knowing that there is no need to stay under the radar, and an inspiration to me, providing many tools to take teaching/coaching and learning to a higher level! I love being part of a movement that makes my college a place people are proud to be a part of teachers and students!

- *English*—I have been an educator since 2010. In the past couple of years, I found myself becoming complacent and the fire I once had was nearly extinguished. Now it is October 2019, and I am beyond grateful for this enlightening opportunity and newfound drive this academy has given me. I have learned some lifelong valuable lessons that I have used daily in and outside the classrooms. It has taught me to "Keep it Simple" if I truly want to be an effective teacher. I have learned that learning is a reciprocated relationship and that I am not there to serve as an answer key but to serve as a facilitator to the learning experience.

  This academy has taught me that if I continuously encourage my students, then the progress will happen. I have evolved from a teacher who simply taught to one who now teaches with intention! I have learned to chunk until I can't chunk anymore. The quality of one lesson is more valuable than the quantity of ten. I thank this academy for reigniting my light, my fire, and my passion. For this, I will proudly carry my newest motto I learned from session one, "Today I will do what others won't so tomorrow I can do what others can't!"

- *History*—Even though I have more than twenty-five years of experience, I learned many new techniques from ILA and I have already incorporated them into my current courses with success. I feel excited and renewed!

- *Speech*—ILA has given me much more than just tools for enhancing student learning in my courses. It has inspired me to make sure that I'm doing everything possible to ensure every one of my students succeeds.

- *Computer Science*—I would have to say that I have gained many insights and suggestions for improving both my leadership and teaching experiences. The class has and still is achieving its goal by allowing me as an instructor to learn, benefit, and even enjoy this learning experience.

- *Radiology*—ILA has really opened up my eyes and taught me how to successfully incorporate active learning strategies and student engagement!

- *English*—ILA has given me strategies to effectively reach at-risk students from a variety of demographics. Because of ILA, I have also implemented several new hands-on activities in my classes that get students out of their chairs and away from their devices. They actually are having fun while learning critical thinking and writing skills. From my observations, these learning activities have promoted overall participation. Perhaps the strongest assets I have implemented as a result of ILA are the tutorial videos for my module objectives. Because of ILA, I am a much more confident and student-oriented instructor with a desire to help all students succeed.

- *Economics*—The ILA experience has provided me with countless strategies for making my classroom more learning-centered and student-friendly.

- *Air Conditioning and Repair*—Having participated in many different types of professional development, I can honestly say that ILA has been one of the most informative and useful courses I have been involved in.

- *Allied Health*—I am not sure I would've thought about how our activities tie into the bigger picture of life skills if not for ILA—seems like an obvious tie in now. ILA is a fabulous program. I think my coworkers might be tired of "Well, in ILA I learned . . ." LOL!

- *Instructional Dean*—Our college is pleased to have had over forty faculty participate in the ILA. The challenging and invigorating curriculum has provided the basis for academic transfer, career technical, and nursing/ allied health faculty to explore ways to enhance student retention and engagement. Several of our faculty have confirmed that they have, indeed, experienced tremendous improvement in their students' successful completion rates and have shared their ILA experience and teaching strategies with their colleagues departmentally and college-wide.

  While the faculty in the first cohort were working to restructure their courses to better meet the needs of their students, many of them found that their feelings about teaching became restructured as well. One of our faculty members proclaimed that she had grown tired of herself as a teacher but that the ILA experience energized her and renewed her faith in herself and in her students. Being able to observe and participate in the final presentations for the first cohort was exciting because I could feel the instructors' excitement and envision the difference they make in the lives of our students every day. We are thankful for the opportunity for our faculty to participate in ILA and look forward to supporting more ILA cohorts.

- *Psychology*—I made a twenty-minute video about how to study for my general psych class, right after I started ILA. It's all about growth mindset, as well as Bloom's taxonomy, how to take notes, the difference between copying down information and taking notes, reading versus studying, you know, the usual. This semester, I posted it as usual. Today, the first day of class, a nontraditional student posted this comment: "I just wanted to say if my teachers had explained to me how to study the way you just did then I would have finished my masters twenty-five years ago."

- *Psychology*—Just wanted to thank you for motivating me with your story of doing 10,000 push-ups with your grandson over the course of a year through daily chunking of just thirty each day! On November 16 I started doing my push-ups, and on Monday of this week I had performed over 10,000 push-ups! So, I have benefited more from ILA than I expected!

- *Instructional Dean* (regarding one of his most at-risk and resistant instructors)—I've never seen anyone make as big of a change in the success of their students as XXX has. He has definitely drank the Kool-Aid and it is some powerful stuff. Thank you for ILA!

***

Congratulations on making it this far in the book! Hopefully, you have gained some bits of knowledge to assist you in your journey as an educator. However, it is the inspiration to put that knowledge into action that is the ultimate goal of this book. As educators and teacher-leaders, everything we do to improve ourselves translates into a greater opportunity to help others.

This goal of empowering others is aspirational and the challenges immense, but this is who we are and this is what we do as professional educators—we take the least advantaged and work with a relentless passion and purpose to empower with them with advantages needed for success. This is not just a professional obligation but a moral imperative for all those who have an influence over others.

The learning-college concept championed by Dr. Terry O'Banion reiterated the importance of learning and growth for everyone employed at an institution. Focusing on what is possible through at-scale, proven instructional and support strategies grounded in cognitive science and the neurology of learning makes it much easier to muster up the courage, resilience, and determination to persist in efforts to constantly improve the quality of learning.

For faculty of community colleges, an environment where educational equity is a form of social justice, this requires a renewed commitment to applying those concepts and strategies so crucial to deeper and more meaningful learning. Our work contributes to more completely developed students proficient in those basic life skills essential to success in the workplace. It therefore benefits us, our students and their families, our colleagues, our institution, and our society. Ultimately, quality of life is increased for all as a more skilled and educated workforce is created for the community.

Right now, there are too many people in this country who depend on the ability of higher education to adapt and overcome the challenges of the twenty-first-century classroom. In order for this country to continue to pride itself in equal opportunity for all, higher education must find a way to scale-up proven strategies, and it must do so right now. It should not be an option for faculty to forego strategies shown by research to improve student success and increase confidence levels.

Today, we need teacher-leaders more than ever—not just in positions of leadership but in all classrooms, serving as warriors for student success. It is time for the teacher-leaders already doing their part to become more vocal and to be comfortable making things happen instead of waiting for them to happen. Fostering this leadership throughout the faculty ranks will allow higher education to maximize learning.

It is time to expand QEPs so they can have an impact on all students and all employees. It is time to use the accrediting agency's requirement of "constant improvement based on data" as a forcing function to unite all employees on the common goal of "inspiring and facilitating learning." More than ever, higher education needs to cultivate a culture of evidence and action, using the research prowess of advanced-degree professionals to help create an environment of innovation and creativity. This is an environment where the three Cs dominate—where Connection, Collaboration, and Celebration guide us all!

As seen from the evidence in this book, an ILA experience can have a profound effect on building leadership and problem-solving skills throughout the faculty ranks. This, in turn, has a profound effect on all students, and effects can be transformative in those who need a quality education the most: the underserved and underprepared.

Get started today by selecting faculty to participate in an ILA program and then using these faculty to facilitate your institution's or system's own ILA. If you would like more information on how you or your faculty can develop an ILA, please contact me at InstructionalLeadershipAcademy@gmail.com.

***

As a final reflection/review self-assessment, you should be able to articulate how the following acronyms/concepts contribute to your continual development as an instructional leader:

- Q-TIP
- KISS
- T.A.S.E.
- CC-MVP
- I-CAN
- ILA
- PSS (appreciations)
- Kaizen
- Encouragement
- T-P-S
- Chunking
- 2-10-2
- Self-discipline
- Intentional teaching
- Three pillars of effective instruction
- Three C's for success

- Adapt & Improvise
- Control or Compensate
- Mindset over Skillset
- Growth vs. Fixed mindset
- Proactive vs. Reactive
- Logical action vs. Emotional reaction

- Never, ever ask permission to lead
- Doing nothing not an option
- Disappointment vs. Discipline
- Progress vs. Excuses
- Education vs. Initiation
- Extreme ownership

Appendix A

 Professional Educator Commitment Statement

Recognizing that I volunteered to serve as an Alabama Community College System (ACCS) professional educator, fully knowing the challenges of my chosen profession and that my students and the mission of the ACCS would take priority over my own personal comforts, I will always endeavor to uphold the prestige and honor of the ACCS family.

Acknowledging an ACCS professional educator must tackle each level of the learning domains, I must arrive at the cutting edge of the classroom by online and/or traditional instruction. I accept the fact that my community expects me to be a leader and lifelong learner of innovative teaching strategies, constantly striving to improve the quality of activities used to engage the student in critical thinking, while accepting responsibility for the results of the training I provide. Students will, as a result of their interaction with me, as well as with my colleagues, develop lifelong learning strategies and problem-solving skills which extend well beyond the confines of the classroom.

Faithfully will I maintain accountability to my fellow educators and students. I will always keep myself mentally alert for new ways to inspire and facilitate learning with a diverse student population, while promoting the dignity of work, value of education, and the merit of service. Excellence for me is not a destination, but an enthusiastically contagious attitude of high expectations backed by a system of training, support, and accountability that empowers students to develop more successful life skills!

Gallantly will I show my state I am a specially selected and well-trained professional committed to instilling the principles of personal responsibility needed for my students to succeed in life and develop into more productive, contributing members of society. I will strive to consistently mirror the positive can-do attitude and grit required of my students. Since my students are expected to move past their comfort zone and self-perceived limitations, this I shall also expect of myself as I constantly strive to 'Lead by Example' in pursuit of the advancement of equity and social justice! 'Doing nothing' in response to any variable impeding student learning is not an option, as the economic viability of this state depends on my courageous and relentless pursuit of total student development.

My courtesy to administrators, staff, and students alike, combined with neatness of dress and care of equipment, shall set the example for others to follow. I will always support my colleagues, for despite our diversities we share common goals and passions for student learning and success. Where others see a crisis, we see an opportunity for a persistent, growth mindset to accomplish that which others may find too difficult - allowing us to achieve results others find too elusive!

Energetically will I meet the deterrents that hinder learning and success for both myself and my students. I shall endeavor to conquer any obstacles in the learning environment, for I am professionally trained for and mentally focused on providing a truly equal opportunity for all students to achieve the American Dream through higher education. When confronted with my own errors or my students' mistakes, I choose to create opportunities to learn and improve. Active engagement and persistent support will always take precedence over passive transmission of knowledge.

Readily will I display the tenacity and integrity required to persist in achieving the ACCS vision where "*education works for all*", even against the most demanding of obstacles and resistance. I believe in my students and refuse to give up on them. I expect them to perform at a higher standard and I will constantly strive to provide them with a level of training, support, and encouragement that exceeds these standards.

My commitment to uphold the academic integrity of ACCS is fueled by my passion to increase the quality of life for each and every student!!

ACCS Instructional Leadership Academy, 2018   T. Holland

Figure D.1 Professional Educator Commitment Statement. *Source*: Author created.

Appendix B

ACCS INSTRUCTIONAL LEADERSHIP TEAM OATH

Realizing I have been chosen to be a part of an elite team of educational leaders, I will always strive to uphold the honor of this voluntary position.
The mission of this team is to provide the leadership necessary to instill a culture of constant and never-ending improvement across all instructional areas, while infusing the learning environment with an enthusiastic and contagious, positive, can-do attitude of 'whatever it takes'.
The welfare and training of the faculty and staff on my team are my responsibility, and I will always strive to lead them beyond their self-perceived limitations.
My passion, purpose, and persistence will be unsurpassed in post-secondary education, and will be fueled by my desire to provide an equal opportunity for ALL students to succeed through higher education!

Figure D.2   ACCS Instructional Leadership Team Oath. *Source*: Author created.

WCC Department of Biology

Program Mission Statement

The Department of Biology at Wallace Community College provides a curriculum designed to address the diverse interests of today's student population. The mission of this department is to support a program that provides a quality education for transfer biology majors, allied health and medical pre-professionals, and general education students. The department must also serve as a resource of biological knowledge for the community. Above all, the program encourages students to be life-long learners and to place their knowledge of biology in a frame of reference enabling them to become productive, active participants in our society. In support of this mission, the Biology Department maintains an ongoing effort to provide a modern, well-equipped physical plant and a diverse, articulate, scholarly, up-to-date faculty dedicated to providing the best possible two-year education in biology.

Appendix C

WALLACE COMMUNITY COLLEGE STUDENT CREED

As a student of Wallace Community College, I believe in...

S - E - R - V - E

STRIVING for educational excellence by setting high but realistic goals; to diligently work to stretch my intellectual, physical, emotional and social limits; and to apply my time and mind to achieve academic excellence and complete my educational goals;

ENCOURAGING those around me by setting an appropriate example for all to follow;

RESPECTING the individuality and diversity of instructors and fellow peers;

VIEWING the application of knowledge that I obtain as power to succeed.

EXHIBITING integrity by remaining honest and true in all of my life endeavors.

I PLEDGE to uphold and honor the values in this creed as I progress forward in my life.

I PLEDGE to rid my life of behavior that may weaken the spirit of our community.

I PLEDGE always to strive to be better than I was yesterday!

WCC Diplomats, 2014

Figure D.3 Wallace Community College (WCC) Student Creed. *Source*: Author created.

Appendix D

ILA Course Redesign on LMS: Requirements for Implementation in Highest Enrollment Course

1. Provide your own short **personal survey** (—four to six questions) for implementation after your first major exam in each section, each term. Use all survey results (including institutional survey) as an opportunity to improve both the response rate *and* positive perceptions.
2. Identify key questions (—four to six questions) from the **institutional survey** which you will use to monitor data, which may or may not be the same as the ones given after the first exam.
3. Provide a list of *instructor-made* **unit objectives** for each of your four to six units. This list will include everything the student must be able *to do* to successfully complete each of the end-of-unit summative assessments.
4. Provide a warm, positive, and encouraging **welcome video** to your course on your LMS.
5. Provide a short (—five to ten minutes) *instructor-made* **lecture video** for *each* unit objective for all units.
6. Provide a list of **frequent assessment** exercises used for each unit, connecting each to the related objective(s). Your list will grow and be adjusted over time.
7. Provide a list of **active-learning activities** for each unit which support the core competencies of critical thinking and communication, connecting each to the related objective(s). Your list will grow and be adjusted over time.

8. Provide a specific system for early, intrusive **interventions** to proactively address at-risk student performance. (*who*, *when*, and *what* will be discussed)

9. Provide students with a short list of **expectations** (reiterate the need for them to show up prepared - having looked up objectives before watching the lecture video accompanying each objective), as well as a list of what they can expect of you.

Appendix E

Figure D.4 **Pinkard House.** *Source*: Author created.

References

Adler, Mortimer J. *The Paideia Proposal: An Educational Manifesto*. New York: Simon & Schuster, 1982.

American Association of Community Colleges. *Reclaiming the American Dream: A Report from the 21st Century Commission on the Future of Community Colleges*. Washington, DC: American Federation of Teachers, AFL-CIO, 2012.

American Council on Education. *2017 American College President Study*. https://www.acenet.edu/Research-Insights/Pages/American-College-President-Study.aspx.

Bailey, T., Jaggers, S. S., & Jenkins, D. *Redesigning America's Community Colleges: A Clearer Path to Student Success*. Cambridge, MA: Harvard University Press, 2015.

Baird, A. & Parayitam, S. "Employer's Ratings of Importance of Skills and Competencies College Graduates Need to Get Hired: Evidence from the New England Region of USA." *Education + Training* 61, no. 5 (2019): 622–634.

Berkeley Center for Teaching and Learning. University of California Berkeley. https://teaching.berkeley.edu/considerations-large-lecture-classes.

Berrett, D. "Teaching Revival: Fresh Attention to the Classroom May Actually Stick This Time." *Chronicle of Higher Education*. March 9, 2015. https://www.chronicle.com/article/teaching- revival/.

Billy Graham Quotes. BrainyQuote.com, BrainyMedia Inc, 2021. https://www.Brainyquote.com/quotes/billy_graham_113622.

Cabrera, A. & Phillips, J. "It's Time to Celebrate High-Quality Community Colleges." *Diverse Issues in Higher Education*. July 23, 2019. https://diverseeducation.com/article/150345/.

Center for Community College Student Engagement. *Making Connections: Dimensions of Student Engagement (2009 CCSSE Findings)*. Austin, TX: The University

of Texas at Austin, Community College Leadership Program, 2009. https://docplay
er.net/2911039-Making-connections-dimensions-of-student-engagement-2009-fin
dings.html.

Civitas Learning. *What Really Works: A Review of Student Success Initiatives.* 2019.
https://media.civitaslearning.com/wp-content/uploads/sites/3/2020/02/Civitas_Lea
rning_What_Really_Works_Report.pdf.

Costa, A. *Toward a Model of Human Intellectual Functioning in Developing Minds*:
A Resource Book for Teaching Thinking. Revised edition, edited by A. Costa.
Alexandria, VA: Association for Supervision and Curriculum Development, 1981.

Diamond, R. "Why Colleges Are So Hard to Change." *Inside Higher Ed.* September
8, 2006. https://www.insidehighered.com/views/2006/09/08/why-colleges-are-so
-hard-change.

Family of Vince Lombardi c/o Luminary Group LLC. "Famous Quotes by Vince
Lombardi." *Famous Quotes by Vince Lombardi*, 2021. http://www.vincelombardi
.com.

Fink, L. *Creating Significant Learning Experiences: An Integrated Approach to
Designing College Courses.* San Francisco, CA: John Wiley & Sons, 2003.

Finkelmeyer, T. "Campus Connection: Online Videos Replace Live Lectures . . . and
Students Thrive." *The Cap Times.* October 21, 2012. https://madison.com/ct/news
/local/ education/campusconnection/campus- connection-online-videos-replace-li
ve-lectures-and-students-thrive/article_f1043ba2-1a1f-11e2-92a9-0019bb2963f4
.html.

Flaherty, C. "The Dangers of Fluent Lectures." *Inside Higher Ed.* September 9, 2019.
https://www.insidehighered.com/news/2019/09/09/study-how-smooth-talking-pro
fessors-can-lull-students-thinking-theyve-learned-more.

Gardner, J. *On Leadership.* New York, NY: The Free Press, 1990.

Glazer, R. "CVS Lost $2 Billion With 1 Decision—Here's Why They Were Right."
Forbes. April 21, 2020. https://www.forbes.com/sites/robertglazer/2020/04/21/cvs
-lost-2-billion-with-1-decision-heres-why-they-were-right/?sh=6934a9f7689c.

Goldrick-Rab, S., Baker-Smith, C., Coca, V., Looker, E., & Williams, T. *College and
University Basic Needs Insecurity: A National #RealCollege Survey Report.* The
HOPE Lab, 2019.

Hart, B. & Risley, T. "The Early Catastrophe." *Education Review* 77, no. 1 (2004).
https://www.gsa.gov/graphics/pbs/The_Early_Catastrophe_30_Million_Word
_Gap_by_ age_3.pdf.

Hart Research Associates. *It Takes More Than a Major: Employer Priorities for
College Learning and Student Success: An Online Survey Among Employers
Conducted on Behalf Of: The Association Of American Colleges And Universities.*

Washington, DC: Hart Research Associates, 2013. https://www.aacu.org/sites/def
ault/files/files/LEAP/2013_EmployerSurvey.pdf.

Haskins, R. "Three Simple Rules Poor Teens Should Follow to Join the Middle
Class." *Brookings*. March 13, 2013. https://www.brookings.edu/opinions/three
-simple-rules-poor-teens-should-follow-to-join-the-middle-class/.

Jaschik, S. & Lederman, J., eds. "2019 Survey of College and University Presidents."
Inside Higher Ed. Inside Higher Ed. and Gallup, 2019.

Kinnamon, J. & O'Banion, T. "Creating a Culture of Leadership." *League for Innovation in the Community College*. March 2021. https://www.league.org/occasional-p
aper/creating-culture-leadership.

Kolb, D. A. *Experiential Learning: Experience as the Source of Learning and Development*. Englewood Cliffs, NJ: Prentice-Hall, 1984.

Marti, E. *America's Broken Promise: Bridging the Community College Achievement
Gap*. Albany, NY: Hudson Whitman Excelsior College Press, 2016.

Mercogliano, C. "Title." Life Learning Magazine, Nov/Dec 2013. https://www.life
.ca/lifelearning/quotes-about-unschooling-life-learning.htm.

Merisotis, J. "In the Work of the Future, Abilities Matter Most and the Learning
Never Stops." *Lumina Foundation*. December 9, 2020. https://www.luminafoundat
ion.org/news-and-views/in-the-work-of-the-future-abilities-matter-most-and-the-l
earning-never-stops.

Nater, S. & Gallimore, R. *You Haven't Taught Until They Have Learned: John
Wooden's Teaching Principles and Practices*. Morgantown, WV: Fitness Information Technology, 2010.

O'Banion, T. *A Learning College for the 21st Century*. Westport, CT: American
Council on Education/Oryx Press Series on Higher Education, 1997.

———. *Bread and Roses: Helping Student Make a Good Living and Live a Good
Life*. Chandler, AZ: League for Innovation in the Community College and Roueche
Graduate Center, National American University, 2016: 41.

———. *Launching a Learning-Centered College*. Mission Viejo, CA: League for
Innovation in the Community College, 1999. https://files.eric.ed.gov/fulltext/ED43
2315.pdf.

———. "What Kind of Tuition-Free College Education?" *Community College Week*.
September 27, 2015.

———. *13 Ideas That Are Transforming the Community College World*. Washington,
DC: Rowman & Littlefield Publishers, 2019.

Opper, I. *Teachers Matter: Understanding Teachers' Impact on Student Achievement*. RAND Corporation, 2019. https://www.rand.org/pubs/research_reports/RR
4312.html.

Payne, R. *A Framework for Understanding Poverty*. Highlands, TX: aha! Process, 2005.

Pillsbury, P. "The Impact of Teacher Effectiveness on Student Achievement." *Education News*. March 11, 2016. https://www.targetsuccess.biz/wp/?p=888.

Price, P. "Are You as Good a Teacher as You Think?" *Thought + Action* (Fall, 2006): 7–14.

Ray, J. & Marken, S. "Life in College Matters for Life After College." *Gallup*. May 6, 2014. https://news.gallup.com/poll/168848/life-college-matters-life-college.aspx.

Rimer, S. "At M.I.T., Large Lectures Are Going the Way of the Blackboard." *New York Times*. January 12, 2009. https://www.nytimes.com/2009/01/13/us/13physics.html?auth=link- dismiss-google1tap.

Rothenburg, P. *White Privilege: Essential Readings on the Other Side of Racism*. New York: Worth Publishers, 2002.

Ryback, R. "The Science of Accomplishing Your Goals." *Psychology Today*. October 3, 2016.

Salisbury, D. "Dopamine Impacts Your Willingness to Work." *Research News @ Vanderbilt*. May 1, 2012. https://news. vanderbilt.edu/2012/05/01/dopamine-impacts-your-willingness-to-work/?utm _source=vuhomepage&utm_medium=vuhomeslider&utm_campaign=0503- dopamine-drive.

Sanders, W. L. & Rivers, J. C. *Cumulative and Residual Effects of Teachers on Future Student Academic Achievement*. Knoxville, YN: University of Tennessee Value-Added Research and Assessment Center, 1996.

Strauss, V. "The Surprising Thing Google Learned about its Employees – and What it Means for Today's Students." *Washington Post*. December 20, 2017.

Supiano, B. "Can a New Approach to Teaching Fix Inequality?" *The Chronicle of Higher Education*. May 7, 2018. https://www.chronicle.com/article/traditional-teaching-may-deepen-inequality-can-a-different-approach-fix-it/.

Wallas, G. *The Art of Thought*. Kent: Solis Press, 2014. First published 1926.

West Monroe Partners. *Closing the Technology Leadership Gap*. January 2018. https ://www.westmonroepartners.com/perspectives/signature-research/it-soft-skills.

Willink, J. & Babin, L. *Extreme Ownership*. New York City: St. Martin's Publishing Group, 2015.

———. *The Dichotomy of Leadership*. New York City: St. Martin's Publishing Group, 2018.

Wingspread Group on Higher Education. *An American Imperative: Higher Expectations for Higher Education*. Racine, WI: Johnson Foundation, 1993.

Yee, K. *289 Interactive Techniques*. 2020. CC BY-NC-SA. https://www.usf.edu/atle/documents/handout-interactive-techniques.pdf.

Zull, J. *The Art of Changing the Brain*. Sterling, VA: Stylus Publishing, 2002.